Beyond the End of History:
Rejecting the Washington Consensus
by
Keith Preston

Beyond the End of History:
Rejecting the Washington Consensus
by
Keith Preston

ISBN-13: 978-1-910881-25-5

Black House Publishing Ltd
Kemp House
152 City Road
London
United Kingdom
EC1V 2NX

www.blackhousepublishing.com
Email: info@blackhousepublishing.com

Contents

Introduction   1

American Imperialism vs. The Identity of the World's Peoples   5

The Nietzschean Prophecies: 15

Nietzsche the Visionary   27

Our Struggle Is Neither Moral Nor Intellectual, But Physical   39

Ernst Junger   45

Emma Goldman: A Life Worth Living   65

Democracy as Tyranny   97

The Iron Fists Masquerading as Invisible Hands   113

Philosophical Anarchism and the Death of Empire   125

Zionism and the Power Elite   209

Anti-Imperialists of the World, Unite!   223

References   241

Introduction

In 1989, the neoconservative political scientist Francis Fukuyama published an article titled "The End of History?" in the journal of international relations *The National Interest*. Fukuyama expanded upon the ideas presented in this article in a book issued three years later titled *The End of History and the Last Man*. The context of Fukuyama's analysis involved the end of the Cold War, the collapse of the Soviet Union, and the supposed triumph of the American and Western European model of "democratic capitalism" as the supposed final end of human political and economic evolution. The presumption behind Fukuyama's thesis was that democratic capitalism was the most advanced form of political economy that humanity would ever achieve. Consequently, any further political evolution would simply be a matter of waiting for the rest of the world to catch up with the Western model.

It was also during 1989 that the English economist John Williamson coined the term "The Washington Consensus" to describe the neoliberal economic model that has emerged during the post-Cold War era of economic globalization. This alleged "consensus" represents a collection of policy prescriptions favored by the American foreign policy and economic elites based in Washington, D.C. and by Washington-dominated international institutions such as the World Bank, International Monetary Fund, and World Trade Organization. Over the past three decades, these policy prescriptions have in turn been adopted by Western elites as the expected model for economic development in the underdeveloped nations, and have served as the framework for the advancement of the global economy on an international scale.

However, during this time the overconfidence of Fukuyama's prediction has become apparent. Not only has considerable resistance to the economic model that Washington seeks to impose emerged, but the wider Western model of political economy has also been met with skepticism among large elements of the developing world. This is evidenced by the growth of fundamentalism throughout the Islamic world, the leftward turn of Latin America, the rise of Putinism in Russia, and the emergence of the "Asian Way" in East Asian nations such as China, South Korea, Singapore and Indonesia. Even in the Western nations, political parties rejecting the neoliberal consensus have emerged on both the Left and Right, and these parties are growing in popularity.

The essays presented in this collection represent a variety of themes pertaining to discontent with the currently dominant world order, and examines the ideas of a variety of thinkers, both past and present, that have offered critical analysis of the liberal democratic capitalist model of political economy, and its related cultural corollaries. The opening essay, "American Imperialism vs. The Identity of the World's Peoples," explains the role of Americanization in imposing a global monoculture that is having the effect of eradicating traditional forms of cultural identity, and provides an overview of the resistance that is rising in opposition to this model. The next three essays revisit the work of two of the most prescient critics of the values of modernity from past times. "The Nietzschean Prophecies," explores the remarkable accuracy with which Nietzsche foretold the future of Western civilization as it would unfold over the subsequent two centuries. "Nietzsche the Visionary" revisits the work of Nietzsche and offers speculation about what a model of civilization guided by Nietzschean values might involve. "Ernst Junger: The Resolute Life of an Anarch" discusses a leading literary figure associated with the "conservative revolutionary" movement that emerged during the Weimar Republic, and his later development of the concept of the "Anarch."

These are followed by four essays examining the work of past and present anarchist thinkers, and that offer core criticisms of the dominant political, economic, and philosophical values of the present age. The first of these, "Our Struggle is Neither Moral nor Intellectual, But Physical" explores the implications of postmodern nihilism and cultural relativism, and affirms a Stirnerite approach to political theory. This followed by an overview of the thought of the classical anarchist Emma Goldman with a highlighting of those ideas within Goldman's outlook that would no doubt contradict certain presumptions of the Left in its contemporary form. The next two essays review the work of Hans Hermann Hoppe, an anarchist of the Right, and left-wing anarchist Kevin Carson. Hoppe's critique of the political model of liberal democracy is presented alongside Carson's critique of the economic model of state-capitalism in a way that challenges the fundamental assumptions of prevailing political values.

Three subsequent essays analyze imperialism as it is presently manifested in the forms of the Anglo-American-Zionist-Wahhabist axis in the political realm, and global capitalism in the economic realm. These works likewise call for anarchist movements to reclaim the position they held a century ago as the world's foremost and most feared revolutionary forces. Essentially, all of these essays constitute an effort to think modernity through to the other side in a way that challenges the progressive, liberal, democratic, and capitalist consensus. However, none of these works are conventionally "right-wing" in the sense of advocating a restoration of values of a reactionary, conservative, bourgeois, traditionalist, Christian, or racist nature. Instead, the essays contained in this collection are genuinely forward-looking and consider what the development of a genuine post-modernity might involve.

Keith Preston
Richmond, Virginia, United States

August 20, 2016

American Imperialism vs. The Identity of the World's Peoples

Lecture given in Washington, D.C. on October 31, 2015

I was very happy when I was asked to speak to this gathering on the topic of the conflict between American imperialism and European identity, and indeed the identity of virtually all of the world's peoples.

I have been an outspoken critic of American imperialism for several decades now, and as someone who has his political origins on the far Left, for much of that time I was mostly concerned about the relationship between the United States and the underdeveloped world. However, after spending some time in Europe off and on for the past fifteen years, I've also come to realize that much of the criticism that can be voiced concerning the relationship between the United States and the underdeveloped world is also quite applicable to the relationship between the United States and Europe.

I will explain why that is in a moment, but first let me say that I consider American imperialism to be the bastard child of European colonialism, and it was a child that grew up to be a monster that ended up eating its father. I will explain what I mean by that in a moment as well. But I also think a bit of historical perspective is necessary in order to fully understand this question.

Two hundred years ago, most of the peoples around the world were still in the hunter and gatherer stage in terms of their level of social evolution. This is something that most contemporary people have no awareness of. It's certainly something that my students are surprised to hear when I tell them about it. But during the thousands of years that civilization has existed, within the broader context of all of humanity, civilization has still been the exception rather than the rule, at least until very, very recently. While many of the criticisms of European colonialism that are frequently voiced are indeed quite legitimate in my view, it is also true that a major part of the legacy of European colonialism is that it brought the virtues of Western civilization to many other parts of the world. Now, I am not someone who thinks that white, Western civilization is all that there is and that everything else is garbage. That would be a totally ahistorical perspective, in my view. But I would argue that the legacy of European colonialism is comparable to the legacy of Alexander the Great, who brought the virtues of classical Greek civilization to what in the fourth century B.C. (or B.C.E. if we want to be PC about it, I guess I don't need to worry about that here), but what in the fourth century B.C. was most of the known world.

When I say that American imperialism is the bastard child of European colonialism, what I mean by that is that on one hand America is very much a product of European colonialism. We Americans did get our start as British colonies, as we know. However, it is also true that during the middle part of the twentieth century, the Europeans happened to engage in a particularly fratricidal war, which was probably the most tragic episode in world history, and one of the long terms results of this war was that the old European colonial empires essentially came to an end because their European mother counties had largely been laid to waste during the course of the war.

Now, I have a longstanding debate with a number of friends who are conservatives in the American sense, that is, loyal Republicans who can't enough of FOX News, we all know the kinds of folks I'm talking about, the kind of people who think that the America of the 1950s was the apex of human civilization. These mainstream conservative types are often a bit bewildered when I explain to them that the reason America achieved what amounted to world dominance in the postwar era is because all of its competitors had been wiped out in the war. All that was left was Communism, which was a severe aberration, and the Third World which was largely mired in a pre-industrial state. With economic and geopolitical competitors of that type, of course the United States achieved world dominance. And, in fact, the United States stepped in and essentially picked up where the older European colonial empires left off. During the Cold War period, many of the former European colonies in Asia and Africa became American clients, and along with the American puppet states in Latin America, which represented the United States' traditional sphere of hegemony, all of these nations collectively became outposts of the American empire.

However, I would argue that American imperialism is different in character from European colonialism. European colonialism, in my view, was very much comparable to the old Roman empire of antiquity. The Roman Empire was certainly interested in exercising political, military, and economic hegemony over their subject peoples. However, the Roman Empire normally allowed its subject peoples to retain their own local cultures, traditions, religions, and ethnic identities. The Romans were mostly just concerned with collecting taxes and preventing rebellions, and not trying to transform their subject peoples in a fundamental way. Now, the subjects of the empire were expected to participate in the state cult of the emperor, but for most of the peoples of the Roman Empire this was not a problem since they were polytheists anyway. In fact, that's what got the Christians into so much trouble with the Roman authorities. As monotheists, they could have only one god. The Jews were actually exempt from participation in the state cult, by the way, but the Romans refused to extend that privilege to the Christians as well. I guess they figured once was enough.

But as far as the difference between American imperialism and European colonialism is concerned, I think something I observed the first time I ever went to Europe illustrates this dichotomy quite well. When I first ventured to Europe, one of the first things that I noticed was how old everything was: the architecture, the designs of the streets and the sidewalks, the public buildings, the art, the museums. Yet everywhere in the midst of this very old European cultural experience, I saw signs of Americanization. I recall, for example, observing scenery where these very old cathedrals would be intermixed with signs advertising American fast food restaurants, like McDonald's, or Burger King, or Kentucky Fried Chicken. As an American this was no big deal to me personally because I was already used to seeing this crass commercialism everywhere I went, but I recall thinking at the time that if I were a European I would be extremely offended by this form of cultural imperialism that was all around.

I think this experience illustrates very well a crucial difference between American imperialism and more traditional forms of imperialism or colonialism. American imperialism has a quasi-religious quality to it in the sense that it is not just about to whom taxes get paid, but instead it is about changing the way that people live in a much wider sense, changing the way they think, and altering their identity in very fundamental ways. And I think this is true of American imperialism as it pertains to Europe as much as it pertains to other parts of the world. But we see examples of this everywhere. A friend of mine, a national-anarchist by the name of Welf Herfurth, tells the story of visiting Saigon in Vietnam, supposedly a Communist nation, and observing Vietnamese youngsters on the streets of Saigon trying to emulate the mannerisms of American rap singers. Today in Japan, for the first time ever, the Japanese are starting to have a problem with obesity. Now, when we think of the Japanese we normally don't think about fat people. We think of healthy people who have traditionally enjoyed comparative long life expectancies because of their healthy diets of fish and rice.

However, due to the importation of American fast food culture into Japan, the Japanese are now starting to experience problems with obesity and the health difficulties that result from this.

American imperialism is not merely about exercising political hegemony, it is about facilitating what is thought to be a moral transformation of other peoples and cultures. And as I said, I believe there is a quasi religious mentality associated with this kind of moral crusading. One thing that is distinctive about Christianity is that it teaches that temptation is just as great a sin as acting on temptation. For example, Christianity teaches that hating someone is as great a moral failure as murdering them, or that desiring another man's wife is the same as actually adulterating the wife of another. Most ethical or religious philosophies teach that the essence of virtue is the process of overcoming temptation or refusing to give in temptation, not that merely experiencing temptation and succumbing to temptation are one and the same. I believe that the morality that drives the ideology of the contemporary Western world is a secularization of this kind of traditional Christian blurring of the distinction between thoughts and actual deeds. For example, it has always seemed to me that the real problem that liberals and leftists have with racism, or homophobia, or patriarchy, or whatever Ism or Archy or Phobia happens to be on the chopping block this week, is not necessarily any tangible or identifiable harms that are associated with these as much as the mere idea that someone, somewhere, somehow might think racist or homophobic thoughts. It is the impurity of their hearts and not the malevolence of their deeds that is somehow the real problem. The greatest fear of the Left is that someone might be hiding away in a broom closet thinking about racism.

This is the morality that I also believe guides the American Empire. In fact, when the Islamists refer to American imperialists as the modern Crusaders, I think they have a point, not necessarily in the way they mean it, but it is an apt analogy. As an illustration, in a speech delivered in Chicago in June of 2014, Hillary Clinton suggested that if she were to become President of the United States that feminist ideology would be a central component part of her approach to foreign policy, and we can only imagine where that will eventually lead. Earlier this year, we observed the spectacle of President Obama traveling to Kenya in order to lecture their president on gay rights. And, of course, we remember the uproar a few years ago when a number of political forces in the Western world were calling for a boycott of the 2014 Winter Olympics in Russia over Russia's failure to, I don't know, endorse gay marriage or whatever the problem was. In 1980, the United States under President Carter boycotted the Olympics in Moscow because of the Soviet Union's invasion of the sovereign state of Afghanistan. Less than thirty-five years later, we saw Americans and others calling for a boycott of the Olympics in Russia in the name of gay rights, which I suppose says a great deal about the direction that the Western world has gone in during the past third of a century. And we see that this liberal crusader mentality has produced disaster all over the world.

Recall, for example, the so-called "Freedom Agenda" of the former Bush administration, and that was part of the ideological rationale for the war in Iraq. I suppose we can gauge how well that worked out by observing what a paradise Iraq is today. Remember the military action against Libya in 2011, led by the Obama administration, and ostensibly under the pretext of defending human rights, which led to the creation of the failed state that Libya is today. Recall the so-called "Arab Spring" and the efforts of the United States to undermine secular governments in Arab nations, in the name of spreading democracy, which is supposedly something that all people everywhere want, irrespective of their history, culture, or traditions, I guess because Francis Fukuyama told us so, or whatever. But the real impact of the "Arab Spring", as Mr. Putin recently pointed out, was the coming to power of Islamists in some countries and the growth of terrorist organizations in others. So we are able to plainly see that all of this crusading for democracy and human rights has actually led to a reduction of democracy and human rights, or at least a reduction in humans.

Now, aside from the loss of blood and treasure that has been generated by American military imperialism, we are also able to observe the loss of identity that is taking place because of American economic and cultural imperialism. In nation after nation around the world, American television, popular music, popular culture, fashion, media, fast food, and consumer culture are increasingly everywhere. It's as if the ambition is for the entire planet to become one giant, universal Wal-Mart. And what is happening is that the unique identities of people all over the world are being eradicated.

There are essentially three kinds of identity that are acceptable according to the value system on which American imperialism is implicitly based. One of these is the identity of a subject to state. Notice that I didn't say "citizen". I said "subject". There is the identity of the worker or the professional, whereby someone's identity comes to be defined by their place in the economy. And there is the identity of the consumer, the role of the individual as a participant in the marketplace. No other form of identity is acceptable within the context of this particular paradigm. Not ethnicity, not nationality, not race, not culture, not religion, not history, not tradition, not community, not ancestry, not family, and apparently, not even gender. Instead, the ambition is to create masses of helots that function merely as deracinated, working, consuming, tax-paying, obedient drones without any connection to the past, no regard for the future, no folklore, no distinctiveness, and no serious aspirations. That is the vision that is implicit in the rhetoric and in the practice of the American Empire.

Now, the question that emerges from this critique of the American Empire and its impact on the identities of the world's peoples is the matter of how to go about building resistance. This question in turn raises some very fundamental geopolitical questions. I have a generally optimistic view because already we see significant pockets of resistance developing all over the world. I interpret present day international relations largely in terms of what I call "Team A" versus "Team B". Team A is the dominant coalition with the framework of the international power elite, or the international plutocracy, or international capitalism, or whatever you want call it. This dominant coalition is what I call the Anglo-American-Zionist-Wahhabist axis consisting of the United States as the senior partner, along with England, Israel, Saudi Arabia, the other Gulf States, and most of the member states of NATO and the European Union as junior partners.

As far as the present day relationship between Europe and the United States is concerned, I'm inclined to think that it was ironically Mao Tse-tung who had the best analysis of that. In the early 70s, Maoist China developed what they called the "Three Worlds Theory," which is not the same thing as the idea of the First, Second, and Third World that you found in Western political theory during the same period. Instead, the Maoist model argued that the world order of the time consisted of the First World, which was the United States and its satellites, including Western Europe, the Second World, which was the Soviet Union and its satellites, and the Third World of what they considered to be exploited nations. And I would suggest that a modified version of this theory is still applicable, with the modification being that the Second World has disappeared, and that most of the former Soviet satellites have become American satellites with Russia losing its superpower status.

And out of this situation is emerging what I call Team B. The foundation of Team B is what I refer to as the triangular resistance, that is, three distinctive blocks of nations that are emerging in opposition to American imperialism. The most significant of these is the emergence of the so-called BRICS, that is, the economic alliance of Brazil, Russia, India, China, and South Africa. There is also what is called the Resistance Block in the Middle East, which consists of Iran, Syria, Hezbollah, a variety of Iraqi and Palestinian groups, the Houthi in Yemen. The third pattern of resistance consists of what I call "resistance nations" or resistance movements in Latin America that resist their own incorporation into the American Empire. This block also includes Brazil, Venezuela, Cuba, Ecuador, Bolivia, and Argentina with varying degrees of consistency, as well as the wider set of Latin American populist movements that these nations to some degree represent. In addition to these three blocks of resistance, there are also outliers like Belarus, North Korea, Zimbabwe, and the Kurdish independence movement that has recently emerged. There are also a variety of non-state actors around the world reflecting a wide range of identities that are resistant to incorporation into the American empire and its program of global liberal capitalist imperialism. So resistance is building everywhere even as the weaknesses of the American empire become increasingly obvious.

In particular, Russia, China, and Iran have emerged as bulwarks against U.S. imperialism, and we have in recent times seen a greater cooperation between these nations, for example, in the currency swap agreement between Russia and China, or the collaboration between Russia and Iran in the war against ISIS, and I have seen discussion recently concerning the possibility of Iran joining the BRICS alliance.

Ultimately, however, we also need an independent and self-assertive Europe. If I could give any advice to the European nations it would be to break out from underneath the American Empire, dissolve NATO, and claim self-determination for themselves and this includes military self-determination as well as political, economic, and cultural self-determination. The United States is on its way to becoming a failed state, with a $19 trillion national debt, the largest national debt in world history, and a society where virtually all of its institutions are increasingly dysfunctional. This is not system that will go on forever. Those of us who are Americans should be preparing ourselves for a post-America. Meanwhile, the Europeans should, in my view, strive to reclaim their own heritage and destiny. Ultimately, however, the salvation of Europe is dependent upon the abolition of the American Empire.

The Nietzschean Prophecies:

Two Hundred Years of Nihilism and the Coming Crisis of Western Civilization

Among the many great and enormously influential thinkers of the nineteenth century, it is Friedrich Wilhelm Nietzsche (1844–1900) who arguably stands the highest in terms of possessing both the most profound and penetrating criticisms of Western civilization as it was in his time, and the most prescient insights and predictions as to what the future course of the evolution of the West would involve. In our own day, Nietzsche has been a popular topic of academic discourse for some time, and the reading of his works has long been a popular pastime among trendy undergraduates. Yet in Nietzsche's day, he remained obscure and his works were not widely read or accepted until after his death. Even with the abundance of Nietzsche scholarship that has been produced in the more than a century since his passing, his core ideas remain widely misunderstood or misinterpreted. Indeed, Nietzsche has been largely appropriated by the academic Left, a great irony considering his own considerable contempt for the politics of the Left, and the prevailing academic philosophy of postmodernism includes the philosophy of Nietzsche as a direct ancestor in its genealogical line.

No thinker is more important or relevant to the ideas of the Conservative Revolution than Nietzsche. While Marx continues to retain his status as the most influential radical thinker of the nineteenth century, it was Nietzsche who was the more revolutionary of the two in the actual implications of his thought. Nietzsche also stands as a polar opposite of the conservative counter-revolutionaries that arose in opposition to the spread of the influence of the Enlightenment. Nietzsche is no mere traditionalist in the vein of Edmund Burke, Joseph de Maistre, or Louis de Bonald. His outlook involves a dramatic departure not only from traditional Western thought as it had unfolded since the time of the Socratics, but from the intellectual culture of even the most advanced or revolutionary thinkers of his own time.

The Historical Context of Nietzsche's Thought

An adequate understanding of Nietzsche is impossible without recognition of the historical context in which he wrote. Nietzsche's core works were produced between 1872 and 1888. By that time, the intellectual revolution of the Enlightenment was well-established among Western intellectual elites and among the rising educated middle classes. The Enlightenment intellectual revolution and its outgrowths were existential in nature. The most important aspect of the impact of the revolution was what Nietzsche characterized as the "death of God". Advancements in human knowledge in a wide variety of areas had the effect of undermining the credibility of traditional theological views on cosmology, moral philosophy, the meaning of human existence, and so forth. The overthrow of the Christian world view that had dominated Western civilization for fifteen hundred years left subsequent thinkers with a number of ultimately profound questions.[1] If the purpose of an individual's life is not to achieve salvation in an afterlife, then what is the purpose of life? If the king or established political authorities do not rule by divine right, then what is the basis of political legitimacy? How should society be organized? If morality is not to be understood according to the teachings of the Church, the Bible, or traditional religious authority, then what is the basis of justice, morality, truth, or "right and wrong"? Do such concepts have any intrinsic or objective meaning at all? If the observable universe was not the product of special creation by a divine power, and if humanity was not "created in the image of God," then what is the meaning

---

1   Peter Gay, *The Enlightenment: The Rise of Modern Paganism* (New York: W. W. Norton and Co., 1966), 8–9, 62–63.

of existence? Does it have any meaning beyond itself? If history is not guided by divine providence, then how is the process of historical unfolding to be understood? These are the questions that Western thinkers have been grappling with since the older, theological view of the universe and existence was demolished by the intellectual innovations of the Enlightenment.

The New Religion of Reason and Progress

Western civilization existed for millennia prior to the rise of Roman Christianity, so it is unsurprising that anti-Christian, Enlightenment intellectuals found inspiration in the classic works of antiquity. The Enlightenment thinkers (the "*philosophes*") developed a world view and philosophical outlook relatively similar to that which prevailed among the great thinkers of Greco-Roman intellectual culture.[2] The traditional Christian emphasis on faith, revelation, mystery, and divine authority was rejected in favor of a new emphasis on the efficacy of human reason and ability to engage in rational criticism. The Enlightenment view of the universe mirrored the human-centered outlook of the Greeks, with the ideas of the *philosophes* reflecting the Greek adage that "man is the measure of all things" to a much greater degree than Christian thought had ever done. It was the view of the *philosophes* that human reason and rational thought alone possessed the capability for the discernment of profound insight into the workings of the universe through the use of science. This confidence had been generated by the scientific revolution of the seventeenth century. Human reason was likewise capable of discerning the workings of society and of discovering ways by which society and humanity could be improved upon. Out of this conviction emerged an intellectual optimism that expressed great confidence in the possibility and inevitability of progress. This intellectual framework that was bequeathed to subsequent generations of Europeans by the great thinkers of the Enlightenment formed the foundation for most of modern thought.

---

2   *Ibid.*, 59–127.

The concept of progress was a dominant feature of every major aspect of nineteenth-century thinking, whether in the areas of philosophy, politics, or science. Thinkers of the German Idealist school, such as Immanuel Kant and G. W. F. Hegel, attempted to retain the notion of justice, morality, and virtue as concepts possessing transcendent characteristics in a manner similar to that found in earlier Christian approaches to moral philosophy. Hegel developed a philosophical doctrine known as "historicism" that characterized the process of human historical development as one by which reason unfolds towards a higher state of rational unity that contains within itself the collection of prior expressions of, and resolved contradictions within, human thought. Hegel gave a metaphysical and quasi-theological gloss to his philosophical system in a way that is still debated and subject to various interpretations. Yet, this linear, progressive view of history postulated by Hegel established the framework for historical interpretation that would dominate Western thought for the next century.[3]

Karl Marx and Friedrich Engels developed a materialist conception of Hegel's interpretation of history as a dialectical process. The core component of the Marxist interpretation of history is a kind of economic determinism. According to Marxism, history is the manifestation of the struggle between competing socio-economic classes. Other aspects of human life such as politics, religion, culture, family, and philosophy are merely expressions or outgrowths of the material foundations of a given society. Marxism regards history as an evolutionary process whereby class conflict serves as the dialectical process whose impact is the advancement of humanity to a higher stage of social development.[4]

---

3   Georg W. F. Hegel, *The Philosophy of History*, trans. J. Sibree (Amherst, NY: Prometheus Books, 1991).

4   Karl Marx and Friedrich Engels, *The Communist Manifesto* (New York: International Publishers, 1948).

The nineteenth-century idea of progress was further strengthened by the scientific advances of the time. Evolutionary thinking became dominant in the natural sciences as the older, religious views on the origins of humanity and the universe fell into intellectual disrepute. The prevailing model of evolutionary theory of the era was the "developmental" model. This framework suggested that the evolutionary process was a manifestation of a linear drive towards a particular end. The analogy often used was that of the growth of an individual. The conventional view was that evolution transpires in a way that demonstrates direction and purpose. This particular rendition of evolution, most famously represented by the theories of Jean-Baptiste Lamarck, was exploded by Charles Darwin. Darwin argued that evolution takes place through a process of adaption by means of natural selection.[5]

Darwin's actual theory indicated that the process of natural biological evolution exhibits a great deal of randomness, and unfolds in a haphazard way with no specific outcome being inevitable regarding the ends of the evolutionary process. The actual implications of authentic Darwinian evolutionary theory severely detracted from the established "developmental" model of biological and social evolution.[6] Yet the publication of Darwin's work had the effect of popularizing evolutionary thinking, even if his ideas were misunderstood or misinterpreted. Subsequent thinkers would attempt to find justification for their preferred social or political views in Darwinian evolutionary biology.[7] Marx considered Darwin to have found a scientific justification for his own views on socio-economic evolution, and Darwin was also appropriated by racists and proponents of chauvinistic nationalism. Indeed, efforts to interpret human social evolution within the context of a pseudo-Darwinian biological framework became rather open-ended in nature. Proponents of social reform,

5   Peter J. Bowler, *The Non-Darwinian Revolution: Reinterpreting a Historical Myth* (Baltimore: Johns Hopkins University Press, 1988), 9–10, 43–44, 24–28, 40–45.

6   *Ibid.*, 9–14.

7   *Ibid.*, 132–58.

humanitarians, advocates of predatory capitalism, utopians, racial supremacy theorists, and proponents of class warfare all appealed to Darwin as a justification for their beliefs, all of which were rooted in fundamental misunderstandings of Darwin's actual ideas.[8] It was the philosophy of Nietzsche that provided the interpretive framework of human history that was the most compatible with the implications of genuine Darwinism.

The Revolt Against Reason and Progress: The Philosophy of Nietzsche

If Darwinian evolutionary biology exploded the nineteenth-century idea of progress in the realm of the natural sciences, it was the thought of Nietzsche that provided the most far-reaching assault on the presumptions of the time in the world of philosophy. Nietzsche is perhaps most well-known for his statements concerning the "death of God," but the meaning of the "death of God" in Nietzschean philosophy involves a good deal more than mere conventional atheism. Other prominent intellectual atheists had come before Nietzsche such as Diderot, Baron d'Holbach, and (by implication) Hume, and he was by no means the inventor of modern atheism.[9] While Nietzsche was certainly an "anti-theological" thinker in the sense of rejecting a theistic world view in a conventional religious sense, his notion of the "death of God" was also intended as a critique of the intellectual presumptions of his own era, including those of intellectual elites who had rejected conventional religious faith. While Nietzsche was an atheist, materialist, and rationalist of a kind comparable to the most radical Enlightenment thinkers, his outlook sharply diverges from the Enlightenment tradition with regards to the role of reason in human life and thought.

Nietzsche regarded the Enlightenment emphasis on reason as having the effect of denying the role of the passions in forming human character, and shaping human action and human societies.

---

8   *Ibid.*, 166–73.

9   Gay, *The Enlightenment*, 63–64, 103, 105, 407–19.

He contrasted the Enlightenment's orientation towards reason with the earlier manifestations and emphasis on the passions he considered to have been made manifest by the Renaissance. He compared these two eras within the framework of his famous Apollonian/Dionysian dichotomy. The Apollonian aspect of human essence is the rational, logical, prudent, and restrained. The Dionysian is the instinctual, impulsive, and emotive. Nietzsche was not a skeptic of the passions in the manner of Hobbes or Burke, who regarded human passion and feeling as prone towards dangerous excesses and in need of restraint. Instead, he counseled human beings to live dangerously. Nietzsche regarded the passionate and the irrational (or non-rational) as the foundation of all high cultures, which he in turn considered to be apex of human existence. The Greeks had emphasized and explored the passions, rather than having feared or shunned them, and for this reason the Greeks had produced the highest of hitherto existing human civilizations. Nietzsche vehemently opposed the rising egalitarian sentiments and trends towards mass society and mass democracy of his era. Only an elite motivated by the passions can produce a high culture. An egalitarian society would be a society of weak and fearful mediocrities concerned only with comfort and safety.

The "death of God" was intended as an attack on philosophical idealism of the kind retained by Kant and Hegel as much as it was an attack on the Christian faith. Nietzsche's philosophy insisted that there is no transcendent or metaphysical foundation for ethics, morality, or justice. Values of this kind are mere human constructions. They have no meaning aside from what human beings, individually or collectively, assign to them. Nietzsche likewise rejected the view of history represented by Hegel's historicism. One of Nietzsche's earliest works, *The Use and Abuse of History*, is an attack on Hegel.[10] The linear view of history contained within Hegel's philosophical system had

---

10 Werner J. Dannhauser, "Friedrich Nietzsche," in History of Political Philosophy, 3rd ed., ed. Leo Strauss and Joseph Cropsey (Chicago: University of Chicago Press, 1987), 829–31.

many precedents in Western thought, with roots going back as least as far as Aristotle. According to Nietzsche, history has no purpose. It is merely a series of events that have no meaning in and of themselves, other than subjective meanings adopted by individuals and human groups relative to their own time, place, and experiences. Nietzsche's philosophy was an attack on virtually the entire legacy of Western metaphysics since the time of Plato.

Nietzsche regarded the nineteenth-century idea of progress, and the myriad of ideologies, movements, and causes of the time that were a manifestation of this idea to be superstitions every bit as much as the theological superstitions that dominated the Christian era. His parable of the madman found in *The Gay Science* is to be interpreted in this way.[11] Nietzsche is ridiculing the intellectuals of his time who believe they have attained a superior state of enlightenment, and who regard themselves as the progenitors of a higher civilization. He is instead arguing that the thinkers of his time have not yet fully recognized the consequences of the "death of God" for Western civilization. Instead, they are simply trying to replace old dogmas and pieties with new ones. Among these new gods are socialism, liberalism, utopianism, humanism, nationalism, democracy, pseudo-scientific racism of the kind represented by thinkers such as Houston Stewart Chamberlain,[12] and the anti-Semitism of his former friend Richard Wagner. Such efforts are dismissed by Nietzsche as methods of avoiding or postponing the existential crisis that Western civilization would ultimately have to face. Nietzsche attacked even the conservatives of his era for making too many concessions to rising egalitarian movements such as democracy and socialism, and for retaining their allegiance to the corpse of Christianity. He dismissed the traditional European aristocracies as weak and in a state of decay, and he also opposed the rising nationalist movements of his time as symptomatic

---

11   *Friedrich Nietzsche, A Nietzsche Reader*, ed. and trans. R. J. Hollingdale (London: Penguin Books, 1977), 202–3.

12   Houston Stewart Chamberlain, *Foundations of the Nineteenth Century*, 2 vols., trans. John Lees (New York: Howard Fertig, 1968 [1899]).

of the egalitarian mass societies of mediocre individuals he saw on the horizon. Nietzsche presciently suggested that the twentieth century would be a time of great wars between the rising ideological mass movements of his own time, and that the existential crisis of civilization would be fully realized only in the twenty-first century.

Nietzsche's prophecy that the twentieth century would be a time of war on an unprecedented scale between polarized ideological forces found its realization in the Great War and then the Second World War, and the destructiveness of the latter surpassed even the shocking brutality of the former. The suffering and death generated by the two world wars, and the invention of weapons technology with the capacity to destroy all of mankind demolished the nineteenth-century faith in progress and pushed postwar intellectuals towards a confrontation with the nihilistic implications of modern science and philosophy of the kind Nietzsche had previously written about. Existentialism, with its implicitly or explicitly Nietzschean roots, became the prevailing philosophical outlook for intellectuals in the mid to late twentieth century. Existentialism represents an effort to confront the crisis of nihilism suggested by Nietzsche and the serious problems this crisis poses for human ethics and the question of meaning. If existence has no meaning, then what is the basis for proper human behavior? If God is dead, is everything permitted, as Dostoevsky suggested? The struggles of existentialist thinkers with these questions are famously illustrated, for instance, by the efforts of the feminist-existentialist Simone de Beauvoir to establish a framework of ethics in the face of the meaninglessness of existence by pointing to the commonness of the human experience, and the possibility of creating shared virtues and values that advance human interests in the realm of lived experience, even if these values ultimately have no objective or cosmic foundation or meaning.[13] Her companion Jean-Paul Sartre argued that one could create one's own meaning by participating in the social or political activities

---

13   Simone de Beauvoir, *The Ethics of Ambiguity* (Secaucus, NJ: Citadel Press, 1948).

of one's time or even by embracing the irrational by, for example, becoming a devout Christian or a militant Communist. Sartre himself chose the latter.

The Future

Nietzsche predicted that it would be well into the twenty-first century before Western thought fully confronted the crisis of nihilism. It would thus far appear that he was correct. Western thought since the Enlightenment has attempted to compensate for the loss of the old faith by replacing the discredited Christian world view with new faiths and new pieties. As these have become increasingly difficult to justify within a framework of rationality and a belief in inevitable "progress," Western intellectuals have increasingly retreated into the irrational. This is illustrated by the curious phenomena of the present efforts by Western intellectual elites to embrace postmodernism, with its accompanying moral and cultural relativism, while simultaneously embracing the egalitarian-universalist-humanist moralistic zealotry popularly labeled "political correctness" and espousing with great piousness such liberal crusades as "human rights," "anti-racism," "gay liberation," feminism, environmentalism, and the like. Such an outlook, which combines extreme moralism in the cultural and political realm, complete moral relativism in the philosophical or metaphysical realm, and at times even falls into subjectivism in the epistemological realm,[14] is fundamentally irrational, of course. That such an outlook has become so deeply entrenched indicates that Western intellectuals are desperately working to avoid a full confrontation with the crisis of nihilism.

Vilfredo Pareto argued that civilizations die when their elites lose faith in their own civilization to such a degree that the will to survive no longer exists. Western political and cultural elites presently exhibit abiding contempt for the legacy of their civilization, as demonstrated by their attachment to anti-Western

---

14 Michel Foucault, *Madness and Civilization: A History of Insanity in the Age of Reason* (New York: Vintage Books, 1965 [1961]).

ideologies such as "multiculturalism" and support for political policies, such as permitting mass immigration into the West from the Third World, that ultimately mean the demographic overrun and death of Western civilization. The presumption of present-day elites is that dramatic demographic alteration can transpire without consequences of significance, or that the overthrow of Western civilization itself may even be desirable. The prevalence of such attitudes once again indicates that cultural nihilism has become rather deeply entrenched. Yet this nihilism has been thus far masked by liberal-humanist platitudes of escalating silliness. It remains to be seen what will eventually bring this crisis to the forefront. Genuine threats to the survival of Western civilization itself may well force such a confrontation. These might include the threat of nuclear terrorism, economic collapse, or ecological catastrophe, the depletion of resources on which civilization has become dependent, or confrontation with an ideological rival that poses an existential threat. As demographic change on a magnitude that threatens cultural dispossession becomes increasingly imminent, and as the consequences of such become increasingly undeniable, perhaps a belated cultural awakening and renewal will begin. Otherwise, it may well be the case that Western modernity and post-modernity will eventually suffer the same fate as the classical Greco-Roman civilization of antiquity.

Nietzsche the Visionary

A Reflection on the Nature of a Civilization Guided by Nietzschean Values

Friedrich Nietzsche suggested in the nineteenth century that the crisis of Western civilization generated by modernity's overthrow of the traditional European order and the loss of faith resulting from the torpedoing of traditional theology by advancements in human knowledge would have repercussions that would endure for two centuries. As the twenty-first century now enters its second decade, the confrontation with that crisis becomes ever more imminent.[1] At present, Western civilization continues to exhibit symptoms of advanced decay and the five hundred year position of Western Europe and its colonial offspring as the dominant centers of power on the earthly stage is steadily being eclipsed by the rise of new great powers represented by such nations as Russia, China, India, and Brazil. Likewise, mass immigration from the Third World into the West threatens to erode the demographic majority of indigenous European peoples in their traditional homelands by the middle to latter part of the century. The egalitarian ethos that provides the foundation of the self-legitimating ideology of the Western ruling classes becomes ever more absurd in its pronouncements and oppressive in its practices with each passing decade.

Future historians will likely look back on the contemporary West as a madhouse where the classic virtues of heroism, high culture, nobility, self-respect, and reason had almost completely disappeared,

---

1   Keith Preston, "The Nietzschean Prophecies: Two Hundred Years of Nihilism and the Coming Crisis of Western Civilization," *The Radical Tradition: Philosophy, Metapolitics & the Conservative Revolution*, edited by Troy Southgate (Primordial Traditions, 2011).

along with the characteristics of adulthood generally. The present era is the era of the Last Man. The legacy of mass democracy and the values of therapeutic liberalism has been the creation of a culture of infantilism. The morality of *ressentiment* is now the public morality. The guiding principles of contemporary liberal democracies are an all-pervasive consumerism and loudly proclaiming one's own status as an official victim of historic or cosmic injustices, whether real or imaginary. Self-indulgence has been surpassed only by self-pity as the guiding principle of an individual's relationship to the wider society. The commercial values of capitalism, the egalitarian values of Marxism, the psychological values of therapeutic culture, and the tendency toward mob rule inherent in mass democracy have been synthesized by modern societies in such a way as to make the wider and more fundamental values related to the preservation and perpetuation of civilization itself virtually impotent. Perhaps even more dreadful has been the exportation of these manifestations of cultural degeneration to nearly every corner of the globe. The Americanization process generated by globalization brings with it a cancer that threatens the survival of ancient cultures that have thus far endured for millennia.

Nietzsche was one of the great visionaries who recognized this process as it was unfolding even in its early stages. In contrast to the notion of progress that dominated so much of nineteenth century thought, Nietzsche regarded much of the history of Western civilization itself as a process of degeneration and decline. The advent of Platonic thought marked a degenerative departure from the time of the pre-Socratics, whom he regarded as representing the peak era of classical civilization. The Christian conquest of the classical world was still further degeneration and, indeed, the time when cultural rot really began to take root. Modernity carried the degenerative process even further to the point where, in the latter part of the nineteenth century, Western civilization had reached the terminal stage. Nietzsche correctly predicted that the twentieth century would be a time of great warfare between mass ideological movements and that this great convulsion of

Western civilization would be the prelude to the confrontation with the crisis of nihilism in the twenty-first century.[2]

The most poignant question raised by Nietzsche's philosophy involves the matter of what will emerge on the other side of Western civilization's historical trajectory once modernity and post-modernity have finally expired. It would appear that there are two primary routes which the unfolding of Western history may take. One of these is the extinction of Western civilization itself resulting from the combined forces of a loss of international power, internal rot, and demographic overrun. The other would be some sort of cultural renewal and awakening. It is this latter option for which the vision of Nietzsche provides inspiration. What would a future post-postmodern Western civilization actually look like? What would be its guiding values, mores, social structures, and political institutions? Nietzsche himself was rather vague on what his ideal type of society might be. So Nietzsche's own preferences or inclinations regarding such questions have to be inferred rather than directly discerned.

It is clear enough that Nietzsche was not and would not today be any kind of conventional "conservative." Indeed, Nietzsche had little regard for the conservatives of even his own time. He regarded the European nobility as decadent and unwilling to fight to retain its historic and traditional place when confronted with the rising egalitarian movements of the era. His admonition that men should aspire to greater cruelty is to be interpreted in light of his criticisms of the weakness of the noble classes. Nietzsche was a firm believer in Pareto's later axiom that he who becomes a lamb will be devoured by the wolves. He presciently saw that the European elite lacked the resolve to effectively counter the dangers posed by the growing ideological extremisms of the era. Nietzsche was the anti-Marx. He held even the conservative icon Bismarck in contempt for his embrace of egalitarian measures like universal suffrage and extensive welfare state legislation. Nietzsche also disdained the embrace of nationalism by modern

---

2   *Ibid.*

conservatives and opposed Bismarck's project of unification of Germany's previously sovereign regions under a centralized national regime. Instead, Nietzsche considered nationalism to be a manifestation of the same egalitarian tendencies of mass society as movements like socialism and communism.[3]

Contrary to the popular vulgarized interpretation of Nietzsche's thought as a forerunner to Fascism and National Socialism, Nietzsche was greatly alarmed by the growth of the modern state and of the tendency towards militarism resulting from the mass armies made possible by the modern state's powers of conscription. The form of the state that began to emerge in the nineteenth century exemplified Hobbes' characterization of the absolute ruler as an all-encompassing Leviathan. The massive growth of the state was the end result of the growth of mass political participation through democratic suffrage and of mass political movements reflecting popular ideological enthusiasm. This was a criticism of the modern state that would be revisited by twentieth century elite theorists such as Jose Ortega y Gasset. As Michael Kleen has observed:

The State was a temple in which the masses worshipped themselves. In exchange for catering to their needs and flattering their egos, the masses placed their collective will under the auspices of the State where they flourished like never before in history. For both Nietzsche and Ortega, that arrangement was Janus-faced, because although the masses grew in ever-increasing numbers—high art, music, education, and individualism in general suffered. European culture began to decay. Violence and militarism (especially of the uniform variety) became the order of the day.[4]

---

3   Werner J. Dannhauser, "Friedrich Nietzsche," *History of Political Philosophy*, edited by Joseph Cropsey and Leo Strauss. Chicago and London: University of Chicago Press, 1963, 1972, Third edition, 1987, pp. 829-831.

4   Michael Kleen, "Nietzsche and Ortega Juxtaposed," *Strike-the-Root.Com*, August 18, 2010. Archived at http://www.strike-the-root.com/nietzsche-and-ortega-juxtaposed

Clearly, a society which reflected Nietzschean ideals would rollback the growth of the modern Leviathan state and would eschew the national chauvinisms and aggressive militarism which characterized much of right-wing and left-wing politics alike during the twentieth century. In his own predictably unique way, Nietzsche might be said to have embraced a kind of pan-European cosmopolitanism. Says Michael Kleen:

> Unfortunately, Nietzsche did not leave a well thought out alternative to the modern state. Instead, he left his readers to infer his preference based on the political arrangements he criticized. In *Human, All-Too Human* (1878), however, he touched on nationalism and the nation state, proposing that it would be a benefit to Europeans to abolish nations and breed a "European man" that would contain the best qualities of all peoples living on the continent. He envisioned a noble class that freely exchanged ideas across Europe. Based on his other arguments, we can surmise that Nietzsche was *not* advocating something along the lines of a European Union or a transnational state, but perhaps a collection of thousands of municipalities along the lines of the ancient Greek *polis*.[5]

This inference regarding what Nietzsche's preferred political model might have been seems apt enough given his suggestion that pre-Socratic classical civilization constituted the apex of Western cultural achievement.

Given Nietzsche's pronounced hostility to the state, it is interesting to note his disdain for the anarchist movements of his era. He apparently regarded these as secularized versions of Christian utopian other-worldliness.[6] This is a fair criticism given the strident millenarian strands to be found within classical

---

5   Michael Kleen, "Nietzsche and the State," *Strike-the-Root.Com*, July 15, 2010.
     Archived at http://www.strike-the-root.com/nietzsche-and-state

6   Charles Bufe, "Introduction," *The Philosophy of Friedrich Nietzsche*, by Henry Louis
     Mencken. San Francisco: See Sharp Press. Originally published in 1908.

anarchism, the influence of Rousseau-inspired egalitarianism on classical anarchist thought, and the embrace of anarchism by Christian moralists like Tolstoy. Nietzsche might be said to be a manifestation of a non-egalitarian anarchism, or an "anarchism of the Right," just as he is more widely known as an exponent of "atheism of the Right" with his strident critique of Christian slave-morality. It is also doubtful that Nietzsche would be particularly enamored of modern libertarian thought, with its roots in classical liberalism, its embrace of Enlightenment rationalism, and its vulgar reduction of social life to that of *homo economicus*. The rise of the classical bourgeoisie in the eighteenth and nineteenth centuries was accompanied by all of the social and political trends that Nietzsche detested: mass democracy, the centralized nation-state, imperialism, and massive national armies. If he regarded the hereditary European nobility as decrepit, he would have regarded the rising bourgeoisie upper middle class as even more degenerate than the aristocracy it aimed to replace. If the Christian foundations of the *ancien régime* represented a deterioration of classical civilization to Nietzsche, how much more deplorable would he have found the *economism* of the bourgeoisie.

Indeed, Nietzsche's contrast of the Appollonian and the Dionysian foreshadows the latter critique of the rationalization of modern life advanced by Weber. For Nietzsche, rationality leaves no space for the passions. Though his own atheism and materialism were clearly derivative of latter Enlightenment thought, Nietzsche himself was an admirer of the Renaissance, not the Enlightenment. One can only imagine the contempt Nietzsche would have for contemporary Western societies and their institutionalization of the morality of *ressentiment* and their preoccupation with safety and security. As Nietzsche counseled men to live dangerously, he would no doubt regard, for instance, the present trend towards redefining long established childhood games and toys as menacing hazards or ordinary foods as the near-equivalent of poisons as an affront to authentic virtue. He would no doubt regard the now all-pervasive institutionalization of what has been termed "political correctness" to be the ultimate in the elevation of slave-morality and the inversion of nobility. Nietzsche would likely regard contemporary therapeutic culture as a form of human degeneration that even he might have been previously inclined to regard as impossible. He would no doubt observe the circus-like atmosphere of contemporary American politics and wonder, "How can this be?" If he were a contemporary man, Nietzsche might well observe the present state of Western culture and repeat the words of Christ at Gethsamane: "*Let this cup pass from me!*"

A Nietzschean civilization would be one where men were once again not only invited but encouraged to live dangerously. Clearly, such a society would be an aristocracy, but not just any kind of aristocracy. It is doubtful that Nietzsche would have seriously regarded the hereditary nobility as a manifestation of his own ideal. An authentically Nietzschean aristocracy would certainly maintain more stringent requirements for admission than mere accident of birth. A Nietzschean aristocracy would therefore be an aristocracy of merit rather than inheritance, but it would not be the pseudo-aristocracy of the bourgeoisie elites for whom prowess at money-making represents the highest human type. Nor would it be the New Class bureaucratic elite that emerged in the twentieth century and from which much of the contemporary upper middle class is drawn.[7] It is this class that is at present challenging the domination of the traditional bourgeoisie.[8] Nietzsche would have certainly regarded the New Class as even more degenerative than the bourgeoisie itself. Nor would the aristocracy of merit be comprised of a set of totalitarian dictators of the kind normally identified with Fascism, Communism, or National Socialism. The political institutions of a prototypical Nietzschean society would be neither feudal nor capitalist nor social democratic nor totalitarian.

---

7   Alvin W. Gouldner, *The Future of Intellectuals and the Rise of the New Class*. New York: Continuum Publishing Service, 1979.

8   Scott Locklin, "Social Classes: The Upper Middle Class," *AlternativeRight.Com*, August 17, 2010. Archived at http://www.alternativeright.com/main/blogs/zeitgeist/social-classes-the-upper-middle-class/

It is clear that in such a society economic values would play a secondary role to cultural and aristocratic values. The commercial class and the political class would not be allowed to merge in the way that they have in modern bourgeoisie societies. As Nietzsche advocated a frank atheism, it also obvious that religious institutions would likewise play a secondary role and remain separated from the state in the same manner as contemporary liberal societies. This does not necessarily mean that society as a whole would espouse atheism. Atheism may well retain its present status as the dominant perspective of intellectual elites with the common people and a minority of elites practicing the religion most compatible with their own cultural identity and familial ancestry. The renewed interest in recent times among Western peoples in primordial faiths and the growth of various forms of paganism may be an indication of a revival of non-Christian traditional Western faiths in the future. Christianity may well have to share space on the cultural stage with Odinism or Asatru at some point in the future just as it now increasingly has to share space with Wicca, Islam, Eastern mysticism, Deism, the myriad of "New Age" sects, and so forth. Tradition would certainly be an important aspect of a society organized as an aristocracy of merit, but tradition would not be an end unto itself. Nietzsche was, after all, a revolutionary whose thinking was more radical in its implications than even the thought of Marx. Tradition in a civilization guided by the ideals of Nietzsche would be regarded as a continuum that connects the present with the past and which regards the present as a bridge from the past to the future. Tradition would likewise be considered as a force which provides the individual with a sense of place within the context of these wider historical forces. Yet such a reverence for tradition would not imply stasis. Tradition would be regarded as pathway in an ongoing journey and not a final endpoint.

The most compelling question that arises from speculation on the nature of a Nietzschean society is the one that considers from where a revolutionary aristocracy would arise. Just as an aristocracy of this kind would not be one whose claim to merit was rooted in mere financial acumen, so would such an aristocracy necessarily be more than a band of political opportunists who happened to seize power through guile, connivance, and manipulation.

Though Nietzsche advised men to increase their cruelty, it does not necessarily follow that a Nietzschean aristocracy would be devoid of the traditional principle of *noblesse oblige*. The Nietzschean elites are not tyrants. The demise of institutions which Nietzsche abhorred such as mass democracy, the modern state, the domination of commercial interests, decrepit religious denominations, and mass armies would no doubt strengthen other institutions, including many that are at present being smothered by the forces of modernity. The most obvious among these are the family, tribe, clan, and community. Still others are guilds, fraternities, cultural organizations, educational institutions that exist independently of the wider political apparatus of mass democracy, philanthropies, localized associations for the pursuit of community activities, law, science, art, athletics, professions, labor associations, farmers association, citizen posses, regional militias, and many more possible examples. Within each of these kinds of human social arrangements, there would likely arise an elite comprised of individuals of superior ability and virtue who came to be regarded by the larger community specifically and the wider society generally as deserving of their position due to their greater merit.

Perhaps areas of social life requiring highly specialized levels of expertise would be governed by appointees from scholarly institutions devoted to learning and the cultivation of virtue and wisdom on the part of their individual devotees. Erik von Kuehnelt-Leddihn was fond of pointing to the traditional Chinese civil service examination system as one reflecting the ideals of meritocracy. The scholars who comprised the Mandarin class were drawn from the ranks of those demonstrating superior skill and ability. This was not a hereditary class but one where even the lowliest peasants with remarkable talents could achieve self-advancement.

Indeed, Kuehnelt-Leddihn observed that one of the weaknesses of the Right was its failure to offer a utopia of its own as a counter to the utopias proposed by the Left.[9] It is in the thought of Nietzsche that a very generalized blueprint for the intellectual backdrop of a "Utopia of the Right" can be found. With the emergence of contemporary ideologies like National-Anarchism, a glimpse becomes available into what the future of civilization might be once the era of the Last Man has passed. As one anonymous commentator has suggested:

> I think that the future will be a world of dizzying social complexity, replete with small city-states with governments ranging the gamut from democratic to monarchical to theocratic, surrounded by vast hinterlands filled with eco-villages and wild ranges where hunter gatherer humans chase wild game and forage for nuts and berries, while vast trade fleets of ultra-light zeppelins transfer goods and services all over the planet, and transhumanist consciousnesses zip through endless, decentralized computer networks maintained by industrial syndicates a million workers strong, who build satellites and launch them into orbit to maintain a global network of communication so primitivists can use cell-phones to trade furs for plastic-composite bows... and so on.[10]

The decline of existentialism and postmodernism may well represent the final breath of Western philosophy and the fulfillment of Nietzsche's prophecy of the 21st century as the time when Western civilization would have to face the crisis of nihilism. This dissolution of Western philosophy corresponds with the dissolution of Western civilization itself.[11] The pronounced decadence of present day Western elites who

---

9   Erik von Kuehnelt-Leddihn, *Leftism Revisited: From De Sade and Marx to Hitler and Pol Pot*. Washington, D.C.: Regnery Gateway, 1990.

10   I am grateful to Michael Parish for this insight.

11   Chris George, "Wisdom and Vision," *New Kind of Mind*, April 11, 2011. Archived at http://www.newkindofmind.com/2011/04/wisdom-and-vision.html

actively seek to undermine and destroy their own civilization is the manifestation of the suicidal nihilism of the Last Man. The seemingly inevitable demographic transformation of the West over the next century may well mark the dawn of a new "post-Western West" out of which new primordial myths will arise.

Our Struggle Is Neither Moral Nor Intellectual, But Physical

The notion that there is any inherent relationship between one's views on moral philosophy and one's views on political philosophy is an idea that I tend to be rather skeptical of. For example, political conservatives can be either devout Christians who cling to one or another conception of divinely decreed morality or materialists and moral skeptics. Likewise, political liberals can be found among both adherents of the Social Gospel and secular humanists. For those such as I who reject the state entirely, the question remains of what sort of approach to moral philosophy, if any, serves as the basis for our political perspective.

Much of classical anarchist thought is implicitly rooted in the egalitarian humanist thought of the likes of Jean-Jacques Rousseau and the progressive, evolutionary view of history formulated by G. W. F. Hegel and some of the social Darwinists, notably Herbert Spencer. According to this view, human nature is essentially benign but has been corrupted or stifled by less than optimal social institutions or lack of education. As human knowledge increases and social institutions evolve, the benign, benevolent, and cooperative qualities of human nature will, according to this theory, eventually shine through. This kind of uniquely naive utopianism emerged during the eighteenth and nineteenth centuries, a time of immensely rapid political, economic, and scientific development. The achievements of that era unfortunately led to the foolish belief that virtually anything is possible so long as human beings maintained the proper commitment and applied themselves. Today, when we hear leftists talk about their ideals of a "world without hunger" or a "world without hate," and their constant rhetoric about "commitment," "awareness," and "raising consciousness," we know that the ghost of Rousseau walks among us. The problem, of course, is that not a shred of evidence exists to support this sort of outlook. There is no indication of human moral improvement, however defined, throughout the ages. The recently expired twentieth century produced some of the worst horrors in history—world wars, genocides, and nuclear weapons. Is this any sort of improvement over the cannibals and perpetrators of human sacrifice of ancient times?

Some anti-statists, such as the disciples of Murray Rothbard and Ayn Rand, attempt to justify their beliefs with some sort of "natural law" theory. This is largely a more consistent and well-developed version of the Lockean philosophy employed by the American revolutionaries. According to this view, the inalienable right of individuals to life, liberty, property, or the pursuit of happiness has somehow been decreed by nature. While this may have been a useful myth at the time of the ascendancy of classical liberalism, its seems on its surface to be little more than an arbitrary, quasi-religious, mystical doctrine that simply asserts what it wishes to prove. Historically, natural law doctrines have just as often been used to justify various types of authoritarianism, such as the "natural" superiority of some races over others or Catholic opposition to "unnatural" acts like contraception, than any sort of liberty.

Other anti-statists are utilitarian ethicists who defend liberty on the grounds that it brings about the "best" results. While it is certainly important to be able to demonstrate that anarchism is workable in practice and that free market economics produces results which most people would find favorable, utilitarianism as a moral outlook seems rather arbitrary as well. Why the greatest good for the greatest number? Why not the greatest good for the smartest, the strongest, the healthiest, the most creative, or the most attractive, or the members of some particular racial or religious group? The Benthamite calculus involving the attempt to weigh the overall balance of pleasure over pain seems impossible to measure in the real world. Why prioritize pleasure? What about people who argue that "suffering is good for the soul"? And why should I care if everyone else is miserable so long as I am happy?

Those who attempt to make a religious case for liberty seem to have the weakest position of all. Even if one accepts religious belief as legitimate, this says nothing about the problem of power. No religious denomination that has ever obtained political power has ever created anything even remotely approaching a free society. An occasional religious anarchist or libertarian can be found, but most seriously religious people tend towards theocracy more than anything else. Even those who support formal church/state separation usually believe that the state should legislate or regulate with regards to matters of personal or religious "morality" (abortion, homosexuality, drug use, pornography, etc.). Many espouse statist economic views and/or a militarist/imperialist foreign policy outlook as well.

The natural tendency of nearly all human beings is to favor themselves over others. Most people develop the views on politics, philosophy, ethics, morality, etc., that are most consistent with their own needs and desires and the interests of their peer groups or culture of origin. Most people exhibit very little capacity for independent thinking or moral perception beyond self-interest and the influence of peers and leaders. Because different individuals and groups have conflicting interests and value systems, social conflict inevitably results. Hobbes believed that the only solution to this dilemma was an all-powerful state that would restrain the predatory inclinations of individuals and competing social forces for the sake of preserving order and civilization. The problem with Hobbes' position should be obvious enough. Who restrains the restrainers? Hobbes saw the choices as either chaos or tyranny. He opted for the latter.

I largely agree with Hobbes' analysis but I reject his conclusion. There seems to me to be a third way between absolutism and disorder. I am referring to the "spontaneous order" described by

Hayek that naturally accompanies freedom and decentralization. Because human beings are predators by nature, no one should ever hold power over another. Freedom allows individuals the means to cooperate with others for the sake of their own mutual self-interest without resorting to force or coercion. Anarchism is the political philosophy most capable of accommodating the greatest diversity of value systems, thereby minimizing the harm generated by social conflict. The idea of dispersion of power inherent in anarchism serves to erect a safeguard against the disasters that typically accompany concentrations of power. The result is a natural, organic order that tends towards the stabilization and harmonization of society. However, I do not regard this realization as grounds for any sort of objective morality. None of this has anything to say concerning the matter as to whether economic prosperity, social peace, and individual freedom are desirable ends in and of themselves. The conservative icon Russell Kirk regarded liberty as defensible only as a means to "virtue," however defined. Some argue that peace and prosperity breed weakness, mediocrity, and selfishness. Mussolini maintained that war is good because it advances the strong and eliminates the weak thereby contributing to the overall improvement of the species.

Like Bertrand Russell, I tend to regard moral questions as matters of subjective individual emotions and opinions. Ultimately, existence is predicated on Stirner's amoral war of each against all. Does this absence of any objective morality mean that "everything is permitted" as Nietzsche insisted? While there may be no abstract, metaphysical, cosmic source of moral imperatives, human beings are still bound by natural and physical laws (though some postmodern thinkers seem to deny even this). Means have to be consistent with the ends one wishes to pursue. Machiavelli regarded "morality" as a matter of simple expediency in the maintenance of power. The flip side of this, and a matter of supreme importance for anarchists, involves those who would resist power. Here a type of "reverse Machiavellianism" comes into play where the moral means is that which furthers resistance to power. The implication of this is that our struggle against the state is neither moral nor intellectual but physical. Does this mean that "might makes right"? No, it means that "might makes might" with "right" being an individual value judgment. Those among us who have decided that freedom and anarchism are "right," for whatever reason, need to acquire the might necessary to achieve our objectives.

This is a question that I struggled with for some years. When I first started out in this fight, I was a much more an orthodox leftist than I am now and I held views not unlike the Rousseauian-Hegelian perspective described above. When I became interested in free market economics, I was initially attracted to Rothbard's natural rights theory but eventually dismissed it as wishful thinking. The way I finally worked it out was when I watched a documentary on public television concerning the early 1960s trial of Nazi mass murderer and war criminal Adolf Eichmann. I kept asking myself, what made me right and what made Eichmann wrong? The matter of sheer self-interest? I would not want to live under a Nazi state. Natural sympathy? I had a certain empathic regard for those exterminated in the ovens and gas chambers. Logical principles? I could see no basis for the extermination programs as far as matters of expediency were concerned. Yet Eichmann's self-interest and sympathies were clearly much different from mine and irrationalism is a core tenet of Nazism.

The theologian C. S. Lewis once remarked:

> What was the sense in saying the enemy [i.e., the Nazis] were in the wrong unless Right is a real thing which the Nazis at bottom knew as well as we did and ought to have practised? If they had no notion of what we mean by right, then, though we might still have had to fight them, we could no more have blamed them for that than for the colour of their hair.

Yet, as Noam Chomsky has repeatedly pointed out, the Nazi archives provide ample evidence of the Nazis' conviction of the rightness of their cause. The key part of Lewis' statement is "we might still have had to fight them." Questions of self-interest, natural sympathies, and practical social considerations are in and of themselves sufficient reason to resist phenomenon such as Nazism. No objective morality is necessary.

As mentioned, our struggle against the state is primarily physical in nature. If someone is motivated to fight the state because they believe in "natural rights" or that anarchism will produce "the greatest good for the greatest number," then more power to them. Myths can be a source of inspiration in any conflict. However, the real issue involves the need for our anarchist popular organizations, intermediary institutions, citizen militias, economic enterprises, common law courts, and other forms of organization needed to obtain the resources, influence, and raw social power, in the Nockian sense, to bring down the state and prevent its return by violent means if necessary. All of the moral theory and academic analysis in the universe will be insufficient if we cannot physically resist our enemies.

Ernst Junger

Ernst Junger: The Resolute Life of an Anarch

Perhaps the most interesting, poignant and, possibly, threatening type of writer and thinker is the one who not only defies conventional categorizations of thought but also offers a deeply penetrating critique of those illusions many hold to be the most sacred. Ernst Junger (1895-1998), who first came to literary prominence during Germany's Weimar era as a diarist of the experiences of a front line storm trooper during the Great War, is one such writer. Both the controversial nature of his writing and its staying power are demonstrated by the fact that he remains one of the most important yet widely disliked literary and cultural figures of twentieth century Germany. As recently as 1993, when Junger would have been ninety-eight years of age, he was the subject of an intensely hostile exchange in the "New York Review of Books" between an admirer and a detractor of his work.[1] On the occasion of his one hundredth birthday in 1995, Junger was the subject of a scathing, derisive musical performed in East Berlin. Yet Junger was also the recipient of Germany's most prestigious literary awards, the Goethe Prize and the Schiller Memorial Prize. Junger, who converted to Catholicism at the age of 101, received a commendation from Pope John Paul II and was an honored guest of French President Francois Mitterrand and German Chancellor Helmut Kohl at the Franco-German reconciliation ceremony at Verdun in 1984.

---

1   Ian Buruma, "The Anarch at Twilight", *New York Review of Books*, Volume 40, No. 12, June 24, 1993. Hilary Barr, "An Exchange on Ernst Junger", *New York Review of Books*, Volume 40, No. 21, December 16, 1993.

Though he was an exceptional achiever during virtually every stage of his extraordinarily long life, it was his work during the Weimar period that not only secured for a Junger a presence in German cultural and political history, but also became the standard by which much of his later work was evaluated and by which his reputation was, and still is, debated.[2]

Ernst Junger was born on March 29, 1895 in Heidelberg, but was raised in Hanover. His father, also named Ernst, was an academically trained chemist who became wealthy as the owner of a pharmaceutical manufacturing business, finding he was successful enough to essentially retire while he was still in his forties. Though raised as an evangelical Protestant, Junger's father did not believe in any formal religion, nor did his mother, Karoline, an educated middle class German woman whose interests included Germany's rich literary tradition and the cause of women's emancipation. His parents' politics seem to have been liberal, though not radical, in the manner not uncommon to the rising bourgeoisie of Germany's upper middle class during the pre-war period. It was in this affluent, secure bourgeoisie environment that Ernst Junger grew up. Indeed, many of Junger's later activities and professed beliefs are easily understood as a revolt against the comfort and safety of his upbringing. As a child, he was an avid reader of the tales of adventurers and soldiers, but a poor academic student who did not adjust well to the regimented Prussian educational system. Junger's instructors consistently complained of his inattentiveness. As an adolescent, he became involved with the Wandervogel, roughly the German equivalent of the Boy Scouts.[3]

It was while attending a boarding school near his parents' home in 1913, at the age of seventeen, that Junger first demonstrated his first propensity for what might be called an "adventurist" way

---

2   Nevin, Thomas. *Ernst Junger and Germany: Into the Abyss*, 1914-1945. Durham, N.C.: Duke University Press, 1996, pp. 1-7. Loose, Gerhard. *Ernst Junger*. New York: Twayne Publishers, 1974, preface.

3   Nevin, pp. 9-26. Loose, p. 21

of life. With only six months left before graduation, Junger left school, leaving no word to his family as to his destination. Using money given to him for school-related fees and expenses to buy a firearm and a railroad ticket to Verdun, Junger subsequently enlisted in the French Foreign Legion, an elite military unit of the French armed forces that accepted enlistees of any nationality and had a reputation for attracting fugitives, criminals and career mercenaries. Junger had no intention of staying with the Legion. He only wanted to be posted to Africa, as he eventually was. Junger then deserted, only to be captured and sentenced to jail. Eventually his father found a capable lawyer for his wayward son and secured his release. Junger then returned to his studies and underwent a belated high school graduation. However, it was only a very short time later that Junger was back in uniform.[4]

Warrior and War Diarist

Ernst Junger immediately volunteered for military service when he heard the news that Germany was at war in the summer of 1914. After two months of training, Junger was assigned to a reserve unit stationed at Champagne. He was afraid the war would end before he had the opportunity to see any action. This attitude was not uncommon among many recruits or conscripts who fought in the war for their respective states. The question immediately arises as to why so many young people would wish to look into the face of death with such enthusiasm. Perhaps they really did not understand the horrors that awaited them. In Junger's case, his rebellion against the security and luxury of his bourgeoisie upbringing had already been ably demonstrated by his excursion with the French Foreign Legion. Because of his high school education, something that soldiers of more proletarian origins lacked, Junger was selected to train to become an officer. Shortly before beginning his officer's training, Junger was exposed to combat for the first time. From the start, he carried pocket-sized notebooks with him and recorded his observations on the front lines. His writings while at the front

---

4   Loose, p. 22. Nevin, pp. 27-37.

exhibit a distinctive tone of detachment, as though he is simply an observer watching while the enemy fires at others. In the middle part of 1915, Junger suffered his first war wound, a bullet graze to the thigh that required only two weeks of recovery time. Afterwards, he was promoted to the rank of lieutenant.[5]

At age twenty-one, Junger was the leader of a reconnaissance team at the Somme whose purpose was to go out at night and search for British landmines. Early on, he acquired the reputation of a brave soldier who lacked the preoccupation with his own safety common to most of the fighting men. The introduction of steel artifacts into the war, tanks for the British side and steel helmets for the Germans, made a deep impression on Junger. Wounded three times at the Somme, Junger was awarded the Iron Medal First Class. Upon recovery, he returned to the front lines. A combat daredevil, he once held out against a much larger British force with only twenty men. After being transferred to fight the French at Flanders, he lost ten of his fourteen men and was wounded in the left hand by a blast from French shelling. After being harshly criticized by a superior officer for the number of men lost on that particular mission, Junger began to develop contempt for the military hierarchy whom he regarded as having achieved their status as a result of their class position, frequently lacking combat experience of their own. In late 1917, having already experienced nearly three full years of combat, Junger was wounded for the fifth time during a surprise assault by the British. He was grazed in the head by a bullet, acquiring two holes in his helmet in the process. His performance in this battle won him the Knights Cross of the Hohenzollerns. In March 1918, Junger participated in another fierce battle with the British, losing 87 of his 150 men.[6]

Nothing impressed Junger more than personal bravery and endurance on the part of soldiers. He once "fell to the ground in tears" at the sight of a young recruit who had only days earlier

5   Nevin. p. 49.

6   *Ibid.*, p. 57

been unable to carry an ammunition case by himself suddenly being able to carry two cases of missiles after surviving an attack of British shells. A recurring theme in Junger's writings on his war experiences is the way in which war brings out the most savage human impulses. Essentially, human beings are given full license to engage in behavior that would be considered criminal during peacetime. He wrote casually about burning occupied towns during the course of retreat or a shift of position. However, Junger also demonstrated a capacity for merciful behavior during his combat efforts. He refrained from shooting a cornered British soldier after the foe displayed a portrait of his family to Junger. He was wounded yet again in August of 1918. Having been shot in the chest and directly through a lung, this was his most serious wound yet. After being hit, he still managed to shoot dead yet another British officer. As Junger was being carried off the battlefield on a stretcher, one of the stretcher carriers was killed by a British bullet. Another German soldier attempted to carry Junger on his back, but the soldier was shot dead himself and Junger fell to the ground. Finally, a medic recovered him and pulled him out of harm's way. This episode would be the end of his battle experiences during the Great War.[7]

In Storms of Steel

Junger's keeping of his wartime diaries paid off quite well in the long run. They were to become the basis of his first and most famous book, *In Storms of Steel*, published in 1920. The title was given to the book by Junger himself, having found the phrase in an Old Icelandic saga. It was at the suggestion of his father that Junger first sought to have his wartime memoirs published. Initially, he found no takers, antiwar sentiment being extremely high in Germany at the time, until his father at last arranged to have the work published privately. *In Storms of Steel* differs considerably from similar works published by war veterans during the same era, such as Erich Maria Remarque's *All Quiet on the Western Front* and John Dos Passos' *Three Soldiers*. Junger's book

---

7   *Ibid.*, p. 61

reflects none of the disillusionment with war by those experienced in its horrors of the kind found in these other works. Instead, Junger depicted warfare as an adventure in which the soldier faced the highest possible challenge, a battle to the death with a mortal enemy. Though Junger certainly considered himself to be a patriot and, under the influence of Maurice Barrès[8], eventually became a strident German nationalist, his depiction of military combat as an idyllic setting where human wills face the supreme test rose far above ordinary nationalist sentiments. Junger's warrior ideal was not merely the patriot fighting out of a profound sense of loyalty to his country or the stereotype of the dutiful soldier whose sense of honor and obedience compels him to follow the orders of his superiors in a headlong march towards death. Nor was the warrior prototype exalted by Junger necessarily an idealist fighting for some alleged greater good such as a political ideal or religious devotion. Instead, war itself is the ideal for Junger. On this question, he was profoundly influenced by Nietzsche, whose dictum "a good war justifies any cause," provides an apt characterization of Junger's depiction of the life (and death) of the combat soldier.[9]

This aspect of Junger's outlook is illustrated quite well by the ending he chose to give to the first edition of *In Storms of Steel*. Although the second edition (published in 1926) ends with the nationalist rallying cry, "Germany lives and shall never go under!", a sentiment that was deleted for the third edition published in 1934 at the onset of the Nazi era, the original edition ends simply with Junger in the hospital after being wounded for the

---

8   Maurice Barrès (September 22, 1862 - December 4, 1923) was a French novelist, journalist, an anti-semite, nationalist politician and agitator. Leaning towards the far-left in his youth as a Boulangist deputy, he progressively developed a theory close to Romantic nationalism and shifted to the right during the Dreyfus Affair, leading the Anti-Dreyfusards alongside Charles Maurras. In 1906, he was elected both to the Académie française and as deputy of the Seine department, and until his death he sat with the conservative Entente républicaine démocratique. A strong supporter of the Union sacréi(Holy Union) during World War I, Barrès remained a major influence of generations of French writers, as well as of monarchists, although he was not a monarchist himself. 9. Nevin, pp. 58, 71, 97.

9   Nevin, pp. 58, 71, 97.

final time and receiving word that he has received yet another commendation for his valor as a combat soldier. There is no mention of Germany's defeat a few months later. Nationalism aside, the book is clearly about Junger, not about Germany, and Junger's depiction of the war simultaneously displays an extraordinary level of detachment for someone who lived in the face of death for four years and a highly personalized account of the war where battle is first and foremost about the assertion of one's own "will to power" with clichéd patriotic pieties being of secondary concern.

Indeed, Junger goes so far as to say there were winners and losers on both sides of the war. The true winners were not those who fought in a particular army or for a particular country, but who rose to the challenge placed before them and essentially achieved what Junger regarded as a higher state of enlightenment. He believed the war had revealed certain fundamental truths about the human condition. First, the illusions of the old bourgeoisie order concerning peace, progress and prosperity had been inalterably shattered. This was not an uncommon sentiment during that time, but it is a revelation that Junger seems to revel in while others found it to be overwhelmingly devastating. Indeed, the lifelong champion of Enlightenment liberalism, Bertrand Russell, whose life was almost as long as Junger's and who observed many of the same events from a much different philosophical perspective, once remarked that no one who had been born before 1914 knew what it was like to be truly happy.[10]

A second observation advanced by Junger had to do with the role of technology in transforming the nature of war, not only in a purely mechanical sense, but on a much greater existential level. Before, man had commanded weaponry in the course of combat. Now weaponry of the kind made possible by modern technology and industrial civilization essentially commanded man. The machines did the fighting. Man simply resisted this

---

10   Schilpp, P. A. "The Philosophy of Bertrand Russell". Reviewed Hermann Weyl, *The American Mathematical Monthly*, Vol. 53, No. 4 (Apr., 1946), pp. 208-214.

external domination. Lastly, the supremacy of might and the ruthless nature of human existence had been demonstrated. Nietzsche was right. The tragic, Darwinian nature of the human condition had been revealed as an irrevocable law.

Storms of Steel was the first of several works based on his experiences as a combat officer that were written by Junger during the 1920s. *Copse 125* described a battle between two small groups of combatants. In this work, Junger continued to explore the philosophical themes present in his first work. The type of technologically driven warfare that emerged during the Great War is characterized as reducing men to automatons driven by airplanes, tanks and machine guns. Once again, jingoistic nationalism is downplayed as a contributing factor to the essence of combat soldier's spirit. Another work of Junger's from the early 1920s, *Battle as Inner Experience*, explored the psychology of war. Junger suggested that civilization itself was but a mere mask for the "primordial" nature of humanity that once again reveals itself during war. Indeed, war had the effect of elevating humanity to a higher level. The warrior becomes a kind of god-like animal, divine in his superhuman qualities, but animalistic in his bloodlust. The perpetual threat of imminent death is a kind of intoxicant. Life is at its finest when death is closest. Junger described war as a struggle for a cause that overshadows the respective political or cultural ideals of the combatants. This overarching cause is courage. The fighter is honor bound to respect the courage of his mortal enemy. Drawing on the philosophy of Nietzsche, Junger argued that the war had produced a "new race" that had replaced the old pieties, such as those drawn from religion, with a new recognition of the primacy of the "will to power".[11]

Conservative Revolutionary

Junger's writings about the war quickly earned him the status of a celebrity during the Weimar period. *Battle as Inner Experience* contained the prescient suggestion that the young men who had

11   Nevin, pp. 122, 125, 134, 136, 140, 173.

experienced the greatest war the world had yet to see at that point could never be successfully re-integrated into the old bourgeoisie order from which they came. For these fighters, the war had been a spiritual experience. Having endured so much only to see their side lose on such seemingly humiliating terms, the veterans of the war were aliens to the rationalistic, anti-militarist, liberal republic that emerged in 1918 at the close of the war. Junger was at his parents' home recovering from war wounds during the time of the attempted coup by the leftist workers' and soldiers' councils and subsequent suppression of these by the Freikorps. He experimented with psychoactive drugs such as cocaine and opium during this time, something that he would continue to do much later in life. Upon recovery, he went back into active duty in the much diminished German army. Junger's earliest works, such as *In Storms of Steel*, were published during this time and he also wrote for military journals on the more technical and specialized aspects of combat and military technology. Interestingly, Junger attributed Germany's defeat in the war simply to poor leadership, both military and civilian, and rejected the "stab in the back" legend that consoled less keen veterans.

After leaving the army in 1923, Junger continued to write; producing a novella about a soldier during the war titled *Sturm*, and also began to study the philosophy of Oswald Spengler. His first work as a philosopher of nationalism appeared in the Nazi paper *Volkischer Beobachter* in September, 1923. Critiquing the failed Marxist revolution of 1918, Junger argued that the leftist coup failed because of its lacking of fresh ideas. It was simply a regurgitation of the egalitarian outlook of the French Revolution. The revolutionary left appealed only to the material wants of the German people in Junger's views. A successful revolution would have to be much more than that. It would have to appeal to their spiritual or "folkish" instincts as well. Over the next few years Junger studied the natural sciences at the University of Leipzig and in 1925, at age thirty, he married nineteen-year-old Gretha von Jeinsen. Around this time, he also became a full-time political writer. Junger was hostile to Weimar democracy and its commercial bourgeoisie society. His emerging political ideal was one of an elite warrior caste that stood above petty partisan politics and the middle class obsession with material acquisition. Junger became involved with the the Stahlhelm, a right-wing veterans group, and was a contributor to its paper, *Die Standardite*. He associated himself with the younger, more militant members of the organization who favored an uncompromised nationalist revolution and eschewed the parliamentary system. Junger's weekly column in *Die Standardite* disseminated his nationalist ideology to his less educated readers. Junger's views at this point were a mixture of Spengler, Social Darwinism, and the traditionalist philosophy of the French rightist Maurice Barrès, opposition to the internationalism of the left that had seemingly been discredited by the events of 1914, irrationalism and anti-parliamentarianism. He took a favorable view of the working class and praised the Nazis' efforts to win proletarian sympathies. Junger also argued that a nationalist outlook need not be attached to one particular form of government, even suggesting that a liberal monarchy would be inferior to a nationalist republic.[12]

In an essay for *Die Standardite* titled "The Machine," Junger argued that the principal struggle was not between social classes or political parties but between man and technology. He was not anti-technological in a Luddite sense, but regarded the technological apparatus of modernity to have achieved a position of superiority over mankind which needed to be reversed. He was concerned that the mechanized efficiency of modern life produced a corrosive effect on the human spirit. Junger considered the Nazis' glorification of peasant life to be antiquated. Ever the realist, he believed the world of the rural people to be in a state of irreversible decline. Instead, Junger espoused a "metropolitan nationalism" centered on the urban working class. Nationalism was the antidote to the anti-particularist materialism of the Marxists who, in Junger's views, simply mirrored the liberals in their efforts to reduce the individual to a component of a mechanized mass society. The humanitarian rhetoric of the

---

12   *Ibid.*, pp. 75-91.

left Junger dismissed as the hypocritical cant of power-seekers feigning benevolence. He began to pin his hopes for a nationalist revolution on the younger veterans who comprised much of the urban working class.

In 1926, Junger became editor of *Arminius*, which also featured the writings of Nazi leaders like Alfred Rosenberg and Joseph Goebbels. In 1927, he contributed his final article to the Nazi paper, calling for a new definition of the "worker," one not rooted in Marxist ideology but the idea of the worker as a civilian counterpart to the soldier who struggles fervently for the nationalist ideal. Junger and Hitler had exchanged copies of their respective writings and a scheduled meeting between the two was canceled due to a change in Hitler's itinerary. Junger respected Hitler's abilities as an orator, but came to feel he lacked the ability to become a true leader. He also found Nazi ideology to be intellectually shallow, many of the Nazi movement's leaders to be talentless and was displeased by the vulgarity, crassly opportunistic and overly theatrical aspects of Nazi public rallies. Always an elitist, Junger considered the Nazis' pandering to the common people to be debased. As he became more skeptical of the Nazis, Junger began writing for a wider circle of readers beyond that of the militant nationalist right-wing. His works began to appear in the Jewish liberal Leopold Schwarzchild's *Das Tagebuch* and the "national-Bolshevik" Ernst Niekisch's *Widerstand*.

Junger began to assemble around himself an elite corps of bohemian, eccentric intellectuals who would meet regularly on Friday evenings. This group included some of the most interesting personalities of the Weimar period. Among them were the Freikorps veteran Ernst von Salomon, Otto von Strasser, who with his brother Gregor led a leftist anti-Hitler faction of the Nazi movement, the national-Bolshevik Niekisch, the Jewish anarchist Erich Muhsam who had figured prominently in the early phase of the failed leftist revolution of 1918, the American writer Thomas Wolfe and the expressionist writer

Arnolt Bronnen. Many among this group espoused a type of revolutionary socialism based on nationalism rather than class, disdaining the Nazis' opportunistic outreach efforts to the middle class. Some, like Niekisch, favored an alliance between Germany and Soviet Russia against the liberal-capitalist powers of the West. Occasionally, Joseph Goebbels would turn up at these meetings hoping to convert the group, particularly Junger himself, whose war writings he had admired, to the Nazi cause. These efforts by the Nazi propaganda master proved unsuccessful. Junger regarded Goebbels as a shallow ideologue who spoke in platitudes even in private conversation.[13]

The final break between Ernst Junger and the NSDAP occurred in September 1929. Junger published an article in Schwarzchild's *Tagebuch* attacking and ridiculing the Nazis as sell outs for having reinvented themselves as a parliamentary party. He also dismissed their racism and anti-Semitism as ridiculous, stating that according to the Nazis a nationalist is simply someone who "eats three Jews for breakfast." He condemned the Nazis for pandering to the liberal middle class and reactionary traditional conservatives "with lengthy tirades against the decline in morals, against abortion, strikes, lockouts, and the reduction of police and military forces." Goebbels responded by attacking Junger in the Nazi press, accusing him being motivated by personal literary ambition, and insisting this had caused him "to vilify the national socialist movement, probably so as to make himself popular in his new kosher surroundings" and dismissing Junger's attacks by proclaiming the Nazis did not "debate with renegades who abuse us in the smutty press of Jewish traitors."[14]

Junger on the Jewish Question

Junger held complicated views on the question of German Jews. He considered anti-Semitism of the type espoused by Hitler to be crude and reactionary. Yet his own version of nationalism

---

13   *Ibid.*, p. 107.
14   *Ibid.*, p. 108.

required a level of homogeneity that was difficult to reconcile with the sub national status of Germany Jewry. Junger suggested that Jews should assimilate and pledge their loyalty to Germany once and for all. Yet he expressed admiration for Orthodox Judaism and indifference to Zionism. Junger maintained personal friendships with Jews and wrote for a Jewish owned publication. During this time his Jewish publisher Schwarzchild published an article examining Junger's views on the Jews of Germany. Schwarzchild insisted that Junger was nothing like his Nazi rivals on the far right. Junger's nationalism was based on an aristocratic warrior ethos, while Hitler's was more comparable to the criminal underworld. Hitler's men were "plebian alley scum". However, Schwarzchild also characterized Junger's rendition of nationalism as motivated by little more than a fervent rejection of bourgeoisie society and lacking in attention to political realities and serious economic questions.[15]

The Worker

Other than *In Storms of Steel*, Junger's *The Worker: Mastery and Form* was his most influential work from the Weimar era. Junger would later distance himself from this work, published in 1932, and it was reprinted in the 1950s only after Junger was prompted to do so by Martin Heidegger.

In *The Worker*, Junger outlines his vision of a future state ordered as a technocracy based on workers and soldiers led by warrior elite. Workers are no longer simply components of an industrial machine, whether capitalist or communist, but have become a kind of civilian-soldier operating as an economic warrior. Just as the soldier glories in his accomplishments in battle, so does the worker glory in the achievements expressed through his work. Junger predicted that continued technological advancements would render the worker/capitalist dichotomy obsolete. He also incorporated the political philosophy of his friend Carl Schmitt into his worldview. As Schmitt saw international relations as a

---

15   *Ibid.*, pp. 109-111.

Hobbesian battle between rival powers, Junger believed each state would eventually adopt a system not unlike what he described in *The Worker*. Each state would maintain its own technocratic order with the workers and soldiers of each country playing essentially the same role on behalf of their respective nations. International affairs would be a crucible where the will to power of the different nations would be tested.

Junger's vision contains a certain amount of prescience. The general trend in politics at the time was a movement towards the kind of technocratic state Junger described. These took on many varied forms including German National Socialism, Italian Fascism, Soviet Communism, the growing welfare states of Western Europe and America's New Deal. Coming on the eve of World War Two, Junger's prediction of a global Hobbesian struggle between national collectives possessing previously unimagined levels of technological sophistication also seems rather prophetic. Junger once again attacked the bourgeoisie as anachronistic. Its values of material luxury and safety he regarded as unfit for the violent world of the future.[16]

The National Socialist Era

By the time Hitler came to power in 1933, Junger's war writings had become commonly used in high schools and universities as examples of wartime literature, and Junger enjoyed success within the context of German popular culture as well. Excerpts of Junger's works were featured in military journals. The Nazis tried to co-opt his semi-celebrity status, but he was uncooperative. Junger was appointed to the Nazified German Academy of Poetry, but declined the position. When the Nazi Party's paper published some of his work in 1934, Junger wrote a letter of protest. The Nazi regime, despite its best efforts to capitalize on his reputation, viewed Junger with suspicion. His past association with the national-Bolshevik Ersnt Niekisch, the Jewish anarchist Erich Muhsam and the anti-Hitler Nazi Otto

---

16   *Ibid.*, pp. 114-140.

von Strasser, all of whom were either eventually killed or exiled by the Third Reich, led the Nazis to regard Junger as a potential subversive. On several occasions, Junger received visits from the Gestapo in search of some of his former friends. During the early years of the Nazi regime, Junger was in the fortunate economic position of being able to afford to travel outside of Germany. He journeyed to Norway, Brazil, Greece and Morocco during this time, and published several works based on his travels.[17]

Junger's most significant work from the Nazi period is the novel *On the Marble Cliffs*. The book is an allegorical attack on the Hitler regime. It was written in 1939, the same year that Junger re-entered the German army. The book describes a mysterious villain that threatens a community, a sinister warlord called the "Head Ranger". This character is never featured in the plot of the novel, but maintains a foreboding presence that is universal (much like "Big Brother" in George Orwell's *1984*). Another character in the novel, "Braquemart", is described as having physical characteristics remarkably similar to those of Goebbels. The book sold fourteen thousand copies during its first two weeks in publication. Swiss reviewers immediately recognized the allegorical references to the Nazi state in the novel. The Nazi Party's organ, *Volkische Beobachter*, stated that Ernst Jünger was flirting with a bullet to the head. Goebbels urged Hitler to ban the book, but Hitler refused, probably not wanting to show his hand. Indeed, Hitler gave orders that Junger not be harmed.[18]

Junger was stationed in France for most of the Second World War. Once again, he kept diaries of the experience. Once again, he expressed concern that he might not get to see any action before the war was over. While Junger did not have the opportunity to experience the level of danger and daredevil heroics he had during the Great War, he did receive yet another medal, the Iron Cross, for retrieving the body of a dead corporal while under heavy fire. Junger also published some of his war

---

17   *Ibid.*, p. 145.

18   *Ibid.*, p. 162.

diaries during this time. However, the German government took a dim view of these, viewing them as too sympathetic to the occupied French. Junger's duties included censorship of the mail coming into France from German civilians. He took a rather liberal approach to this responsibility and simply disposed of incriminating documents rather than turning them over for investigation. In doing so, he probably saved lives. He also encountered members of France's literary and cultural elite, among them the actor Louis Ferdinand Celine, a raving anti-Semite and pro-Vichyite who suggested Hitler's harsh measures against the Jews had not been heavy handed enough. As rumors of the Nazi extermination programs began to spread, Junger wrote in his diary that the mechanization of the human spirit of the type he had written about in the past had apparently generated a higher level of human depravity. When he saw three young French-Jewish girls wearing the yellow stars required by the Nazis, he wrote that he felt embarrassed to be in the Nazi army. In July of 1942, Junger observed the mass arrest of French Jews, the beginning of implementation of the "Final Solution." He described the scene as follows:

> "Parents were first separated from their children, so there was wailing to be heard in the streets. At no moment may I forget that I am surrounded by the unfortunate, by those suffering to the very depths, else what sort of person, what sort of officer would I be? The uniform obliges one to grant protection wherever it goes. Of course one has the impression that one must also, like Don Quixote, take on millions."[19]

An entry into Junger's diary from October 16, 1943 suggests that an unnamed army officer had told Junger about the use of crematoria and poison gas to murder Jews *en masse*. Rumors of plots against Hitler circulated among the officers with whom Junger maintained contact. His son, Ernst, was arrested after an informant claimed he had spoken critically of Hitler. Ernst Junger

---

19   *Ibid.*, p. 189.

was imprisoned for three months then placed in a penal battalion where he was killed in action in Italy. On July 20, 1944 an unsuccessful assassination attempt was carried out against Hitler. It is still disputed as to whether or not Junger knew of the plot or had a role in its planning. Among those arrested for their role in the attempt on Hitler's life were members of Junger's immediate circle of associates and superior officers within the German army. Junger was dishonorably discharged shortly afterward.[20]

Following the close of the Second World War, Junger came under suspicion from the Allied occupational authorities because of his far right-wing nationalist and militarist past. He refused to cooperate with the Allies De-Nazification programs and was barred from publishing for four years. He would go on to live another half century, producing many more literary works, becoming a close friend of Albert Hoffman, the inventor of the hallucinogen LSD, with which he experimented. In a 1977 novel, *Eumeswil*, he took his tendency towards viewing the world around him with detachment to a newer, more clearly articulated level with his invention of the concept of the "Anarch". This idea, heavily influenced by the writings of the early nineteenth century German philosopher Max Stirner, championed the solitary individual who remains true to himself within the context of whatever external circumstances happen to be present.

Some sample quotations from this work illustrate the philosophy and worldview of the elderly Junger quite well:

"For the anarch, if he remains free of being ruled, whether by sovereign or society, this does not mean he refuses to serve in any way. In general, he serves no worse than anyone else, and sometimes even better, if he likes the game. He only holds back from the pledge, the sacrifice, the ultimate devotion ... I serve in the Casbah; if, while doing this, I die for the Condor, it would be an accident, perhaps even an obliging gesture, but nothing more."

---

20   *Ibid.*, p. 209.

"The egalitarian mania of demagogues is even more dangerous than the brutality of men in gallooned coats. For the anarch, this remains theoretical, because he avoids both sides. Anyone who has been oppressed can get back on his feet if the oppression did not cost him his life. A man who has been equalized is physically and morally ruined. Anyone who is different is not equal; that is one of the reasons why the Jews are so often targeted."

"The anarch, recognizing no government, but not indulging in paradisal dreams as the anarchist does, is, for that very reason, a neutral observer."

"Opposition is collaboration."

"A basic theme for the anarch is how man, left to his own devices, can defy superior force - whether state, society or the elements - by making use of their rules without submitting to them."

"... malcontents... prowl through the institutions eternally dissatisfied, always disappointed. Connected with this is their love of cellars and rooftops, exile and prisons, and also banishment, on which they actually pride themselves. When the structure finally caves in they are the first to be killed in the collapse. Why do they not know that the world remains inalterable in change? Because they never find their way down to its real depth, their own. That is the sole place of essence, safety. And so they do themselves in."

"The anarch may not be spared prisons - as one fluke of existence among others. He will then find the fault in himself."

"We are touching one a ... distinction between anarch and anarchist; the relation to authority, to legislative power. The anarchist is their mortal enemy, while the anarch refuses to acknowledge them. He seeks neither to gain hold of them, nor to topple them, nor to alter them - their impact bypasses him. He must resign himself only to the whirlwinds they generate."

"The anarch is no individualist, either. He wishes to present himself neither as a Great Man nor as a Free Spirit. His own measure is enough for him; freedom is not his goal; it is his property. He does not come on as foe or reformer: one can get along nicely with him in shacks or in palaces. Life is too short and too beautiful to sacrifice for ideas, although contamination is not always avoidable. But hats off to the martyrs."

"We can expect as little from society as from the state. Salvation lies in the individual."[21]

---

21 Junger, Ernst. *Eumeswil*. New York: Marion Publishers, 1980, 1993.

Emma Goldman: A Life Worth Living

Biographical Overview

The life of Emma Goldman serves as a powerful metaphor for the transformation of Western civilization as it was during the era when traditional society was on its deathbed to what it has become in contemporary postmodern times. Emma Goldman was born a subject of the Russian Empire in 1869 in the Lithuanian city of Kovno. Her family were Orthodox Jews and she was the first child of her mother Taube Bienowitch's second marriage. Taube married Abraham Goldman after her first husband had died of tuberculosis. Emma's father was an inept businessman whose financial failures forced the family into poverty. He was also a violent man who used a whip as a means of disciplining his children. Emma's lifelong disdain for and conflict with authority figures began with Abraham Goldman and these sentiments were enhanced by the trauma she experienced by observing the flogging of a peasant in the streets of the village of Papile as a child.[1]

The Goldman family moved to Prussia when Emma was seven years old and took root in the city of Konigsberg. She was enrolled in a *realschule* and suffered both corporal beatings and sexual molestation at the hands of her teachers and was later denied entry into the *gymnasium* because of her supposed bad behavior. The family later relocated to St. Petersburg, Russia and the poverty generated by her father's failures forced Emma and her siblings to find work so the adolescent Emma found a job

---

1   Drinnon, Richard. *Rebel in Paradise: A Biography of Emma Goldman*. Chicago: University of Chicago Press, 1961, pp. 1-12; Goldman, Emma. *Living My Life*. 1931. New York: Dover Publications, Inc., 1970, pp. 1-28; Wexler, Alice. *Emma Goldman: An Intimate Life*. New York: Pantheon Books, 1984, pp. 1-14.

in a corset shop. Her father objected to her interest in education saying, "Girls do not have to learn much! All a Jewish daughter needs to know is how to prepare gefilte fish, cut noodles fine, and give the man plenty of children." The conflict between Emma and Abraham Goldman grew when he tried to force her into an arranged marriage at age fifteen. Emma was further traumatized by a sexual assault she experienced while still employed at the corset shop. Her interest in politics began when the Russian emperor Alexander II was assassinated in 1861 by members of the Nihilist movement. Her introduction to radicalism occurred a short time later when she discovered Nikolai Chernyshevsky's novel, *What Is To Be Done?*, which features as one of its characters a young woman who escapes her unhappy family life by joining the Nihilists.

After much quarreling between father and daughter, Abraham allowed Emma, then sixteen, to move in 1885 with her sister Helena to the United States where she took up residence in the Rochester, New York home of her sister Lena who had previously gone to the USA with her husband. After an outbreak of anti-Semitism in St. Petersburg, her parents joined the sisters in Rochester as well, where Emma had taken a job as a seamstress in a textile factory. Emma had arrived in America just in time to witness the turmoil surrounding the Haymarket bombing incident in Chicago in 1886 and she became interested in the philosophy of anarchism, a radical political ideology whose notoriety had grown because of the incident. At the age of seventeen, Emma was married to an emotionally troubled young man named Jacob Kershner and the marriage ended after a matter of months.

After relocating to New York City, Emma became personally acquainted with two men through whom she would undergo her formal initiation into the anarchist movement. The first of these was Alexander Berkman, who was like Emma a Russian-Jewish émigré, and who would become her on-again, off-again lover and companion for the remainder of both of their lives. Emma met

Alexander at a café and he invited her to go with him to hear a talk by the German émigré anarchist Johann Most. Having once been elected to the German parliament as a Socialist deputy, Most had become an anarchist after having become convinced of the impossibility of meaningful social reform through the state. Most was not only an outspoken critic of the established political and economic order, but an advocate of revolutionary violence as a means of achieving radical objectives. For holding these positions, Most was imprisoned by the German authorities and later fled to the United States.[2]

A strike broke out in Homestead, Pennsylvania in 1892 at a steel plant owned by the "robber baron" Andrew Carnegie. During the course of the strike, a gunfight that lasted for twelve hours erupted between striking workers and members of the Pinkerton private police agency that had been hired by the factory's manager Henry Clay Frick. During the fight seven guards and nine workers were killed. In retaliation, Berkman and Goldman plotted the assassination of Frick. On July 23, 1892, Berkman inflicted three non-fatal gunshot wounds and one stab wound on Frick, an act for which he was arrested, charged with attempted murder and sentenced to twenty-two years in prison. He would ultimately serve fifteen. The attack on Frick was widely criticized by workers and anarchists, even by Johann Most himself, as a form of foolish, provocative, adventurism. Later in life, Emma would say of the plot, "At the age of twenty-three, one does not reason."

During this same time, Emma attempted to turn to prostitution as a means of making ends meet. Never a particularly attractive woman, she was told by a prospective client that she really was not suitable for the business. Yet her experiences led her to develop a lifelong sympathy for the condition of prostitutes.[3]

---

2   Chalberg, John. *Emma Goldman: American Individualist*. New York: HarperCollins
     Publishers Inc., 1991, p. 15; Drinnon, pp. 6-15, Goldman, pp. 22-53; Wexler, pp.
     23-58.

3   Wexler, pp. 57-66.

One of the worst economic crises in U.S. history emerged during the Panic of 1893 and unemployment rates rose to twenty percent. After giving a speech to a crowd of workers in New York City where she urged a workers revolution against the social injustices of industrial capitalism, Emma was arrested for incitement to riot and sentenced to one year in prison. When she was released after ten months, a crowd of three thousand gathered to greet her. She had begun studying medicine under the tutelage of the prison doctor during her incarceration and upon her release sailed to Europe hoping to further her education in the fields of midwifery and massage therapy. Emma lectured on anarchism and other topics in numerous countries while in Europe and became acquainted with European anarchist leaders such as the Italian Errico Malatesta and fellow Russian Peter Kropotkin. Upon returning to the United States, she found that she was now something of a celebrity and embarked on a cross-country speaking tour, the first ever by an American anarchist leader.[4]

U.S. President William McKinley was assassinated on September 6, 1901 by a Detroit-born Polish-American named Leon Czolgosz, who had been inspired by the assassination of King Umberto I of Italy by an anarchist the previous year. Czolgosz had attended a public lecture by Goldman and tried to visit her a few days later at the home she shared with her then-lover Hippolyte Havel and another anarchist couple, Abe and Mary Isaak. Czolgosz's presence aroused the suspicions of Emma and her companions who suspected him of being a police spy. After Czolgosz was arrested for the McKinley assassination, Goldman, Havel, Abe Isaak and ten other anarchists were arrested and detained for two weeks but were released after no evidence emerged of their actual involvement in Czolgosz's action.

The assassination of McKinley generated an enormous public backlash against anarchists and Goldman temporarily withdrew from public life and lived briefly under a pseudonym. However, she resumed her activism when the U.S. Congress passed the

---

4   Drinnon, p. 60; Wexler, pp. 68-79.

Immigration Act of 1903. The Act came to be known as the Anarchist Exclusion Act as it barred immigration into the U.S. by avowed anarchists. A British anarchist named John Turner was threatened with deportation under the Act and Goldman began to champion his cause through her involvement with the Free Speech League. The case of Turner was taken up by the famed defense attorney Clarence Darrow and went all the way to the U.S. Supreme Court. Turner ultimately lost his deportation case, though he had returned to England on his own volition prior to the court's ruling.[5]

In 1906, Goldman began her own print journal, *Mother Earth*, which featured original writings from anarchists around the world and also republished the works of thinkers who had influenced Emma's own ideas including the anarchist godfathers Proudhon, Bakunin, and Kropotkin, the maverick German philosopher Friedrich Nietzsche, and the pioneer feminist Mary Wollstonecraft. Alexander Berkman was also released from prison in 1906 and subsequently became the editor of *Mother Earth* while Goldman pursued speaking engagements. By this time, Goldman was a well-known public figure and her lectures were well-attended by persons of all class backgrounds and from across the political spectrum. Emma also began an affair with a physician by the name of Ben Reitman during this time and started to speak out on behalf of issues related to contraception. She was again arrested in 1916 for distributing materials promoting birth control. When she refused to pay the $100 fine, Emma was sentenced to two weeks in jail.[6]

When the United States under the presidency of Woodrow Wilson entered the First World War in 1917, Emma Goldman and Alexander Berkman both became outspoken critics of the war and urged draft resistance. Their anti-draft activities led to their arrest under the Espionage Act and they were both sentenced to two years in a federal penitentiary. At the time

---

5   Wexler, pp. 61-115.

6   Wexler, pp. 211-216.

Emma remarked, "Two years imprisonment for having made an uncompromising stand for one's ideal. Why that is a small price." After her release in September of 1919, Goldman faced a deportation hearing the following month. It was at the height of the Red Scare and the young head of the U.S. Department of Justice's intelligence division named J. Edgar Hoover wrote at the time, "Emma Goldman and Alexander Berkman are, beyond doubt, two of the most dangerous anarchists in this country and return to the community will result in undue harm." Emma and Alexander were subsequently deported to their homeland of Russia, which had recently undergone the Bolshevik Revolution. Initially sympathetic to the aims of the revolution, Goldman and Berkman eventually became disillusioned by the new Communist regime's repression of dissent. Their disillusionment increased after nearly a thousand striking workers were massacred at Kronstadt by Trotsky's Red Army. They subsequently left Russia and migrated to Berlin where Emma wrote about her experiences under the Bolshevik regime of Lenin.[7]

Goldman was an early critic of the Bolshevik experiment and Communism, much to the dismay of the prominent intellectuals who came to hear her lecture in London after her move there in 1924. By this time, Communism had achieved hegemony on the Left and anarchism had fallen out of favor among radicals who were dismissive of Emma's anti-Bolshevism. She subsequently turned her attention to writing. Her new works included analytical studies of drama as well as her autobiography, *Living My Life*, with the latter being issued by the American publisher Alfred Knopf with the support of prominent American literary and artistic figures such as Edna St. Vincent Millay, Peggy Guggenheim, Theodore Dreiser, and H.L. Mencken.

In 1934, Goldman received permission to return to the United States to speak about her autobiography and her works on drama on the condition that she refrain from speaking on political topics. While she had often been vilified in the American

---

7   Drinnon, pp. 186-187, Wexler, pp. 230-243.

press during her thirty-five years of living in the United States, Goldman's return generally received a warm welcome from the press with most of the negative attacks originating from the Communist papers. After her American visa expired, Emma took up residence in Canada.[8]

By early 1936, Alexander Berkman was living in Nice, France and was terminally ill with cancer. Emma went to visit him hoping to say her final goodbyes but when she arrived she found that Berkman, not wanting to burden his friends with his care, had shot himself. Later that year, the civil war had begun in Spain and the Spanish anarchist movement began to actually carry out a revolution in certain regions of the country. Emma journeyed to Barcelona to witness the revolution in progress and finally enjoyed the opportunity to briefly experience a society where anarchists had become the dominant political force. However, the revolution did not go well as the anarchists were left fighting a two-front war with the forces of General Francisco Franco and the Communist forces backed by the Soviet Union. After the defeat of the anarchists, Goldman returned to Canada in 1939. Now seventy years old, her health began failing just as World War Two was beginning. Goldman remained true to her lifelong antimilitarist convictions. She described the coming war as a "new kind of madness in the world."

Emma Goldman died on February 17, 1940 in Toronto, Canada at the age of 70 after suffering a series of debilitating strokes. Her remains were interred in Forest Park, Illinois outside of Chicago alongside the graves of the Haymarket martyrs who had inspired Emma to take up the cause of anarchism more than a half century earlier.[9]

---

8   Wexler, pp. 96-164.
9   Drinnon, pp. 298-313.

The Historical Context of Classical Anarchism

The life and work of Emma Goldman cannot be fully understood outside the historical context of the classical anarchist movement that her legacy famously represents. Anarchism was a movement to which Goldman was committed with nothing less than religious fervor. Its core doctrines defined her worldview and political activism, and she was arguably as influential and effective as a propagandist for the cause of anarchism as anyone who ever claimed that political mantle. Nearly a century after the heyday of Goldman's radical activism, only a handful of names from the era of classical anarchism are as definitive of the movement's memory as her own.

Anarchism was a product of the convergence of the intellectual culture of the latter Enlightenment and the socioeconomic conditions generated by the early industrial revolution. Forms of proto-typical anarchist thought began to emerge following the French Revolution of 1789, sometimes as a critical response to the authoritarian turn the revolution took, as was the case with the writings of Jean Varlet. Sylvain Marechal in France and William Godwin in England each developed proto-anarchist philosophies at the end of the eighteenth century as did the German writer Max Stirner with his work *The Ego and Its Own*, published in 1844. The first prominent thinker to refer to himself as an "anarchist" was the French economist Pierre Joseph Proudhon. His contemporary Joseph Dejacque assumed the label of "libertarian" and the terms came to be used interchangeably in European political language. Early anarchists participated in the uprisings that swept Europe in 1848 and suffered from the repression that followed.

Anarchists were subsequently involved in the founding of the International Workingmen's Association in 1864. The IWA was an effort to unite various radical labor currents and included such diverse tendencies as the English trade unions, the anarchist followers of Proudhon, social democrats, and disciples of socialists such as Louis Blanc and Karl Marx. The anarchist section of the IWA came to be led by the Russian Mikhail Bakunin and the organization became polarized into two rival camps, one led by Bakunin and one led by Marx, thereby leading to a split that resulted in the anarchists leaving to form their own organization.

The anarchists subsequently positioned themselves as the most militant wing of the international labor movement, opposing attempts at socioeconomic change through the state or conventional political methods in favor of militant "direct action" aimed at the overthrow of both the state and of capitalism and the replacement of these with self-managed workers associations. The Haymarket incident in Chicago in 1886 which sparked Goldman's interest in the anarchist movement had transpired during the course of a general strike being held throughout the United States and Canada in favor of the eight hour workday. The day the strike began, 1st May, subseqently became an international workers holiday known simply as "May Day." The fusion of anarchism and radical trade unionism came to be known as "anarcho-syndicalism" and anarcho-syndicalists dominated the labor movements through much of Europe (particularly in Spain, France, and Portugal) and Central and South America (particularly Brazil, Peru, Chile, Argentina, and Mexico).

As the anarchist movement grew in prominence so did the militancy of its tactics. Some anarchists came to advocate such concepts as "propaganda by the deed," "illegalism," and "expropriative anarchism" which were labels given to what were essentially acts of terrorism such as bombings, assassinations, and robberies of banks and other institutions regarded as complicit in the oppression of the working class. Emma Goldman's early mentor Johann Most was a foremost proponent of such tactics. During the late nineteenth and early twentieth century, anarchists carried out numerous dramatic assassinations of heads of state and other prominent political figures, thereby contributing to the enduring image of anarchists as violence-prone madmen.

The decline of the classical anarchist movement is attributable to several factors. After the Russian Revolution, the ideology of Communism came to be regarded as the revolutionary wave of the future. The prestige of the Soviet Union as a supposed revolutionary state drew many radicals from all over the world into the ranks of the Communist movement. The repression of the labor and other radical movements in multiple countries during the First World War also damaged the anarchist cause. The rise of fascism and aggressive nationalism presented a powerful challenge to anarchism during the interwar period and later fascist regimes subjected anarchists to heavy handed repression. The anarchist movement was further demoralized by the defeat of the Spanish anarchists at the hands of Franco's army. The patriotic loyalties that arose during the Second World War and the near-cosmic, all-encompassing nature of the war itself eclipsed revolutionary struggles within individual countries. Revolutionary zeal was also mitigated by the incorporation of democratic, liberal, labor, and socialist elements into postwar regimes and the implementation of comprehensive economic, political, and social reforms such as the recognition of labor unions, the eight hour day, universal suffrage, free public education, health and unemployment insurance, old age pensions and the like. Rising living standards that allowed the working class to achieve middle class lifestyles eliminated the desperation generated by the poverty and horrid working conditions of earlier times. Lastly, the dramatic growth of the state and public sector bureaucracies during the twentieth century motivated many to regard anarchism as a romantic anachronism. By the middle of the twentieth century, anarchist movements had all but disappeared from the world political scene.[10]

---

10   Avrich, Paul (1984). *The Haymarket Tragedy*. Princeton: Princeton University Press; Beevor, Antony (2006). *The Battle for Spain: The Spanish Civil War 1936–1939*. London: Weidenfeld & Nicolson; Blin, Arnaud (2007). *The History of Terrorism*. Berkeley: University of California Press; Breunig, Charles (1977). *The Age of Revolution and Reaction, 1789–1850*. New York, N.Y: W. W. Norton & Company; Robert Graham, *Anarchism - A Documentary History of Libertarian Ideas - Volume One: From Anarchy to Anarchism (300CE to 1939)*, Black Rose Books, 2005; Daniel Guerin, *Anarchism: From Theory to Practice* (New York: Monthly Review Press, 1970); Nomad, Max (1966). "The

Anarchism and Other Essays

Anarchism and Other Essays was the first of six books that Emma Goldman wrote during her lifetime. The other five include her study of drama, two books criticizing Communism based on her observations of the early Soviet Union, her own autobiography, and a biography of a fellow American female anarchist, Voltairine De Cleyre. The collection of essays presented in her first work was originally published in 1910 and many of these essays were originally written for Goldman's *Mother Earth* journal. These are not scholarly writings by Goldman but a representation of her efforts to present her own ideas and the philosophy of anarchism as she understood it in practical terms. While Goldman remains one of history's most famous anarchists, she is not typically regarded by historians and scholars of anarchism as one of the philosophy's foremost theorists. Instead, she is considered to have been primarily an activist, agitator, and publicist for the movement rather than a contributor of theoretical innovations to the body of anarchist thought.

To be sure, there have been other anarchists, libertarians, and anti-state radicals who have developed far more elaborate intellectual paradigms and systems of thought. Proudhon's original economic philosophy of mutualism, Kropotkin's far reaching social theory, Rudolph Rocker's studies of culture and nationalism, and Stirner's timeless philosophy of egoism each surpass the works of Goldman in their level of abstraction and intricacy. Goldman preferred the more practical, the more immediate, and the more here and now having once remarked, "I don't care if a man's theory for tomorrow is correct. I care if his spirit of today is correct." Yet it would be a mistake to regard Goldman's work as lacking depth or breadth as a survey of the writings in this collection will reveal. From the vantage point of a century later, Goldman's ideas still stand out in their radical, prescient, and still highly relevant nature. In the opening chapter

---

Anarchist Tradition". In Drachkovitch, Milorad M.. *Revolutionary Internationals 1864 1943*. Stanford University Press; Thomas, Paul (1985). *Karl Marx and the Anarchists*. London: Routledge & Kegan Paul.

in this book, "Anarchism: What It Really Stands For," Goldman summarized the anarchist philosophy in this way:

> Anarchism, then, really stands for the liberation of the human mind from the dominion of religion; the liberation of the human body from the dominion of property; liberation from the shackles and restraint of government. Anarchism stands for a social order based on the free grouping of individuals for the purpose of producing real social wealth; an order that will guarantee to every human being free access to the earth and full enjoyment of the necessities of life, according to individual desires, tastes, and inclinations.

Like Bakunin before her, Goldman identified as anarchism's primary enemies, organized religion, the exploitation inherent in feudal and state capitalist property relations, and the state's apparatus of physical coercion. These ideas remain quite controversial and an understanding of the context in which they arose is vital to the development of an objective critique of the ideas of the classical anarchists.

The virulent anticlericalism of the classical anarchists no doubt seems overbearing and excessive in the contemporary Western industrialized nations where the Church has lost most of its political influence and where, with the sole exception of America's evangelical subculture, religious fervor is almost non-existent. Yet classical anarchism arose in those nations such as France, Russia, Spain, Italy, Portugal, and the Latin America countries where the Church hierarchy was still very much an intricate part of the political establishment and where the religious authorities were very much champions of genuinely oppressive institutions that ignored the sufferings of the beleaguered masses and suppressed political dissent and freedom of opinion. In Goldman's own day, freedom of religious opinion was relatively well established in those nations where the Enlightenment had fully taken root such as England, Holland, and America. Yet in regions of Latin

America, Russia, Eastern Europe, Southern Europe, and the Iberian Peninsula the theocratic Church still held powers not considerably removed from those which it had enjoyed in the pre-modern era, and which the clerics continue to enjoy in much of the Islamic world today.

Goldman's critique of "property" echoes the famous dictum of Proudhon that "property is theft." Such a sentiment no doubt seems incongruous in contemporary industrial and postindustrial societies where the working classes have become a middle class and where even some comparatively disadvantaged people often own private homes, real estate, automobiles, televisions, computers, cellular phones, bank accounts, credit cards, and other luxury items that either did not exist or were available only to the very wealthy or well to do during the era of classical anarchism.

The technological and economic advancements of the mid to late twentieth century transformed the once-starving Western working classes into a middle class whose standards of living rivaled or surpassed that of even the middle classes of the classical proletarian era. But poverty in Goldman's day and in the era of classical anarchism was poverty of the kind now identified with southern hemisphere nations where state-privileged land barons and industrial capitalists amassed fortunes off the sweat and often life-threatening conditions of working people and peasant farmers. The goal of the anarchists was not the centralization of control of all wealth and property into the hands of the state in the manner advocated by the Communists. Rather, the anarchists offered a polar opposite solution to what was then called the "social question" or the "labor question." The anarchists wished to decentralize control over productive wealth in the forms of factories, agricultural plantations, and financial institutions through self-managed and federated communes, collectives, cooperatives, labor unions, industrial syndicates, mutual aid societies, small landowners, family farms, and peoples banks. In this regard, the anarchists rather ironically advanced an economic program not similar to that of romantic medievalists and Catholic distributists such as G. K. Chesterton and Hilaire Belloc who were otherwise their cultural and political polar opposites. Some anarchists, particularly those in the English speaking countries such as Benjamin Tucker and John Henry MacKay, espoused a *laissez faire* economic philosophy that was not dissimilar to that of today's free-market libertarians.

Likewise, the anarchist criticisms of the state advanced by Goldman often sound remarkably similar to those voiced by contemporary American conservatives. Quoted selectively, an uninformed reader or observer might think Goldman to be a member of the contemporary American "Tea Party" movement or a follower of modern libertarian politicians such as Ron Paul. There can be no doubt that the powers of the state have grown exponentially since the era of classical anarchism and that even the early anarchists could hardly have dreamed of the kinds of powers that would later be amassed by the modern totalitarian states. The anarchists criticized the state for its tendency to side with the rich and powerful against the poor and working classes in economic and labor disputes, its suppression of political dissent and freedom of speech, its petty bureaucratic regulations, and its destructive war making capabilities. The anarchists could scarcely have envisioned the soft totalitarianism of the managerial states that now dominate the modern countries and which intrude into every area of life in ways never previously conceived of.

The essays presented in this volume likewise speak to many other contemporary questions and offer a refreshingly radical voice. In an era where centralized mass democracy is frequently touted by political and intellectual elites as the only legitimate form of statecraft and even as the apex of human social evolution, and where aggressive wars are undertaken on behalf of its advancement, Goldman offers an insightful critique of the problems of majoritarianism in the second chapter, "Minorities Versus Majorities." Said Goldman of the masses:

Not because I do not feel with the oppressed, the disinherited of the earth; not because I do not know the shame, the horror, the indignity of the lives the people lead, do I repudiate the majority as a creative force for good. Oh, no, no! But because I know so well that as a compact mass it has never stood for justice or equality. It has suppressed the human voice, subdued the human spirit, chained the human body. As a mass its aim has always been to make life uniform, gray, and monotonous as the desert. As a mass it will always be the annihilator of individuality, of free initiative, of originality. I therefore believe with Emerson that "the masses are crude, lame, pernicious in their demands and influence, and need not to be flattered, but to be schooled. I wish not to concede anything to them, but to drill, divide, and break them up, and draw individuals out of them. Masses! The calamity are the masses. I do not wish any mass at all, but honest men only, lovely, sweet, accomplished women only."

Goldman's anarchist impulses instinctively led her to recognize that most human beings are essentially herd creatures who will always be susceptible to the promptings of peers, leaders, and perceived authorities. Goldman understood that genuine human advancement is not made through the mob but through the efforts of the rare individuals and minorities that are able to rise above the herd and pioneer new paths in intellectual, cultural, and political life, often reaping the scorn of the wider society in the process. It is never the majority who make history but the rare individual with a vision and those precious few who become inspired by that vision.

In an era when terrorism is a prevailing public concern, the third chapter, "The Psychology of Political Violence," offers many important insights that contemporary policy makers might do well to heed. Having been peripherally involved in Berkman's assassination attempt on Frick as a young woman, Goldman understood that political violence, or "terrorism," was quite often an outgrowth of genuine injustices that were not being adequately addressed. Just as the anarchist terrorism of a century ago was driven largely by a lack of effective redress of grievances and despair generated by the deplorable socioeconomic conditions of industrial capitalism and feudal land tenancy as they were during the era, so is much of today's Islamic terrorism generated by the oppression inflicted on the peoples of the Muslim world by the imperial powers of the West and their regional client states in the Middle East. The carnage currently being inflicted on the Palestinian people, for instance, drives some to acts of rage in the same way that Berkman was driven to violence by the massacre of striking workers at Homestead.

The fourth chapter, "Prisons: A Social Crime and Failure," also speaks to contemporary times, particularly domestic American politics as the American state contains within itself approximately one quarter of the world's prison population and imprisons a greater number of its subjects, both numerically and per capita, than any other state in the world. Approximately one in thirty Americans are currently in jail or prison or on probation or parole. An increasingly high number of Americans have criminal records. Unless one wishes to dismiss these statistics as representing nothing more than the unique evil of Americans, it stands to reason that the massive prison population found in the United States results in no large part from the gross overcriminalization of the society as a result of the explosive growth of state intrusion into every other institution and every area of economic, cultural and civil life. Further, such data indicates the ineffectiveness of prisons as reformative institutions generally and the need for rethinking methods of controlling crime and handling offenders.

The fifth chapter in this collection, "Patriotism: A Menace to Liberty," strikes an ominous chord in an era when legislation with the Orwellian name of the PATRIOT ACT has resulted in the dramatic expansion of the domestic American police state by granting the authorities previously forbidden discretionary powers regarding the investigation, detention, and imprisonment of alleged terrorism suspects. Indeed, under the National Defense Authorization Act, the U.S. state may now imprison alleged terrorism suspects indefinitely without trial and the American president now claims the authority to engage in the unilateral assassination of American citizens on the mere suspicion of involvement in terrorist activities. Anyone who observed the disgusting spectacle of the way in which the American invasion of Iraq in 2003 was sold to the public through a combination of invoking unsubstantiated threats supposedly posed by the Iraqi regime and appeals to the sillies pieties (for instance, a U.S. Congressman renaming French Fries as "Freedom Fries" because of the French state's sensible criticism of and abstention from the war effort) cannot help but be impressed by Goldman's analysis of how patriotic sentiments can be twisted to serve the most dubious purposes.

The sixth chapter, "Francisco Ferrer and the Modern School," examines the educational philosophy and practices of the Spanish anarchist Ferrer, who was executed by firing squad in 1909 by the Spanish authorities during a time of martial law on the dubious pretense of his supposed involvement in the plot against King Alfonso XIII. Ferrer was a pioneer at introducing secular and non-sectarian education into Spain at a time when education was very much under the control of the Catholic Church, with the Church in Spain being the most reactionary in Europe. It was Ferrer's efforts at undermining the authority of the Church over Spanish education that likely led to his judicial murder. Of course, during the era of Goldman and Ferrer it was inconceivable that someday the public educational systems of the Western world would be used for the purpose of disseminating and inculcating the most clichéd liberal pieties. Indeed, many Catholic schools in the West are now as liberal in their social and political outlook as their secular counterparts.

But while the ideological paradigm dominating Western education may have dramatically shifted over the past century, the fundamentally authoritarian nature of educational institutions continues. Many contemporary American schools are operated with a level of security and surveillance approaching that of prisons, and the discipline meted out by educational authorities remains as petty, arbitrary, and in defiance of common logic as ever. While education is now universal, the overall quality of the education being provided has deteriorated considerably to the point where persons who would have been regarded as near-illiterates in past times are now granted secondary school degrees or even admitted to institutions of higher learning. The growing interest in alternative forms of education involving home schooling, experimental schooling, and even classroom-free online education has been a response to the pervasive and ongoing problem of how to provide proper education to children and young people in a humane institutional setting. It may be that technology ultimately offers the best hope concerning this question. Perhaps the day will come when technological capabilities simply allow education to take place in front of a computer screen being viewed from the comfort of a family's living room or that of neighbors, relatives, or friends, thereby rendering traditional institutions of schooling as irrelevant and archaic as the horse and buggy.

Chapter seven, "The Hypocrisy of Puritanism," examines the puritanical attitudes towards sexuality that were prevalent during Goldman's day. In another irony, it is unlikely Goldman could have envisioned the Western world that exists a century later that has been shaped as it has by the sexual revolution of the 1960s and 1970s. Goldman, for instance, was a pioneer advocate of contraception, a position that got her thrown in jail during her lifetime. Even the dissemination of medical information regarding sexuality was prohibited under the Comstock Laws of her time. Goldman was also a very early advocate of the rights of homosexuals, a position that was virtually unthinkable even among most radicals during her era. How different she would find the world of today where same-sex marriages are well on their way to becoming fully institutionalized and normalized, where technological innovations have made the most extreme forms of pornography available to all through a simple computer key stroke, where the invention of "the pill" dramatically changed sexual mores, and where not only contraception but abortion on demand are widely regarded not only as inalienable rights but as public entitlements to be funded by the state.

Yet the advent of the sexual revolution has by no means brought about the demise of Puritanism. Instead, the old sexual pieties have been replaced by new, unchallengeable pieties derived from egalitarian values whereby any sort of differentiation on the basis of race, gender, sexual orientation, physical handicap, looks, weight, age, transvestism, transexuality and a number of other things has become the ultimate taboo. In Goldman's era, "racism," "sexism," and "homophobia" were universally accepted and even required whereas any and all sexual expression was taboo. Today, the inversion of this arrangement has become the fact, with any and all expression of non-egalitarian sentiments having become forbidden in the midst of a virtual cornucopia of sexual expression.

Chapter eight, "The Traffic in Women," addresses the issue of prostitution. One of the oddities of the sexual revolution and the wider egalitarian culture of political correctness is that the business of prostitution is one of the few remaining sexual subcultures traditionally regarded as deviant to be excluded from the pantheon of official victim groups and the umbrella of claims to freedom of choice and personal rights. In the contemporary culture, even those who practice sado-masochism are coming to be regarded as yet another oppressed minority entitled to their rights. Virtually all Western industrialized countries have decriminalized homosexual relationships. However, only a few have formally legalized prostitution, notably the Netherlands, Germany, and New Zealand. Indeed, mass immigration from Russia, Eastern Europe, and the "Third World" into Western Europe and North America has brought with it an increase in the amount of what is now called "sex trafficking" (or formerly called "white slavery") including coerced prostitution or prostitution of underage persons sponsored by organized criminal syndicates and unscrupulous pimps.

Yet another irony of the present day is the often criticized practice of criminally prosecuting the prostitute while allowing her customers to go free has been reversed in some countries. In the dystopias of Scandinavia where the soft totalitarian values of political correctness and the therapeutic, paternalistic welfare state are most deeply entrenched, and where feminist movements motivated by strong sentiments of misandry are the most powerful, the prostitute is no longer subject to criminal prosecution but it is instead prostitution clients who have been criminalized. Under such regimes, the prostitute herself (or himself) is supposedly a victim of capitalism and patriarchy whereas it is the client who is the victimizer and exploiter. Yet it is unclear how such legal arrangements are of benefit to the prostitutes themselves. Removing the fear of prosecution may be of benefit to a prostitute who is being coerced into the trade and wishes to request assistance from the authorities, but the majority of prostitutes and other sex workers are not subject to direct physical coercion. Even if the prostitute is permitted to practice her trade above ground, her clients must remain underground and therefore the prostitute is forced underground by default as she must protect her clients. Further, while the criminalization of prostitution clients may deter more respectable, married, middle class, or professional men from patronizing prostitutes, it is unlikely that such criminalization would deter those clients who are the most undesirable from the perspective of the prostitute's well-being, e.g. perverts, criminals, sociopaths, underworld figures, violent predators, and other deviants. Yet it is this class of clientele that the prostitute becomes more dependent on under such a legal regime. It is clear that interests and sentiments other than the well-being of the prostitute are the motivations behind such legal arrangements.

In chapter nine, "Woman Suffrage," Goldman offers some commentary that is shockingly politically incorrect by contemporary standards. While Goldman was a pioneer feminist, and as ardent an advocate for women's rights as just about any figure from history, she actually expressed skepticism of the women's suffragist movement. While she was certainly an ardent believer in the equality of the sexes in terms of intellectual ability and moral capabilities, Goldman was indifferent to the question of women's right to vote largely because of her own skepticism of the state itself. As she regarded the state as a useless institution with no purpose other than the perpetration of oppression, Goldman could hardly become enthusiastic about changes in the law that would allow women greater participation in the state. Indeed, Goldman went further than that, fearing that middle class liberal and socialist women would use the vote to expand the power of the state out of maternal sentiment, particularly in the realm of so-called "victimless crime", laws such as those prohibiting alcohol, drugs, gambling, or prostitution. And could there be a more fierce criticism of the excesses of the modern feminist movement than those expressed in these passages from Emma Goldman?

> Woman demands the same rights as man, yet she is indignant that her presence does not strike him dead: he smokes, keeps his hat on, and does not jump from his seat like a flunkey. These may be trivial things, but they are nevertheless the key to the nature of American suffragists.

> There are, of course, some suffragists who are affiliated with workingwomen — the Women's Trade Union League, for instance; but they are a small minority, and their activities are essentially economic. The rest look upon toil as a just provision of Providence. What would become of the rich, if not for the poor? What would become of these idle, parasitic ladies, who squander more in a week than their victims earn in a year, if not for the eighty million wage-workers? Equality, who ever heard of such a thing?

> Few countries have produced such arrogance and snobbishness as America. Particularly is this true of the American woman of the middle class. She not only considers herself the equal of man, but his superior,

especially in her purity, goodness, and morality. Small wonder that the American suffragist claims for her vote the most miraculous powers. In her exalted conceit she does not see how truly enslaved she is, not so much by man, as by her own silly notions and traditions. Suffrage can not ameliorate that sad fact; it can only accentuate it, as indeed it does.

One of the great American women leaders claims that woman is entitled not only to equal pay, but that she ought to be legally entitled even to the pay of her husband. Failing to support her, he should be put in convict stripes, and his earnings in prison be collected by his equal wife. Does not another brilliant exponent of the cause claim for woman that her vote will abolish the social evil, which has been fought in vain by the collective efforts of the most illustrious minds the world over? It is indeed to be regretted that the alleged creator of the universe has already presented us with his wonderful scheme of things, else woman suffrage would surely enable woman to outdo him completely.

Nothing is so dangerous as the dissection of a fetich. If we have outlived the time when such heresy was punishable by the stake, we have not outlived the narrow spirit of condemnation of those who dare differ with accepted notions. Therefore I shall probably be put down as an opponent of woman. But that can not deter me from looking the question squarely in the face. I repeat what I have said in the beginning: I do not believe that woman will make politics worse; nor can I believe that she could make it better. If, then, she cannot improve on man's mistakes, why perpetrate the latter?

Chapter ten, "The Tragedy of Woman's Emancipation," and chapter eleven, "Marriage and Love," likewise contain reflections from Goldman on relationships between the sexes and the role of women in society. Goldman articulated a view of marriage that was shockingly radical in its day but rather prescient in light of subsequent developments regarding patterns of marriage and divorce. Said Goldman of marriage:

> At any rate, while it is true that some marriages are based on love, and while it is equally true that in some cases love continues in married life, I maintain that it does so regardless of marriage, and not because of it.

> On the other hand, it is utterly false that love results from marriage. On rare occasions one does hear of a miraculous case of a married couple falling in love after marriage, but on close examination it will be found that it is a mere adjustment to the inevitable. Certainly the growing-used to each other is far away from the spontaneity, the intensity, and beauty of love, without which the intimacy of marriage must prove degrading to both the woman and the man.

> Marriage is primarily an economic arrangement, an insurance pact. It differs from the ordinary life insurance agreement only in that it is more binding, more exacting. Its returns are insignificantly small compared with the investments. In taking out an insurance policy one pays for it in dollars and cents, always at liberty to discontinue payments. If, how ever, woman's premium is a husband, she pays for it with her name, her privacy, her self-respect, her very life, "until death doth part." Moreover, the marriage insurance condemns her to life-long dependency, to parasitism, to complete uselessness, individual as well as social. Man, too, pays his toll, but as his sphere is wider, marriage does not limit him as much as woman. He feels his chains more in an economic sense.

> Thus Dante's motto over Inferno applies with equal force to marriage: "Ye who enter here leave all hope behind."

That marriage is a failure none but the very stupid will deny. One has but to glance over the statistics of divorce to realize how bitter a failure marriage really is. Nor will the stereotyped Philistine argument that the laxity of divorce laws and the growing looseness of woman account for the fact that: first, every twelfth marriage ends in divorce; second, that since 1870 divorces have increased from 28 to 73 for every hundred thousand population; third, that adultery, since 1867, as ground for divorce, has increased 270.8 per cent.; fourth, that desertion increased 369.8 per cent.

If the fact that one in twelve marriages ended in divorce in Goldman's own time led her in part to develop such views, it is certain that she would feel vindicated in her ideas by the fact that fifty percent of marriages now end in divorce a century later. Indeed, marriage at present is primarily regarded as merely a matter of romantic attachment that brings with it some desirable economic benefits (hence, the otherwise inexplicable push for the recognition of same-sex marriages among the homosexual community) and a marital arrangement can be easily discarded if it is perceived as no longer serving the interests of one or both partners. With the growing prevalence of both civil unions and non-marital forms of cohabitation and family relationships, it is quite possible that formalized marriage will be seen as an anachronism at some point in the not so distant future.

The final chapter, "The Modern Drama: A Powerful Disseminator of Radical Thought," deals with the role of art and theater as a means of influencing opinion in favor of social change. It is important to remember that at the time this essay was written, there was no "mass media" in the modern sense and certainly no electronic media. There was no television or movie industries and radio, silent films, and even photography or the telephone were embryonic technologies. The power and presence of today's media and its ability to shape the wider society including the course of its politics would have been unthinkable then. As she was in so many other areas of political thought and social analysis, Emma Goldman was a pioneer in exploring how the use of cultural forms could be employed to disseminate political ideas and change social norms. Her work in this area preceded more thorough developments of this topic by later thinkers from across the political spectrum including the Italian Communist Antonio Gramsci, the neo-Marxist theorists of the Frankfurt School (particularly Max Horkheimer's critique of the "culture industry"), the neoliberal social theorist Friedrich von Hayek, the Objectivist philosopher Ayn Rand, the French situationists, Michele Foucault and his postmodern hermeneutics, and Alain De Benoist, godfather of the European New Right.

Emma Goldman: Proponent of Nietzschean Aristocratic Radicalism

"Nietzsche was not a social theorist, but a poet, a rebel, and innovator. His aristocracy was neither of birth nor of purse; it was the spirit. In that respect Nietzsche was an anarchist, and all true anarchists were aristocrats."[11]

There can be no doubt that Emma Goldman possessed as much sympathy for the truly oppressed and downtrodden as any person ever did. Yet her sense of empathy for the toiling masses did not blind her to the limitations of ordinary human capabilities. Unlike the Bolshevik leader Trotsky, who once remarked that under Marxism the average human type would reach the heights of an Aristotle or a Goethe, Goldman seemed to recognize a natural stratification of persons with regards to their innate intellectual, moral, and creative faculties. In a similar vein, Goldman once remarked that anarchists are born and not made, a comment that was no doubt a reflection of her realization that most people do not possess the instinct for freedom that so comprehensively defined her worldview. Though Goldman was without question a thinker of the radical Left, her instincts about the limitations of the masses in many ways place her within the

---

11   Goldman, *Living My Life*, pp. 194.

tradition of aristocratic radicalism associated with Nietzsche, Jose Ortega y Gassett, Ernst Junger, and H.L Mencken. Emma understood how easily the average person can be manipulated by institutional authority, particularly that of the state:

> The powers that have for centuries been engaged in enslaving the masses have made a thorough study of their psychology. They know that the people at large are like children whose despair, sorrow, and tears can be turned into joy with a little toy. And the more gorgeously the toy is dressed, the louder the colors, the more it will appeal to the million-headed child. An army and navy represent the people's toys.

Goldman likewise understood that the free association of individuals is the foundation of the good society.

> My lack of faith in the majority is dictated by my faith in the potentialities of the individual. Only when the latter becomes free to choose his associates for a common purpose, can we hope for order and harmony out of this world of chaos and inequality.

These sentiments from Goldman place her far away from the contemporary proponents of political correctness who never tire in their efforts to abridge the freedom of association in the name of creating "rights" for those considered to be in some way disadvantaged or unequal. While Emma clearly had no truck with bigotry of any kind, whether racial, religious, sexual, national, cultural, class, or otherwise, and was light years ahead of her time in her defense of the oppressed, downtrodden, marginalized, alienated, and persecuted, it is inconceivable that she would accept uncritically the shallow orthodoxies advanced even by many contemporary persons who would claim her legacy.

After her death in 1940 and the decline of the classical anarchist movement around the same time, Emma largely faded into obscurity as far as the historical memory was concerned. Yet it was with the cultural upheavals of the 1960s and 1970s that a renewed interest in her work began. There was also a growth of renewed interest in anarchism during this time, and anarchist ideas began to find their way into the ranks of the student rebels of the New Left, the counterculture, and the punk rock subculture of the 1970s. In particular, the growth of the feminist movement in the 1970s brought with it a new appreciation for Goldman's work and ideas and many of her writings were reprinted and brought to a larger audience than even that enjoyed by Emma during her own lifetime.

It is clear enough that Emma Goldman was far ahead of her time in terms of advocating the sweeping social changes that took place in the Western world in the late twentieth century. The liberalization of laws pertaining to birth control, abortion, divorce, homosexuality, sexual expression, free speech, and the rights of the criminally accused, resistance to military conscription and imperialist war, the humane treatment of prisoners, opportunities for women in the academic and professional worlds, the rights of immigrant migrant workers, civil rights for ethnic and racial minorities, and care for the environment were all issues that found much wider audiences in the 1960s and 1970s and which have a direct linear relationship to Goldman's career as a radical activist and writer.

The contemporary academic Left has sought to appropriate Goldman's legacy and in such circles she is often depicted as a prototype for the contemporary clichéd figured of the feminist-Marxist. Yet there are clearly many aspects of Emma's work that would make contemporary leftists very uncomfortable. Some of these have already been discussed: her opposition to mass democracy, her recognition of the limitations of the average person driven primarily by herd instinct, and her admiration of Nietzsche. Likewise, her early prescient criticisms of Bolshevism might well apply with equal force to present day proponents of Cultural Marxism, who like their Bolshevik forbears seek total conformity of thought and work to silence their critics with ridicule, slander, institutionalized censorship and, increasingly, with formal political repression. Her criticisms of the suffragettes as self-absorbed, privileged class women with little real concern for the truly disadvantaged, who use their political influence to not only expand the state but to promote misandry, and who demand equal rights while rejecting equal responsibilities could just as easily apply to many of today's feminist organizations, much to the embarrassment of radical feminists who attempt to claim her mantle.

Above all, it is the uncompromising anarchism of Emma Goldman that continues to set her apart from the faux radicals of the present era, such as the privileged class youths, self-styled victims, and mentally unstable elements who populate the Occupy movement and who claim the banner of "anarchism" but speak the language of left-wing statism if not outright Marxism. Indeed, much of Emma's legacy no doubt overlaps more easily with the libertarian disciples of Ron Paul than it does with the "left" of the present era. The ever growing power of the modern state makes Goldman's anarchist critique of political authority ever more relevant.

The Need for a New Anarchism

It was the rising standards of living of the working classes in the Western world and the taming of the excesses of capitalism through the counterbalancing of capitalist power with that of the social democratic state that were as much as anything else responsible for the decline of the classical anarchist movement and its strident militancy. However, an era is being approached when neither capitalism nor the welfare state will be able to deliver the goods. The advent of the global economy and the subsequent decline of the socioeconomic position of the working and middle classes in the postindustrial nations combined with the growing fiscal crises in those nations and the inevitability of austerity collectively indicate that economic radicalism will likely reemerge at some point in the future. When citizens are no longer able to depend on either the bosses or the state for their sustenance, alternative means of providing for themselves will have to be explored. Already, in the poorest American cities the spectacle of urban gardening is emerging and the models for alternative economic enterprises advanced by earlier anarchist thinkers may regain their relevance. Numerous examples of successful enterprises of this type already exist, perhaps most famously the federation of cooperatives found in the Mondragon region of Spain or the agricultural self-sufficiency of Italy's Emilia-Romagna region.

The ever greater diversification of the contemporary Western nations through mass immigration and demographic, cultural, and generational change insures that the kind of social cohesion necessary to maintain unitary national states will be increasingly difficult to sustain in the generations ahead. Already, there is a growing interest in separatist breakaway movements in both Europe and North America. Social science data indicates that the seeming mass society of the United States contains within itself a plethora of subcultures that are increasingly segregated and self-contained along ideological, cultural, religious, racial, generational, occupational, and socioeconomic lines. It would appear that some sort of formal or informal radical decentralization is inevitable at some point in the future.

The fact the United States has become a nation-state perpetually at war, and which seeks to involve its allies in such conflicts on an ongoing basis, while generating terrorist reprisals against itself with its heavy handed policies on the periphery and working to reignite longstanding rivalries between itself and Russia and China indicates that the anarchist critique of militarism and the inherently expansionist character of the state is as relevant as ever. Likewise, the ever expanding police state, the massive prison industrial complex, the gross overcriminalization of society, the militarization of law enforcement, the seizure of far reaching state powers under the guise of anti-terrorism laws, and the ever growing nanny state which seemingly recognizes no limits to the areas of individual and social life to which it may intrude continue to make the radical anti-statism of anarchism ever more attractive. The time is indeed ripe for the emergence of a new anarchist movement that champions free associations of people tending to their own affairs against the Leviathan regimes produced by contemporary mass democracy.

The Martial Spirit of Emma Goldman

Nietzsche believed that the advent of modernity had brought with it an age of decadence whereby aristocratic values had yielded to the crass commercialism of bourgeois society and the slave morality of egalitarianism. With the loss of aristocratic values came the loss of the warrior ethos and the willingness of the individual to engage in self-sacrifice or expose himself to danger for the sake of values and ideals higher than mere self-preservation or self-gratification. It was this decadence and loss of the warrior spirit that was expounded upon so eloquently by Ernst Junger in his classic essay, "On Danger." As Junger observed:

> The bourgeois person is perhaps best characterized as one who places security among the highest of values and conducts his life accordingly. His arrangements and systems are dedicated to securing his space against the danger that at times, when scarcely a cloud appears to darken the sky, has laded into the distance. However, it is always there: it seeks with elemental constancy to break through the dams with which order has surrounded itself.

> The peculiarity of the bourgeois' relation to danger lies in his perception of it as an irresolvable contradiction to order, that is, as senseless. In this he marks himself off from other figures of, for example, the warrior, the artist, and the criminal, who are given a lofty or base relation to the elemental. Thus battle, in the eyes of the warrior, is a process

that completes itself in a high order; the tragic conflict, for the writer, is a condition in which the deeper sense of life is to be comprehended very clearly; and a burning city or one beset by insurrection is a field of intensified activity for the criminal. In turn bourgeois values possess just as little validity for the believing person, for the gods appear in the elements, as in the burning bush unconsumed by the flames. Through misfortune and danger draws the mortal into the superior sphere of a higher order.[12]

Yet Emma Goldman is one in whom both the aristocratic spirit and warrior ethos was evident. Clearly, she was a superior individual who dared to rise above the sentiments of the herd and create her own identity as a unique individual. Clearly, she did not mind the presence of danger when there were higher values to be pursued. Throughout her life, she endured persistent rejection, ridicule, scorn, imprisonment, exile, and threats of death for her ideals and experienced much sorrow and tragedy along the way. If indeed the Moroccan proverb is correct when it states, "He who has nothing to die for has nothing to live for," then the life of Emma Goldman was certainly a life worth living.

---

12   Junger, Ernst, *On Danger*, New German Critique No. 59, Special Issue on *Ernst Junger* (Spring - Summer, 1993), pp. 27-32.

Democracy as Tyranny

In the early 1950s a collection of essays was published in a single book titled *"The God That Failed"*. The "god" being referred to was Soviet Communism and the authors were disillusioned former Communist enthusiasts whose god had been tried and found severely flawed. Now, a half century later, Hans Hermann Hoppe provides a penetrating critique of another failed political idol. Hoppe's *"Democracy: The God That Failed-The Economics and Politics of Monarchy, Democracy and Natural Order"*(Transaction Publishers, 2001) may well be the most important book on political philosophy to emerge in the last century and may eventually mark the initiation of a whole new era in political thought. If Hoppe's thesis is correct, and he argues his case quite persuasively, then he has revolutionized modern political philosophy in a manner approaching Copernican dimensions. A native of Germany and a professor of economics at the University of Nevada at Las Vegas, Hoppe continues in the school of "Austrian" economics developed by Ludwig von Mises and his student, Murray N. Rothbard. Mises is probably best known for his critique of state socialist schemes for centralized economic planning arguing that such endeavors are literally scientifically impossible as they contain no mechanism (such as the pricing system of the market) by which consumer demand can be effectively calculated thereby guaranteeing that such plans are destined to be wasteful, inefficient failures with shortages of essential goods, overproduction in other areas, a demoralized, unproductive workforce, long-term economic stagnation and eventual economic collapse. Mises resisted the near universal enthusiasms for Marxism and social democracy of his era and clung steadfastly to the classical liberalism and utilitarianism that had emerged in the eighteenth and nineteenth centuries.

Mises' pupil Rothbard took things a bit further, synthesizing Austrian economics with nineteenth century American individualist anarchism and rejecting utilitarianism in favor of a type of revised Lockean natural law theory from which he derived a position that insisted upon absolute individual private property rights (largely defined according to the Lockean "first discovery/mix with labor" principle). Whereas Mises had accepted conventional parliamentary democracy as a form of government, Rothbard rejected the state entirely insisting that even such functions as crime control, courts and defense could be provided by competing private agencies operating on a free market. While Rothbard rejected liberal democracy, he tended to regard it as an advancement over the monarchical and aristocratic systems of the Old Order.

Not so, says Hoppe. Instead, democracy is dismissed as a degeneration towards even greater centralization, statism, tyranny and societal destruction. Hoppe recognizes that the overall standard of living and life expectancy has risen during the time that democracy has been commonplace but insists that this is in spite of rather than because of the advent of democratic state systems. Improvements in the overall human condition have instead been the result of the growth of the market economy, the division of labor, industrialization, technological advancement, higher productivity, etc. Democracy has contributed to none of this in Hoppe's view. To the contrary, democracy has been an obstacle to continued economic improvement which might have been even greater had not democratic states been in the way. Hoppe describes the history of Western political systems as moving from the comparatively stateless feudal order and independent territories to consolidated nation-states and absolute monarchies to modern centralized welfare-warfare state mass democracies to the current foundations being laid for a future global government. Hoppe regards this as an ominous trend leading to universal statism and the destruction of liberty and prosperity.

Essential to Hoppe's thesis is the concept of "time-preference" which is used as a means of describing the degree to which a person prefers instant or delayed gratificaton. Someone with a "high" time-preference values instant gratification to a larger degree and is less willing to forgo immediate pursuit of pleasures or consumption of goods for the sake of some future goal like savings, investment, health, maintaining resources for unforeseen disasters, etc. Likewise, someone with a "low" time-preference is more willing to endure short-term sacrifices for the sake of some future goal. A person with a "low" time-preference is "future-oriented". The more goals one has for the future the more one must work, save, invest, produce and delay gratification in the present. One must maintain a relatively high level of self discipline, personal responsibility and cooperation with others in the process. Conseqently, in a society where overall time-preferences are low the general level of productivity, responsibility, cooperation and civility will be high.

Hoppe describes government as having the social effect of raising time-preferences and reducing expectations for delayed gratification. Government is characterized as having essentially the same effect on society as natural disasters or crime. Both natural disasters such as floods and earthquakes and crimes such robbery and theft diminish the individual's immediate supply of goods thereby raising time-preferences and reducing the amount of resources available for allocation toward future goals. Government achieves a similar effect through its activities of taxing the resources accumulated by the individual, devaluing the unit of exchange ("money") through inflationary monetary policies and restricting the use of resources through regulations and prohibitions. All of this serves to reduce the overall level of productivity and cooperation by reducing the supply of goods available for savings, investment and exchange. Indeed, government is described as having a worse effect on these values than natural disasters or crime as government aggression against and confiscation of individual resources is continuous and ongoing while natural disasters and crime are sporadic and temporary.

The concept of time-preference is used by Hoppe to compare and contrast the effects of monarchical and democratic governments on society, respectively. Hoppe argues that a monarchical ruler will typically have a lower time-preference and be more future oriented than democratically elected rulers and that the policies enacted by a monarch will typically inspire the general population to more salutary behavior than those implemeted by a democratic government. Under a monarchy, the nation is considered the personal property of the king. The nation is then added to the monarch's own personal estate. Naturally, the monarch wishes to improve the value of and maintain the quality of his estate and the prosperity of his estate is connected to the prosperity of the nation as a whole. The monarch also wishes to increase the wealth of the nation for the sake of his posterity and his legacy. A monarch will not wish to tax his subjects to the degree that overall productivity declines and the wealth of the nation, and therefore the monarch's personal and family wealth, decreases. On the other hand, democratic rulers are merely the trustee managers of publicly owned resources. They cannot use these resources once they leave office nor can they bequeath public resources to their offspring. Therefore, the incentive is great to consume in the present with no regard for the future. Also, the higher taxes are at the present time the more resources will be available for democratic rulers to make use of. The long-term effects of such taxation on wealth creation are irrelevant to politicians whose position is temporary. Similarly, as democratic rulers are not personally liable for debts that they incur, but may instead pass such debts on to future generations of taxpayers, there is no incentive for frugality in the present while there is every incentive for wastefulness and improvidence. This explains why taxes and public debts are much higher under democratic governments than under monarchical ones.

Democracy is described by Hoppe as providing incentive towards irresponsible and predatory behavior among both the political class and the general population. A monarch achieves his position by inheriting it. The question of what the character of a particular monarch will be is largely a roll of the dice. A monarch may be a vicious predator, a harmless mediocrity or perhaps even a relatively competent and fair-minded individual. Democratic rulers, on the other hand, come to power largely on the basis of selling themselves to voters. To be effective at this, a successful politician must be, for the most part, an unscrupulous demagogue. Democratic politicians typically acquire a following for themselves by promising to repress or plunder rival economic or cultural groups for the benefit of their own supporters. Under a democracy, the life, liberty and property of every individual comes up for grabs by everyone at every election. Shifting coalitions of oligopolistic special interests and unconstrained popular majorities form, who constantly square off against one another. A situation is created where A and B conspire against C, B and C conspire against A, C and A conspire against B. Democracy becomes merely a substitute for an all-out multiple factioned civil war. The overall moral quality of society degenerates into a war of each against all. Also, the constant plundering and repression of some for the benefit of others decreases the productivity of those being attacked and simultaneously increases the dependency, unproductiveness, infantilization and irresponsibility of those being subsidized with the fruits of the plunder. The general trend in society will be one of decreased productivity and increased crime, recklessness and incivility. Hoppe demonstrates that this trend is currently being played out in Western, particularly American, civilization.

Democracy damages society in other ways. Under a monarchy, there is a clear distinction between the rulers and subjects. Entry into government is typically limited to the royal family and perhaps a few associates and business partners. Under a democracy, the government is ostensibly composed of "everyone" and is "of the people". Elected officials are "the people's representatives". State policy is "the will of the people" and so forth. By perceiving themselves as somehow magically practicing self-rule, there is a decrease in "class consciousness" among the subjects and therefore less popular objection and resistance to taxes, legislation, public debt and even war. Indeed, wars waged by democratic governments tend to be particularly destructive. Monarchical wars are typically fought for the acquisition of territory by the rulers. The public recognizes this and is resistant to participation in such wars. Consequently, popular opinion limits the ability of the monarch to impose taxation or conscription for the purpose of prosecuting the war effort. Democratic wars, on the other hand, tend to be ideological wars. Wars are fought "to make the world safe for democracy", "to defeat godless communism", to turn back the "yellow peril" or the "red horde", to "rid the world of want and fear" or "to eliminate terrorism". Hence, the entire resources of a nation are mobilized for the sake of the war effort. Citizens view themselves as fighting for their "country" rather than for their government or ruling class. Such wars become "total" wars. The goal becomes the complete annihlation of the enemy rather than the mere acquisition of territory. The distinction between combatants and non-combatants is diminished. Unconditional surrender becomes the overriding military objective. Methods of territorial acquisition and the handling of foreign policy disputes that are available under a monarchy, such as marriage or contract, are unavailable to a democratic state. Therefore, foreign policy is organized primarily on the basis of violence.

Hoppe points out that until the commencement of the First World War in 1914, only a handful of Western nations were democracies-America, France, Switzerland and, nominally, England and the Netherlands. All other European nations were monarchies. Since 1914, monarchy has completely disappeared in favor of universal democratization. The subsequent century has seen a massive growth of government, bureaucratic proliferation, increasingly brutal and all-encompassing wars, exorbitant taxation, inflation and currency devaluation, centralization of government, the accumulation of enormous public debts, a breakdown of family and community solidarity, increased mediocrity among the intellectual classes, the rise of totalitarian ideologies such as communism and fascism and an overall increase in crime, economic dependency on the state, personal irresponsibility and ethnic and cultural strife. Hoppe's prognosis for the future of Western civilization is not pleasant. Mounting public debts, ever increasing state obligations for social insurance payments, increasingly exorbitant health care costs, currency destabilization and tax burdens are leading towards a likely economic meltdown. The ongoing tendency towards world government, increased ethnic strife and attacks on traditional liberties, ever expanding social pathologies and perpetual international warfare can only lead to tyranny, societal disintegration and eventual civilizational collapse. As for efforts to reverse this alarming trend, Hoppe insists that the first order of business is to scrap the idea that the power of government, particularly democratic government, can ever be genuinely limited, whether by a written constitution or otherwise. The principle flaw in schemes for limiting the power of government is that legal and constitutional provisions for such limitations are to be interpreted and applied by agents of the state, namely, judges and lawyers, who possess a powerful self-interest in the expansion of the state. In other words, under a limited government the state is to police and regulate itself. The mice are to guard the cheese and the foxes are to guard the chickens. In Hoppe's view, the primary error of classical liberalism was its acceptance of the idea of the state as a necessary evil, rather than as an unnecessary one.

Hoppe favors elimination of the state completely in favor of a system commonly referred to as "anarcho-capitalism" which he alternately describes as "private property anarchy", "natural order" or "private law society". Under such arrangements, all government functions would be privatized including police, courts, streets and defense. The state's armed forces would be dismantled in favor of private mercenaries, militias and guerillas. The state's monopolistic judicial system would be eliminated in favor of competing arbitration agencies. Government-run police forces would be abolished and private police services would operate on the basis of fee-for-service or private contractual agreements. The construction and maintenance of streets and roads would be the perogative of private companies. All taxation and legistlation would be abolished. As for the question of how such a system is to be achieved, Hoppe advocates the building of localized secession movements which would simultaneously work to secure complete independence for their area. The result would be the proliferation of numerous city-states and sovereign territories akin to present day Liechtenstein, Monaco, San Marino, Hong Kong or Singapore. These new political units would then privatize all government functions and effectively abolish the state.

Professor Hoppe has made a monumental contribution to the world of political philosophy. This work is the first serious effort to provide a critique of modern statist "democracy" from an anarchist perspective. Hoppe does not offer anything particularly new to the anarchist attack on the state in a general sense. He largely repeats the arguments offered by earlier anarchists ranging from Godwin to Proudhon to Tolstoy to Rothbard. These and other writers have recognized that the state is an artificially privileged exploiter class that seeks to monopolize exploitation within a particular territorial jurisdiction. Conventional intellectual arguments used to justify the state such as those derived from "social contract" theory and "implicit consent" theory have been thoroughly refuted by Lysander Spooner and others. Hoppe provides no new insights here. Instead, it is with his attack on democratic states specifically that Hoppe makes his contribution to the overall development of anarchist political philosophy. Most people in modern societies generally recognize the illegitimacy of monarchical, aristocratic, theocratic, fascist, communist and military states. However, democratic states are typically thought of as being somehow different from other types of states and as operating on diametrically opposite principles from other regimes. Hoppe skillfully refutes this common misperception.

It has become a commonplace adage among anti-statists that democracy is simply a system whereby four wolves and a sheep take a vote on what to have for lunch and then the wolves pat themselves on the back for being so enlightened and progressive as to take a vote before devouring the sheep. It is a logical absurdity to equate democracy with freedom in the way that mainstream political philosophers and commentators typically do. A system where individuals and minorities are at the mercy of unconstrained majorities hardly constitutes freedom in any meaningful sense. Still, many contemporary persons continue to regard freedom and democracy as synonymous. Indeed, some even equate freedom with merely possessing suffrage in a multi-party system. Democracy is often invoked to justify the most heinous state crimes. The tyrannical drug war is sometimes justified in the name of democracy with the idea being that if the majority approves then any action against individuals must be acceptable. Warmongers currently screaming for an all-out American assault on virtually the entire Muslim world for the sake of advancing Israeli imperialism often try to justify themselves by claiming Israel is "democratic" while its neighbors are not. (Actually, Israel is a racist theocracy.) Military conscription is often justified in the name of democracy. After all, Switzerland has the draft and they are the world's most democratic nation, right? Democratic states typically recognize no limits on their "right" to levy taxes on their subjects with the rationale being that if "the people" elect the government then the people must be taxing themselves. Both social democrats and traditional conservatives appeal to "democracy" to justify virtually any act of repression ranging from zoning ordinances to gun control legistlation to censorship to eminent domain to asset forfeiture laws.

Anarchists, libertarians and, indeed, anti-statists of any stripe must recognize that the abolition of the state is a profoundly un-democratic project as far as modern statist conceptions of democracy are concerned. The political battles of the future will not be between leftists and rightists or liberals and conservatives but between anti-statists and their democratic statist enemies. It is at this point that the meanings of the various types of "democracy" need to be clarified. Democracy may indeed be a wonderful way of operating a voluntary organization or community like a labor union, a cooperative, a neighborhood association, a church or a birdwatchers' club. However, to operate the coercive apparatus of the state as a "democracy" is to invite disaster. Democratic statism simply provides a popular majoritarian cover to whatever actions are carried out by interest groups currently in control of the state who wish to repress or plunder their economic, cultural or ideological competitors. Often, left-anarchists and anarcho-socialists will present themselves as champions of "direct democracy", "consensus democracy" or "participatory democracy". However, this type of democracy is fundamentally different from the centralized, authoritarian, special interest/party politics variety of "democracy" on which modern states are organized. Essential principles of any genuine democracy are voluntarism and decentralization. Membership in participatory democratic communities must be voluntary. The rules and norms of such communities must be consensual in nature. Minorities must not be coercively bound by majoritarian preferences and such communities must be small enough for direct face-to-face deliberation to take place and for dissenters to migrate if they so desire. As an anarcho-capitalist, Hoppe seems to oppose democratic institutions of any type, voluntary or otherwise. Yet, Hoppe's model of an anarchical system is a decentralized collection of private, voluntary communities governing themselves according to their own contractually agreed upon rules. His ideal model of social organization is relatively similar to that employed by shopping malls, planned residential communities and traditional "company towns". But there is no reason why voluntary communities could not form on the principle of either individual private property ownership or voluntary communal ownership and manage themselves in a manner similar to historic New England town meetings.

One flaw in Hoppe's analysis is his failure to differentiate as thoroughly as necessary between the republican ideal of classical liberalism and the all-encompassing centralized statism of modern "democracy". Hoppe regards classical liberal republicanism largely as an initial phase of the conversion from monarchy to democracy. He sees modern democracy as an outgrowth of republicanism. This perspective seems woefully inadequate. Classical liberalism arose in the eighteenth century as an antidote to the tyranny of the ancien regime. The solution to the problems of the Old Order was to be the establishment of a decentralized, confederal republic ordered on the principles of inalienable individual rights, constitutionally limited government and wide separation of powers, both vertically and horizontally. Democracy was to be used merely for administrative purposes within a larger framework of severely limited governmental power. This system, which found its purest expression in the American Revolution, is the diametrical opposite of the authoritarian, centralized, bureaucratic, unconstrained, special interest, state-corporate, welfare-warfare mass democratic states of the modern era. Modern states are not an outgrowth of but a specific repudiation and overthrow of the classical liberal republican ideal.

The pertinent question involves the matter of what forces brought about the demise of republicanism. Hoppe attributes the growth of the modern state to the monopolistic legal order of a constitutional state whereby the constitution is to be enforced by an arm of government, the extension of the franchise and the subsequent creation of more and more interest groups looking to feed at the state's trough and the natural tendency of government to expand over time. However, the initial expansion of statism largely came about as a result of the growth of business corporations and the seizure of power by these corporations. Classical liberal thinkers like Adam Smith and Thomas Jefferson predicted that if the then-nascent corporate class was to continually grow in power and influence the result would be the subversion and destruction of the republican system. The creation of the U.S. constitutional system was in and of itself a coup against the more decentralized and libertarian Articles of Confederation by northeastern banking and mercantile interests led by the likes of Alexander Hamilton who preferred a stronger central government for the advancement of commercial interests. The consolidation of federal power over the states in the American Civil War was largely the result of the seizure of the federal government by northern industrial capitalist interests led by Abraham Lincoln who wished to suppress their southern feudal competitors and subordinate the south as an economic colony.

The further growth of the state in the late nineteenth century was primarily rooted in the mercantilist ambitions of early "big business" leaders of the robber baron period. Since the beginning of the twentieth century, capitalist corporations have been central to statist expansion during the Progressive era, the First World War, the Depression and the New Deal era, the Second World War, the Cold War, the Great Society, 1980s Reaganite military socialism and, now, the current laying of the foundations for a global corporate state via the World Trade Organization, International Monetary Fund, the World Bank, NAFTA, etc. As a staunch economic conservative, Hoppe is loathe to fully recognize the role of capitalist power in the fostering of statism. However, any serious attack on the state must necessarily include an attack on corporate power as well. While it is true that business corporations operating on a purely contractual basis could be among the many different types of economic organizations that could exist in a stateless economy, the present U.S. corporate system rests heavily on state intervention and many contemporary economic elites have attained their positions as a result of the infrastructure created by corporate statism. The collapse of the U.S. regime would mean the simultaneous collapse of the corporate structure as well. The matter of what will come afterward is the next question needing an answer.

Hoppe is also a very reactionary cultural conservative and his comments denouncing "democrats, socialists, multiculturalists, counterculturalists and alternative lifestylists" are reminiscent of Stalinist diatribes against "Trotskyites, social democrats, petty bourgeoise anarchists, rootless cosmopolitans and bourgeoise degenerates". Similarly, Hoppe's anti-immigration hysteria comes perilously close to resembling the rhetoric of xenophobes and nativists raving about "mongrel hordes." Nonetheless, Hoppe raises some interesting questions even on these points. Anarchists and libertarians frequently assume that the end of centralized monopoly government will automatically usher in the reign of a new millenium of freedom and tolerance. However, anarchism merely implies the existence of a social order based on the principle of voluntary association. Questions of property relations are irrelevant at this point. The division between private and communal property is not as clear as some seem to believe. On one hand, ALL property is private to some degree. State-owned property is, for all practical purposes, the private property of the state. Communal property is the private property of the commune. Likewise, many forms of "private" property are owned collectively in some way. Corporations are owned collectively by investors, shareholders and managers. Family property is owned collectively by husbands, wives and heirs.

The anarcho-socialist vision of decentralized communes and federations of workers' syndicates implies that the communes and syndicates will be the collectively owned private property of the workers and communities. Presumably, these units would be able to establish whatever types of internal rules and regulations they wished and exclude those who did not comply or who were not wanted. The same would obviously be true of the privately owned institutions such as schools or businesses that are favored by free-market libertarians. In an anarchist system, there would be no federal regulatory bureaucracy enforcing "civil rights", "anti-discrimination" or other forms of egalitarian legistlation. Consequently, private communities controlled by the Nation of Islam would be able to exclude whites and Jews, businesses controlled by the Aryan Nations would be able to exclude blacks and Jews, Christian educational institutions would be able to exclude homosexuals and atheists, Jewish institutions would exclude Nazis and so on. Landlords could refuse to rent to tenants whose looks they did not like and employers could "discriminate" on any basis they desired. Even if the anarcho-socialist vision of an economy where all rental housing and industry is owned cooperatively by the tenants and workers was to be fully implemented, it is likely that Jewish housing cooperatives would deny admittance to raving anti-semites and that workers cooperatives would refuse to take in lazy, obnoxious parasites. All of this would be perfectly "legal" and permissable in an anarchist order unless some higher political authority said otherwise in which case the state would have re-emerged. Hoppe argues that the level of discrimination would increase markedly in a stateless society.

Libertarians have often been perplexed by the question of "authoritarian cultures". What about those people and groups that simply do not desire liberty for either themselves or others? The venerable anarchist tradition of decentralization represents the best way out of this dilemma. In a system of small, localized, self-managed communities, persons who chafed under the norms of their community of origin would be able to migrate towards an environment that was hopefully more hospitable. Migration as a seriously viable option has long been demonstrated to be the best protector of individual liberty rather than centralized governments and state courts enforcing legistlated "civil rights", "due process", "constitutional rights" and other arbitrary and vaguely defined concepts that are easily ignored or repealed. The utility of decentralization also gives additional weight to Hoppe's prefered strategy of revolution by secession of small groups.

The best bet for smashing Leviathan seems to be the building of separatist movements at the local and regional level. There are already a good number of small but growing groups of this type in the United States-the League of the South, Republic of Texas, the New England Confederation, Alaskan Independence Party, the Green Panthers and others. If these and other groups of this type were to grow and begin supporting one another a full-on assault on the state would be underway. These movements could support one another even when they are geographically separated or even ideologically opposed. In the southern states, for example, rural conservatives and populists could agitate for "states' rights" or "county supremacy" while black nationalists and separatists could demand separate municipalities for predominately black communities in urban areas. Anarcho-socialists in Vermont or Oregon could align themselves with lassez faireists in Kansas or Texas. Small town Christian fundamentalists could align themselves with anarcha-feminist lesbian separatists in San Francisco. Most of the decentralist, libertarian and anti-state groups in the U.S. have yet to consider the opportunities that such alliances might generate. The rallying cry should be "Secessionists Unite!". After all, this is what made the first American Revolution. Perhaps it will be the basis of a second American Revolution as well.

The Iron Fists Masquerading
as Invisible Hands

Every so often in the history of liberty a book or pamphlet has come along that has revolutionized libertarian thought and practice. One of these is Thomas Paine's "Common Sense" which was largely responsible for popularizing the ideals of the Enlightenment and the American Revolution. Another is Lysander Spooner's "No Treason" which utterly demolishes the absurd "social contract" theory on which constitutionalist states are ostensibly based. Hans Hermann Hoppe's recent work "Democracy: The God That Failed" thoroughly refutes the notion that modern democratic statism can be reconciled with liberty or even represents an improvement upon earlier monarchical states. Now comes Kevin Carson's "The Iron Fist Behind the Invisible Hand". Just as Hoppe has revolutionized modern political philosophy by drawing and expanding upon the work of the late Murray N. Rothbard and his teacher, Ludwig von Mises, Carson has, in the space of twenty-four pages, revolutionized political economy by expounding upon the work of Rothbard and another of his influences, the nineteenth century individualist-anarchist Benjamin R. Tucker.

Historically, anarchists have been divided on the question of markets. Traditional anarcho-socialists have typically rejected the market seeing it as nothing more than a source of predatory competition, concentration of economic power and exploitation. Most classical continental European anarchists, particularly the Kropotkinists, sought to abolish the market altogether in favor of a decentralized collection of autarchist communes based on production for subsistence, although some traditional anarcho-communists accepted the idea of free exchange or barter between independent communal units. Some American and British anarchists, such as Tucker or John Henry MacKay, preferred a lassez faire variation of anarchism consisting of small property owners operating on a stateless free market. Some of the differences between communist and individualist anarchists seem to be more of a cultural than economic nature. Anarcho-communists tended to be concentrated in nations, such as Russia or Spain, where industrial capitalism was far less advanced and the old feudal order remained largely intact. The anarcho-communist ideal was largely based on the concept of the peasant village community collectively operating its own agricultural economy minus the external exploitation of the feudal landlords. In nations where the Industrial Revolution had really taken root and the market economy had really begun to expand, such as England or America, anarchists were more likely to idealize the small merchant, craftsman or farmer, hence the individualist character of Anglo-American anarchism. This dichotomy between communist and individualist anarchists continues to the present day. If anything, the differences have become even more pronounced. While the anarchists of old often argued fervently over ideological differences (Tucker and Johann Most refused to recognize one another as "true" anarchists), a mutual admiration frequently existed between the communist and individualist camps. Tucker was an admirer of the European anarchists Proudhon and Bakunin and translated their works into English and his anarchist journal, Liberty, published the writings not only of anarcho-socialists but also of outright Fabians or Marxists, such as George Bernard Shaw. Today, the two camps largely disavow one another. Most contemporary free market anarchists think of themselves as "anarcho-capitalists", whereas Tucker regarded himself as a socialist, and most anarcho-socialists of today reject free market anarchists as mere apologists for corporate power.

Carson ably demonstrates that the division between contemporary anarchists on economic matters need not be as wide as it seems. Like the anarcho-capitalists, Carson favors a genuinely stateless free market. However, he argues effectively that the economic arrangements that an authentic free market economy would likely produce are remarkably similar to those typically advocated by anarcho-socialists. Serious free market economists, such as Rothbard, have long recognized that the corporatist structure of modern "Big Business" rests on state intervention rather than lassez faire. The state creates the fictitious legal infrastructure of corporate "personhood". The state protects and assists corporations by means of limited liability laws, subsidies, government contracts, loans, guarantees, bailouts, purchases of goods, price controls, regulatory privilege, grants of monopolies, protectionist tariffs and trade policies, bankruptcy laws, military intervention to gain access to international markets and protect foreign investments, regulating or prohibiting organized labor activity, eminent domain, discriminatory taxation, ignoring corporate crimes and countless other forms of state-imposed favors and privileges.

Carson traces the development of modern corporate states all the way back to the late medieval period. In those days, the feudal structure, which originated from the military conquest of traditional agricultural communities and the imposition of an artificial aristocracy of external state-privileged exploiters, was in the process of breaking down. The free cities of the era began to appear as points of light on the broader feudal map. The market economy was growing, innovative technologies were coming into existence and the common people were obtaining more opportunities to claim their rightful status as free individuals. The ruling class was put on the defensive and sought to reestablish itself by fully expropriating traditional peasant lands and militarily conquering the free cities. The dispossessed peasants, no longer having any means of autonomy or self-sufficiency, were forced to migrate towards industrial centers and into the slave-like factory system. The state intervened to make sure that labor discipline was maintained by such methods as severely restricting the freedom of migration and suppressing efforts at self-organization by the laborers. The old feudal elites reinvented themselves as a new industrial capitalist ruling class by means of mercantilist economic policies which tended to concentrate wealth. In early America, for example, it was the northeastern mercantilists consisting of banking, shipping and land magnates led by Alexander Hamilton who initiated the Federalist coup against the libertarian Articles of Confederation and established the centralist presidential state for the purpose of advancing mercantilist commercial interests.

Carson's central thesis is that "capitalism", defined in the traditional Marxist/socialist/left-anarchist sense of separation of labor from ownership and the subordination of labor to capital, would largely be impossible under genuine free market arrangements. Most Americans are accustomed to thinking of capitalism and free enterprise as being one and the same. This is certainly the perspective taught in the state's educational institutions and promoted by the corporate media. Carson lambasts fake populism of the type promulgated by corporate-sponsored afternoon talk radio which ignores the role of corporations, banks and other elite economic interests in fostering statism and instead works to channel the hostility of the working and middle classes away from the elites for whom most state intervention is actually done and towards the lower classes and the urban poor in a type of "divide and conquer" strategy. According to this ideology, the real enemies of free enterprise and proponents of statism are welfare recipients and the residents of homeless shelters and public housing projects. But it is the ruling class that is the primary beneficiary of state intervention. The primary role of such intervention is to redistribute wealth upward and centralize economic power. The tools used to obtain these objectives are as old as modern corporate states themselves. These tools include the state-imposed money monopoly, patents and subsidies.

Under the present system of federal government monopoly on the issuance of legal tender and central banking via the Federal Reserve, interest rates are kept artificially high, an artificial shortage of credit is maintained and access to finance capital is constricted. These arrangements centralize wealth and concentrate economic power in a myriad of ways. Carson argues that under a system of free banking, cooperative banks would be able to form and issue private bank notes as credit against the output of future production. Genuine competition among free banks would dramatically reduce interest rates, perhaps to the cost of administrative overhead. Access to cheap credit would make self-employment possible for nearly any industrious person with marketable skills or services. As the price of capital diminished, interest upon bonds, dividends upon stock and rents upon land and buildings would also fall. The proliferation of new businesses and the increased viability of self-employment would greatly enhance the bargaining power of workers, both individually and collectively. Workers would have a wider variety of potential employers to choose from in addition to greater opportunities to work for themselves. Employers would be forced by market pressures to make their workplaces more attractive to prospective employees. Workers would gain the collective power to demand the right of self-management in the workplace and could pool their credit to buy out their employers if they wished. This greatly enhanced bargaining power would essentially allow workers to control industries, even industries that remained nominally stockholder-owned. The virtual elimination of interest through market competition would also significantly lower mortage payments and credit card debt. The cost of housing would drop and overall workers' savings would increase. Part-time employment would become a more viable option for many workers as would earlier retirement. Involuntary unemployment would also shrink.

Echoing Rothbard, Carson demonstrates how patents are nothing more than government grants of monopoly privilege. The function of patent law is to create monopolies on the marketing of particular products thereby establishing an artificial pricing system where such products are marked up dozens of times beyond their actual market value. This has been particularly true of pharmaceuticals where prices are often marked up 40 times or more. The effect of this arrangement is to eliminate competition and innovation by others seeking to improve upon an original product. Patent privilege pertaining to drugs and medical technologies sharply increases the cost of health care to the average consumer, effectively pricing many of forms of health care out of the range of many consumers. The restrictions on competition involved in patent privileges also constrict economic growth and increase unemployment. International patent privileges established by global trade agreements also tend to concentrate wealth in the advanced nations and stifle growth, competition and innovation in the Third World. Patents serve as a mercantilist tool utilized to maintain lesser developed nations as economic colonies.

Subsidies are probably the most egregious form of state favors to economic elites. Virtually all major U.S. industries are heavily dependent in some way on direct or indirect government financing. Throughout U.S. history, federal subsidies to transportation from the railway system to interstate highways to civil aviation have served to centralize wealth and control over a wide assortment of industries ranging from electrical utilities to petroleum to finance to retail sales. Much is made in some circles about the way large corporate retail chains such as Wal-Mart undercut local small businesses and run them out of the market. But this would be impossible without the massive government subsidies to shipping and transportation that benefit large national chains. So-called "defense spending" frequently amounts to a corporate welfare program. Most defense analysts estimate that a defense budget of approximately $100 billion would be required to effectively defend the territory of the United States. Yet overall military spending is nearly three and a half times that amount and increasing. The primary beneficiaries of such spending are arms manufacturers, the telecommunications industry, defense contractors and petrochemicals industries whose profits are guaranteed via the Pentagon system. This arrangement creates a tremendous concentration of wealth in the hands of de facto state protected monopolies. Tax breaks to corporations that subsidize R&D centralize wealth even further. Carson notes that some free market economists, including Rothbard, object to the characterization of tax breaks as subsidies, an understandable argument, but the problem here is that the burden of making up for this lost revenue is shifted onto the small businessman and rank and file worker.

Carson also engages in a rather thorough analysis of how the state creates an ideological superstructure to conceal its true nature and intentions. Outrageous amounts of "defense" spending are justified by demonizing one local tinpot dictator in the Third World after another, most of whom are the direct creation of U.S. imperialism, subversion, interventionism and aggression. Poor nations with no history of imperial ambition outside of their immediate borders, such as China, are held up as grave threats to world security. Currently, the beleaguered nation of Iraq, which has never acted aggressively against a single American, is attacked as the Second Coming of Nazi Germany and the American public is bombarded with exaggerations and outright lies regarding Iraq's weapons capabilities. Those who criticize and speak out against these lies are denounced as "un-American" under the cover of a pseudo-patriotic ideology while the state controlled media and educational system seeks to remove the authentic patriotism of Jefferson, Madison and Henry from public consciousness. Domestically, corporate sponsored think tanks and other propaganda outlets attack the urban poor as the source of the nation's extensive fiscal problems and pretend that state aid to corporate and financial interests is non-existent. Elite class interests play to public hysteria over crime and scapegoat immigrants, drug users, the homeless and other marginal groups in order to justify the creation of a massive police state apparatus for the purpose of social control.

The implications of Carson's analysis are broad and profound. I have long believed that the development of an entirely new ideological paradigm is necessary if the state is to be effectively combatted. Carson effectively debunks not only the ideology of the ruling class in all its various manifestations-traditional conservatism, neoconservatism, social democracy, welfare liberalism-but also demolishes the positions of various opposition movements as well. His skillful analysis of the impossibility of the centralization of wealth into a class hierarchy without state intervention completely debunks Marxism, which maintains that the market rather than the state is to blame for such centralization. Carson points out that this critique simultaneously debunks the "anarcho-social democracy" of Noam Chomsky to which most contemporary left-anarchists subscribe. "Mainstream" libertarianism is also demonstrated to be grossly inadequate. Carson says of this element:

> Although a few intellectually honest ones like Rothbard and Hess were willing to look into the role of coercion in creating capitalism, the Chicago School and Randoids take existing property relations and class power as a given. Their ideal "free market" is merely the current system minus the progressive regulatory and welfare state-i.e., nineteenth century robber baron capitalism.

Indeed, Carson debunks the U.S. Constitution itself. Among the powers delegated to the federal government by the Constitution are the issuance of patents, subsidy of infrastructure and maintenance of a monopoly on legal tender — precisely the means by which wealth is concentrated and a state-protected ruling class emerges. This demonstrates once and for all that the anti-federalist critics of the creation of the federal government, such as Jefferson and Henry, were correct and that Hamilton and his cronies were traitors to the Revolution just as Lenin and Trotsky betrayed the anti-czarist revolution in Russia.

Carson's analysis is consistent with the work of Rothbard but requires a more thorough application of Rothbardian principles that even Mr. Libertarian himself adhered to. Rothbard recognized the role of the state in creating feudalism and slavery and therefore understood the justice of the compensation of slaves and serfs through the expropriation of the masters and landlords. But Carson has shown that modern corporate states rest on the original expropriation of four centuries ago and the maintenance of this artificial class structure through state intervention ever since. Recognition of this fact necessitates incorporating these factors into modern theories of property rights. Forms of "private" ownership dependent on state intervention are illegitimate according to authentic free market principles. The remaining issue involves the means by which the present unjust order is to be dismantled and replaced with a just one.

It might be useful at this point to consider Hans Hermann Hoppe's application of the traditional anarcho-syndicalist principle to the overtly state socialist regimes of Eastern Europe. Hoppe argued that natural property relations had been so diluted by decades of state socialism that it would be impossible to return Communist state property to its rightful owners according to any objective criteria. Therefore, the syndicalist principle of property rights defined according to usufructuary principles (i.e., use and occupation) was applicable. Interestingly, Hoppe denied that such principles were applicable to the corporate states of the West. However, if such states rest on massive state intervention and expropriation, as Carson ably demonstrates, then such states and their distortions of normal market-based property relations are no more legitimate than those imposed by the Communist mafias of the East. When the present U.S. regime eventually collapses under the weight of its own corruption and mismanagement, most of the corporate and financial infrastructure will likely collapse simultaneously. At that time it will be vital that leaders and popular organizations emerge with constructive plans for the restoration of economic order and normalcy. The alternative will be the chaos that has plagued the former Communist nations and has led to the popular re-election of the old Communist parties, having reinvented themselves as "social democrats," in some instances.

Elsewhere, Carson has written of the need for the development of a popular movement for the dismantling of the state according to a specific hierarchy of priorities. In the interim, those aspects of the state most in need of being attacked are those state practices designed to create an artificially privileged ruling class such as patents, subsidies, the military-industrial complex, the federal money monopoly and the apparatus of the police state. Unlike the so-called "libertarians" of the statist variety (for example, the Cato Institute and the Reason Foundation) who equate liberty with the pseudo-privatization of social security and the state funding of private schools via the voucher system all the while ignoring corporate welfare, military pork and the prison industry, a true anti-state movement must be a populist people's movement against the super-state and its corporate and media allies. This would involve the creation of economic organizations not connected to the state including independent labor unions, credit unions, mutual banks, mutual aid societies, cooperatives and associations of small businessmen, farmers, workers and ordinary taxpayers unified for the purpose of carrying out a formal tax strike. Such institutions would form the basis for economic reconstruction once the statist system disintegrates.

Upon the event of such a systemic collapse, the syndicalist principle will have to be applied far and wide. Collapsed industries would go to the workers with small investors retaining the rights to their shares but no compensation for those who have made millions or billions from state intervention. Agribusiness cartels supported by the state are responsible for the destruction of traditional family farms and the loss of family lands in the process. Consequently, the land holdings of these cartels would be open to homesteading. The federal government owns more than a third of the land in the continental U.S. and this land should be open to homesteaders as well. Public universities would go to the professors, schools to the teachers, streets to the neighborhoods or street repair workers, military bases to the soldiers, public buildings to the bureaucrats, recreational facilities to management agencies and so on. From there each new set of proprietors would be responsible for organizing their own domain according to their own economic needs. Bureaucrats, for example, may sell their buildings or convert their facilities to self-sustaining businesses. Federal courthouses may become the property of the judges and lawyers who then proceed to sell their services as mediators and arbiters, assuming anyone would wish to purchase their services.

The resulting set of economic arrangements would likely be quite diverse. Workers may elect to convert their industries to employee-run cooperatives with individual non-marketable shares being the basis of ownership or, if they wished, they could sell shares to outsiders as well. Productive institutions might well span the whole spectrum from private contractual business corporations to worker owned cooperatives to stockholder owned businesses managed by the workers to collective institutions of the Israeli kibbutzim variety. Intentional communities might be formed that held certain industrial or manufacturing or utility services in common. Small scale enteprenuership would likely expand dramatically and the number of independent craftsmen would increase. Anti-statists need not argue over the details of what a stateless economy would look like. The ideals of free-market libertarians, syndicalists, anarcho-primitivists, municipalists, guild socialists, councilists, mutualists, Georgists, distributists and many other tendencies could be realized in stateless economy. The only requirement is that such arrangements be voluntary and freely chosen. A synthesis of Rothbardian radical free market economics, traditional class struggle anarchism and historic American revolutionary populism provides the ideological vehicle for the achievement of these goals.

Philosophical Anarchism and the Death of Empire

Note: What follows is an effort, however humble, to apply traditional anarchist theory to the world situation we contemporary radicals currently find ourselves in, particularly the emergence of the New World Order, the ongoing dilemma of the Leviathan state, and the uniquely subtle form of totalitarianism that has caught the fancy of the elites of the First World nations, so-called "political correctness."

What I have tried to develop is a kind of "big picture" anarchism, an anarchism that confronts the aforementioned issues head-on, without the distractions that preoccupy most of those in conventional anarchist circles (anti-racism, ecology, popular left-wing causes, particular economic positions, etc.). I have developed something of a reputation for myself as a staunch proponent of jettisoning the conventional "left/right" model of the political spectrum. In this article, I attempt to carry this idea even further. Specifically, I reject the linear, "progressive" view of history implicit in much contemporary political thought in favor of an approach that somewhat approximates the cyclical view suggested by Nietzsche. Additionally, I am increasingly drawn to the view that the most serious intellectual problem of our time, at least with regards to political philosophy and social theory, is the universalist presumption adhered to by virtually all modern political thinkers, whether they be of the liberal, Marxist, conservative, neoconservative, libertarian, or left-anarchist variety. Additionally, the world's two largest religions, Christianity and Islam, along with the increasing monistic humanism that dominates the intellectual culture of the West, include fairly powerful universalist strands as well.

Philosophical Anarchism and the Death of Empire

Lawrence Dennis considered the most negative attribute of the Enlightenment era to be the tendency to interpret the world from the perspective of abstract ideological principles regarded as above and beyond the lived experience of real world human beings. The influence of such thinking on the Jacobins during the period of the French Revolution, the perpetrators of the Napoleonic Wars, and the ideologies of the imperial powers that came to a head in the Second World War (liberalism, fascism, communism) has been previously noted by certain scholars. The French New Right theorist Alain de Benoist goes even further, arguing that the monotheistic orientation of the Judeo-Christian traditions, and the concurrent negating of all other gods and traditions, along with the supplanting by these of the earlier pagan views of divinity, provided the historical foundation for the universalist conceptions of the modern era.[1] Whatever the case may be, it seems clear enough that the key to mounting an effective resistance to the New World Order is the cultivation

---

1   Some clarification on this point is needed. While the term "Judeo-Christian" has become fashionable in modern times, Judaism and Christianity are two separate and distinct traditions. With regards to the question of universalism, Judaism is far less so than Christianity. Foundational Torah Judaism, the type still practiced by some sects like the Neturei Karta, is a profoundly particularistic religion—of the Jews, for the Jews, and by the Jews. Although Gentiles are allowed to convert, Judaism in this form is frequently regarded as being in many ways irrelevant to outsiders. Also, evidence exists that the early Hebrews were henotheistic rather than monotheistic, but simply recognized Yahweh as their ethnic god, in the same way that other eastern Mediterranean peoples recognized Baal. It was the apostate Jew Saul of Tarsus (later known as St. Paul the Apostle) who brought overtly universalistic conceptions into Judaism, apparently against the wishes of some of the earliest disciples of Jesus (Galatians 2:11–14). It could also be argued that the current showdown between Islam and the West, the "clash of civilizations" referred to by Samuel P. Huntington, is best understood as a religious war between two offshoots of Judaism and Christianity— Islam and Humanism. Says Tomislav Sunic: "Undoubtedly, many would admit that in the realm of ethics all men and women of the world are the children of Abraham. Indeed, even the bolder ones who somewhat self-righteously claim to have rejected the Christian or Jewish theologies, and who claim to have replaced them with 'secular humanism,' frequently ignore that their self-styled secular beliefs are firmly grounded in Judeo-Christian ethics. Abraham and Moses may be dethroned today, but their moral edicts and spiritual ordinances are very much alive. The global and disenchanted world, accompanied by the litany of human rights, ecumenical society, and the rule of law—are these not principles that can be directly traced to the Judeo-Christian messianic outlook that resurfaces today in its secular version under the elegant garb of modern 'progressive' ideologies?" ("Monotheism vs. Polytheism, by Alain de Benoist, Introduction and translation by Tomislav Sunic, *Chronicles: A Magazine of American Culture*, April 1996.)

of a cross-cultural ethic whereby a taboo is erected against the insistence that a specific world view be universalized. It would seem that philosophical anarchism is the political paradigm most compatible with the establishment of such a taboo.

The history of human civilization can be divided into three primary phases when considering the evolution of political institutions. The first of these involves an idea that might be described as "the divinity of kings." In the ancient civilizations of Egypt, Babylon, and Rome, the head of state was assigned a godlike status by custom, tradition, law, theology, and popular folklore alike. The early Roman Christians were sent to the lions for the crime of "atheism" which, in the theology of the Roman state religion, meant denial of the divinity of the emperor.[2] When Christianity went on to conquer Greco-Roman civilization, a new political theology evolved in the form of the "divine right of kings," meaning that the king ruled, not as a god himself, but as an earthly appointee of a Divine Other who had been providentially chosen to rule in the political realm just as the Pope ruled in the religious realm. A principal achievement of the Enlightenment of the seventeenth and eighteenth centuries was the demolition of the notion of the divine right of kings. Beginning with the American and French Revolutions of the eighteenth century, a third political paradigm has come to dominate human political life.

Against Democratism

This paradigm that is now nearly universal, at least in the advanced countries, is the paradigm of liberal democracy. It might be said that liberal democracy discards the "divine right of kings" for the "democratic right of the state." Most people

---

2 Mosheim says of second-century Christians: "The simplicity of the worship which the Christians offered to the Deity gave occasion to certain calumnies maintained by both the Jews and the pagan priests. The Christians were pronounced atheists because they were destitute of temples, altars, victims, priests, and of all that pomp in which the vulgar suppose the essence of religion to consist." (Mosheim, Ecclesiastical History, bk. 1, chap. 4, par. 3.)

in the modern world recognize the illegitimacy of fascist, Nazi, communist, monarchical, theocratic, aristocratic, and military forms of government. It is assumed by persons on all points of the political spectrum that a government is only legitimate if periodic elections are held, opposition parties are allowed to organize, and something resembling a "free press" exists. For example, American political culture includes Christian fundamentalists, economic nationalists, and anti-immigration proponents on the "far right," and Marxists, radical feminists, and postmodernists on the "far left." Yet all of these parties claim the banner of "democracy." Those who wish to censor speech that is deemed "hateful" or "obscene" do so under the guise of seemingly venerable democratic notions like "community standards," majoritarian preference, or social equality. Likewise, those who champion "free speech" do so under the seemingly democratic principle of free exchange of ideas and beliefs. Those favoring racial quotas or preferences cite the allegedly democratic principle of equal opportunity while those opposed to such preferences claim that individual responsibility and merit are essential to democracy. Both socialists and "free market" economists claim to be advocates of "economic democracy."

The underlying presumption behind all of these points of view is that virtually any course of action that the state pursues is acceptable so long as the state meets a few bare minimum standards of democracy like "free elections," "free speech," and so on.[3] It is said that the state exists on the basis of a "social contract" and is a reflection of the "popular will." For these reasons, it is widely believed that individuals have an obligation to

---

3   For example, the renowned British historian Paul Johnson, a darling of neo-
     conservatives, says of Jean-Paul Sartre: "Sartre never showed any real knowledge of or
     interest in—let alone enthusiasm for—parliamentary democracy. Having the vote in a
     multi-party society was not at all what he meant by freedom. What did he mean then?"
     (Paul Johnson, Intellectuals [New York: Harper and Row, 1988], 243.) It is interesting
     that a figure as eminent as Johnson apparently cannot conceive of any form of freedom
     greater than run of the mill parliamentarianism. Has he ever read Mill, Spencer,
     Stirner, Proudhon, Mencken, Rothbard, Rand, or even Milton Friedman? Sartre's
     views could be muddled and inchoate at times, to say the least. But Johnson, a former
     Laborite journalist who went to neoconservatism in the 1970s, seems to have no more
     capacity for independent thinking than the typical Soviet commissar.

comply with the decrees of the state, whether in the matter of the payment of taxes, military conscription, weapons confiscation, the prohibition of particular social or cultural practices, or whatever. This common notion is what is meant by the "democratic right of the state." Behind the shield of "democracy," the state may do what it wishes to its subjects, who in turn have no one to blame for their predicament but themselves as they comprise the state, an expression of the "general will." The absurdity and illogic of this view ought to be obvious enough. Clearly, the dominant political paradigm of "democracy" is severely flawed.[4] A new paradigm is surely needed.

Philosophical anarchism holds that the institution of the state is undesirable and unnecessary, and that it should be eliminated in favor of voluntary association and cooperation among groups and individuals. A coherent anarchist would seek to replace the current political paradigm of liberal democracy with a new paradigm in the form of philosophical anarchism or, more specifically, a social order grounded on the principle of voluntary association. The traditional anarchist position regards the state as nothing more than a criminal organization that exists for no genuine purpose beyond the control of territory, the protection of an artificially privileged ruling class, the exploitation of its subjects, and the expansion of its own power. This perspective is consistent with numerous philosophical, ethical, and religious traditions. This was the position of both the classical anarchist theoreticians and modern libertarian-anarchists like Murray Rothbard.[5] The anarchist position on the state is also supported by the sociologist Franz Oppenheimer's landmark study on the origin of the state and its roots in plunder and conquest.[6] Democratists have attempted to respond to the anarchist critique of the state by claiming that their preferred form of state is somehow different from older expressions of the state, usually rooting their claims in some sort of constitutionalist or majoritarian doctrine. Yet, the constitutionalist theory of the state has been comprehensively refuted by Lysander Spooner and his critique of "social contract" theory.[7] And virtually all reasonable political thinkers from Plato and Aristotle onward have recognized majoritarianism as nothing more than a form of mob rule.

The classical liberal economist William Graham Sumner once remarked that the day would come when men would be divided into only two political camps, anarchists and socialists, or, more descriptively of Sumner's views, statists and anti-statists.[8] Sumner's prediction is in the process of being realized as the statist ideology of mass democracy is becoming more and more universalized throughout the modern world. This process has produced some rather silly intellectual offshoots in the form of Francis Fukuyama's "End of History" theory and the "democratic imperialism" of the neoconservatives.[9] So pervasive is democratist ideology that even some anti-statists cannot separate "democracy" from their own critique of the state. For example, many left-wing anarchists claim "direct" or "consensus-

implications even more radical than even he seemed to realize. The best introductions to Rothbard's outlook would likely be his *Man, Economy and State* (1962), *Power and Market* (1970), *For a New Liberty* (1974) and *The Ethics of Liberty* (1982). See also Justin Raimondo's biography of Rothbard, *An Enemy of the State: The Life of Murray Rothbard* (Amherst, NY: Prometheus Books, 2000).

6   Franz Oppenheimer, *The State: Its History and Development Viewed Sociologically*, trans. John M. Gitterman (New Brunswick: Transaction Publishers, 1999).

7   Lysander Spooner, *No Treason: The Constitution of No Authority*.

8   Pierre Lemieux, "Give Me Libertarianism," *Financial Post*, August 29, 2002.

9   Francis Fukuyama, *The End of History and the Last Man* (New York: Free Press, 1992); Joshua Micah Marshall, "Remaking the World: Bush and the Neoconservatives," *Foreign Affairs* 82, no. 6 (November–December 2003); Lee McCracken, "The End of Conservatism," http://www.strike-the-root.com/3/mccracken/mccracken6.html

based" democracy as their ideal.[10] So be it. The voluntary associations that would form the basis of an anarchist social order could indeed have democratic internal structures of some type. But anarchist theory no more mandates that an association have a democratic form of organization than it mandates an autocratic one. Similarly, aside from avowed anti-democrats like Hans-Hermann Hoppe, many libertarians speak of "democratic processes" and "democratic ideals," often going so far as to claim that the current system of electoral democracy is fundamentally legitimate but has only been corrupted by an excess of statism brought on by self-serving public interest groups, crooked politicians, a disproportionate amount of power in the hands of statist intellectuals, etc.[11]

Bob Black has noted that one of the foremost obstacles to the realization of anarchism is the anarchists themselves.[12] Frankly, many professed anarchists could not give a coherent description of anarchist theory or what an anarchist society, realistically speaking, might look like to save their lives.[13] If anarchism is to be

10 I am consistently amazed at the large number of left-libertarians who somehow believe that "decentralized direct democracy" would be the realization their own sociocultural ideals. In many communities, such a system would likely result in the establishment of theocracy or a racialist or nationalist enclave, just as the establishment of conventional parliamentary democracy in contemporary Iraq would no doubt result in a Shiite fundamentalist regime. It is important that anarchists work to develop a critique of modern societies whose depth surpasses that of conventional leftist or left-liberal analysis and emphasis. "Democracy" is not a universal cure-all or absolute, nor is "peace," "justice," "freedom," feminism, environmentalism, anti-racism, or any other left-wing shibboleth. These ideals and tendencies are defined in different ways by different people, many times arising in response to specific historical or cultural situations that are inapplicable to other situations.

11 It should not take a genius of political science to understand that mobocracy and individualism are incompatible, but many libertarians make a tortured effort to reconcile these two.

12 Bob Black, "Anarchism and Other Impediments to Anarchy," http://www.primitivism. com/impediments.htm

13 Keith Preston, "Anarchism or Anarcho-Social Democracy?," http://www. attackthesystem.com/anarchism2.html For most contemporary anarchists, "anarchism" is a muddled utopian ideology implicitly influenced by Rousseauian or Fourierist ideas, often mixed with bits of Dadaist nihilism or a romantic attachment to the Old Left. Contemporary left-anarchism is also heavily influenced by Gramscian cultural Marxism, whereby racial minorities, feminists, and homosexuals take the place of the proletariat as the focus of the class struggle.

defined by the principle of voluntary association, then a system of radical individual autonomy is implied. Individual autonomy of this type should not be confused with either licentiousness or egocentrism. Instead, individual autonomy involves a social order where individual persons choose for themselves the kinds of associations, communities, and institutions they wish to be connected to. Persons with different values, beliefs, interests, or needs will form different kinds of associations. Elitists will form elitist associations. Egalitarians will form egalitarian associations. Socialists will form socialist associations. Racialists will form racialist associations. A continuing theme of traditional anarchism is Kropotkin's concept of "mutual aid," whereby people cooperate with one another towards common ends.[14] But mutual aid can occur only among people with common values and objectives. Consequently, the overarching principle of voluntary association implies that individuals and groups with conflicting interests or goals will naturally separate themselves from one another and practice mutual self-segregation. This in turn implies a radically decentralized social system where different kinds of cultural and ideological groups exercise sovereignty within their own communities. Of course, a social order based on perfect voluntarism or sovereignty may never be achieved in the real world, which is why insightful libertarian theorists including Pierre-Joseph Proudhon, Bertrand Russell, and Paul Goodman have regarded "anarchy" as an ideal, like "peace" and "justice," that humanity can only strive for.[15]

---

14   One of the founding fathers of classical anarchism, Peter Kropotkin was a pioneer if often unrecognized sociologist. Although a formidable social scientist and philosopher, he had a strong inclination towards the delusional utopianism that characterizes much nineteenth-century political thought. His best works are *Mutual Aid*, *The Conquest of Bread*, and *Ethics*.

15   Pierre-Joseph Proudhon, the first thinker to call himself an anarchist, in many ways had more in common with Jeffersonian liberals or Burkean traditional conservatives than the revolutionary socialist tradition that classical anarchism is typically identified with. His application of anarchism was entirely practical, favoring decentralist confederations of local communities, each retaining their own cultural identity, and an economy ordered on worker cooperatives and mutual banks. Bertrand Russell, an unceasing radical during his nearly a century-long life, sometimes expressed sympathy for the ideals of the classical anarchists, but regarded them as impractical. Instead, he clung to the Old Liberalism of his godfather, John Stuart Mill, and the Guild Socialism of G. D. H. Cole and R. H. Tawney. Paul Goodman called himself

It is interesting to explore the objections that anti-anarchists raise against the anarchist position and equally interesting to review the criticisms that different schools of anarchism have of one another. Most reasonable criticisms of the anarchist position are rooted, at least implicitly, in the ideas of Hobbes. In the classical Hobbesian view, human beings left to their own devices exist only in a "state of nature," the essence of which is characterized as "a war of each against all." The Hobbesian "solution" to humanity's predicament is the establishment of a "sovereign" who wields absolute power for the sake of achieving order and making civilization possible.[16] One need not reject Hobbes' overall view of human nature (and I do not) in order to recognize the circular nature of his argument for the supremacy of the sovereign. If human beings cannot be trusted to manage their own affairs in a non-predatory manner, how then is a state comprised of mere human beings to be trusted with power over others? Will not the state, the members of which ostensibly rule on behalf of "order," use its power for predatory purposes of its own? Of course it will. As Errico Malatesta noted:

We do not believe in the infallibility, nor even in the general goodness of the masses; on the contrary. But we believe even less in the infallibility and goodness of those who seize power and legislate, who consolidate and perpetuate the ideas and interests which prevail at any given moment.[17]

... the nature of government does not change. If it assumes the role of controller and guarantor of the rights and duties of everyone, it perverts the sentiment of justice; it qualifies as a crime and punishes every action which violates or threatens the privileges of the rulers and the property owners ... If it appoints itself as the administrator of public

---

a "conservative-anarchist," believing anarchism to require a gradual, evolutionary process.

16   Thomas Hobbes, *Leviathan* (Harmondsworth: Penguin Books, 1985).

17   Errico Malatesta, "Crime and Punishment," http://flag.blackened.net/daver/anarchism/crime_and_punishment.html

services . . . it looks after the interests of the rulers and the property owners and does not attend to those of the working people except where it has to because the people agree to pay.[18]

Throughout history, just as in our time, government is either the brutal, violent, arbitrary rule of the few over the many or it is an organised instrument to ensure that dominion and privilege will be in the hands of those who by force, by cunning, or by inheritance, have cornered all the means of life . . .[19]

Malatesta had no illusions that democracy was an improvement over any other kind of state and essentially agreed with George Bernard Shaw's adage that "democracy substitutes election by the incompetent many for appointment by the corrupt few."[20] Said Malatesta of democracy:

. . . if you consider these worthy electors as unable to look after their own interests themselves, how is it that they will know how to choose for themselves the shepherds who must guide them? And how will they be able to solve this problem of social alchemy, of producing the election of a genius from the votes of a mass of fools?[21]

Democracy is simply a system whereby A and B conspire against C, B and C conspire against A, and A and C conspire against B. As Max Stirner noted, "In a republic, all are masters, and each tyrannizes over the others."[22]

18   Errico Malatesta, *Anarchy*, trans. Vernon Richards (London: Freedom Press, 1974), 22–23.

19   *Ibid.*, 17–18.

20   George Bernard Shaw, *Man and Superman*.

21   Malatesta, *Anarchy*, 53.

22   Max Stirner, *The Ego and His Own*.

Anarchists have never been able to agree among themselves on the question of what an ideal anarchist society would look like. The adherents of virtually all of the schools of anarchism accuse the other anarchist sects of statism and authoritarianism. Anarchists of the leftist or socialist variation are accused of favoring what, in practice, would amount to little more than a decentralized form of social democracy or state communism (and some of this not so decentralized).[23] Libertarian anarchists are condemned for favoring a form of industrialized feudalism that would amount to little more than aristocratic rule by local elites by means of private courts, police, and armies.[24] A newer school of anarchism called "national-anarchism" includes among its adherents believers in racial separatism (as opposed to racial supremacy) and resolute opponents of social practices dear to the hearts of leftists like abortion and homosexuality.[25] Consequently,

23 A particularly grotesque example of left-wing anarcho-statism can be found in the
    Northeastern Anarchist: Magazine of the Northeastern Federation of Anarcho-Communists,
    a publication that favors a global communist government with a central planned
    economy, which will allegedly be anarchistic because the central planners will be
    delegates chosen by local communities. Even this last point is not exactly clear.
    Apparently delegates from factory floors from all over the world are to meet in one big
    workers' parliament to plan production for the whole planet.

24 Hans-Hermann Hoppe even goes so far as to claim that feudal society was stateless, a
    dubious proposition at best.

25 For some in the national-anarchist milieu, the ideal community would be a Nazi-like
    racialist homeland, an arrangement that might be acceptable so long as membership
    was voluntary, but characterizing such an arrangement as anarchistic would certainly
    cause confusion on the part of outsiders. Such arrangements do indeed exist, such as
    the former Aryan Nations compound at Hayden Lake, Idaho. One of the interesting
    things about national-anarchism is its ability to accommodate everything from neo-
    Nazis to radical leftists to Jewish separatists. See my article on national-anarchism at
    http://www.attackthesystem.com/nationalanarchism.html
    I believe national-anarchism to be, in many ways, the most advanced form of
    contemporary anarchist thought. Classical anarchism positioned itself as the most
    radical wing of the international labor movement, the dominant social struggle
    of the day, and incorporated a lot of quasi-Marxist ideas into its overall analysis.
    Neo-anarchism, emerging in the heyday of the New Left of the 1960s, similarly
    attached itself to the black power movement, feminism, environmentalism, and the
    gay movement. Yet, today, these currents have become safely mainstream and, to some
    degree, a reactionary force. Libertarian-anarchism makes the same mistake as the
    Marxists with its narrow economic determinism, its often rigid focus on bourgeois
    class values (much libertarian thought amounts to replacing the proletariat and the
    bourgeoisie with the bourgeoisie and the regulatory welfare state as the antagonists
    in the class struggle), and its universalist and moralistic tendencies rooted in
    Enlightenment rationalism. National-anarchism properly focuses on the most crucial

national-anarchists are accused by their left-wing counterparts of advocating a type of "village fascism". Those of the "primitivist" variant of anarchism are denounced for condemning the bulk of mankind to disease and starvation because of their rejection of modern technology and industrial civilization.[26] And traditional anarcho-syndicalists have long been attacked by individualists for promoting an alternative form of state where the government is simply replaced by labor unions.[27] All of the criticisms that these contending schools of anarchism have of one another are legitimate. Like any other philosophy or ideology, anarchism is imperfect and cannot provide universal solutions to all of mankind's problems.

The differing schools of anarchism each bring to the table a valuable perspective often not found among the other schools. Classical anarchism continues to emphasize the class struggle against international state capitalism, and correctly so, but unfortunately often falls into the trap of economic determinism in the same manner as Marxists and libertarians.[28] Also, many classical anarchist groups resemble nothing quite so much as history clubs or archivist societies, continually adorning their activities with the symbolism of European anarchism of a century ago, an action whose propagandistic value to the modern world is at best quite dubious.[29] Neo-anarchism of the post-New

---

issue of the era—the New World Order—and rejects the universalism common to both the liberal and socialist traditions in favor of particularism and traditionalism, sort of a mixture of Bakunin and Joseph de Maistre.

26 The classic "Unabomber Manifesto" is as good an introduction as any to the primitivist perspective.

27 Unions have shown themselves to be just as oppressive when they come into state power as any other type of organization or institution. The British trade unions that include print workers have been known to censor newspaper articles critical of union activities.

28 For an interesting discussion of the weaknesses of economic determinism, see M. Raphael Johnson, "Economics and Nationalist Theory," *The Idyllic*, August 1, 2003, http://www.theidyllic.com/php/article.php?article=21

29 An experience I had some years ago serves as an illustration of the level of silliness this sometimes involves. I was at a continental anarchist conference in San Francisco in the summer of 1989 and sitting in on a workshop on labor organizing. The program broke down into a shouting match between members of the Industrial Workers of the World (IWW) and the Workers Solidarity Alliance (WSA) over the question of which

Left, post-1960s variety admirably opposes the mistreatment of traditionally disfavored or marginalized social groups—racial minorities, women, homosexuals, the handicapped, and so on. Yet neo-anarchism has also adopted for itself the dogmatic "political correctness" of the liberal establishment with a fervor that approaches self-parody. Libertarian anarchism champions the individual against the state, a refreshing approach given the incipient collectivism and crypto-statism often found on the left wing of anarchism, but sometimes ignores the role of community, culture, and non-economic influences in shaping the human personality.[30] National-anarchism focuses on the long neglected matter of the plight of traditional racial, national, and religious groupings under attack by the forces of modernist multicultural totalitarianism, yet often places a myopic emphasis on race as opposed to class, culture, the state qua the state, and other such matters.[31] Primitivist anarchism of the Zerzanite variety points to the inherently totalitarian potential of advanced technology (as evidenced by such phenomena as the Echelon system), yet ignores the potentially liberatory aspects of technology (which classical anarchists like Kropotkin pointed out) and, predictably, dogmatizes its critique to the level of absurdity.

---

group was most qualified to lead a workers revolution. The IWW is a historical relic composed mostly of students, bohemians, and post-1960s New Leftists. The WSA, which had less than forty members at the time, is the US section of the International Workers Association, which also includes the Spanish CNT described in George Orwell's *Homage to Catalonia*.

30 It should be pointed out that there is a branch of libertarianism called "paleolibertarianism" (after "paleoconservatism") that pays greater attention to the role of non-economic and non-state "intermediary" institutions in social development. While unfortunately holding to a rather narrow bourgeois, Euro-Christian outlook, this tendency admirably works to fill in the gaps in the reductionist materialism and utilitarianism to be found in much libertarian thought. For a critique of paleolibertarianism, see my "Why I Am Not a Cultural Conservative," http:// attackthesystem.com/why-i-am-not-a-cultural-conservative/, and "I'm Still Not a Cultural Conservative," http://www.attackthesystem.com/lancaster.html

31 National-Anarchists are often demonized, quite unjustly in my view, as crypto-Nazis. Actually, national-anarchism has a quite substantive outlook. For a discussion of the important differences between national-anarchism and the traditional right wing, see David Michael, "On a Decisive Break With 'Far Right' Ideology," http://www. nationalanarchist.com/break1.html

Where anarchism differs from other political philosophies is in its provision, through its enduring principles of voluntary association and radical decentralization, of a means for irreconcilable social or political disputes to be handled without tyranny or bloodshed. As this article is being written, an ongoing controversy is taking place in the American state of Alabama concerning the placement of a monument to the biblical "Ten Commandments" in the lobby of a local courthouse by a religiously devout local judge. Secularists and "civil liberties" groups are insisting that such a gesture intolerably compromises the distinction between church and state while religionists are insisting that the mandatory removal of the monument amounts to religious discrimination and persecution.[32] As the courthouse is state property, owned in theory by religionists and anti-religionists alike, there is no objective or principled manner by which the conflict can be resolved. However, in an anarchist social system, individual persons would be free to join whatever associations or communities they wished with members of different communities adopting whatever laws or customs they desired. Some communities might require a particular form of religious observance while others might ban all references to or acknowledgement of religion. Still others might adopt a "live and let live" approach.

Separation of Politics and State

There was a time when nearly all states maintained a particular state religion that every subject was expected to conform to. Those who did not conform faced severe persecution, banishment, imprisonment, torture, and death.[33] The social chaos that resulted from efforts to impose a uniform religious observance motivated some thinkers to consider such notions as "freedom of religion" or "separation of church and state." America was one of the first nations to formally institutionalize such ideas. Today, virtually

---

32   For a comprehensive review of this event, see http://www.reclaimamerica.org/
Pages/10Commandments/MooreTime.asp

33   See Stefan Zweig's classic, *The Right to Heresy.*

all religions are represented in the United States, and most of them conduct their affairs unmolested by the state most of the time. While some gray areas of controversy remain, such as the aforementioned matter of religious displays on state property, most people take for granted that religious pluralism is preferable to the theocratic absolutism of previous eras. Anarchism, properly understood, applies the same principle to politics. Just as the classical liberals Voltaire and Thomas Jefferson wished to separate religion and state, it might be said that traditional anarchism aims to separate politics and state. Instead of a uniform political system being coercively imposed upon all citizens alike, anarchism allows for individuals and groups to form their own voluntary political systems organized according to their own needs. The national-anarchist theoretician David Michael notes that the content of these voluntary political systems (or associations, or communities, depending on what one wishes to call them) might be quite diverse and include communities of a nationalist, communist, Christian, Islamic, or some other variety.[34] It might be appropriate to think of anarchism as a type of meta-system capable of accommodating all sorts of political, economic, and cultural subsystems. Anarchism offers certain political tools—individual autonomy, voluntary association, mutual aid, free federation, radical decentralization, and community sovereignty—that provide diverse social groupings with the means of achieving self-determination.

An anarchist should be wary of teleological theories of society, whereby society is regarded as evolving towards some predetermined or prescribed end. This, of course, is a common characteristic of Marxist views on sociopolitical evolution and, indeed, of much progressive thought, rooted as much of this is in Hegelian metaphysics. Nevertheless, it is possible to make, with reasonable certainty, an elementary set of predictions as to what characteristics an anarchist social order would eventually display. Anarchist theory carries with it certain implications in the realm of economics, law, the prospects of the nation-state system that

---

34 "National Anarchist FAQ," http://www.nationalanarchist.com/faq.html

has been predominant for the past five centuries, and a variety of sociocultural and demographic matters. The first order of business involved in the implementation of the anarchist program is an end to universalism. On this point, many anarchists, particularly those of the leftist-progressive and, to a lesser degree, libertarian schools, miss the boat. The victory of anarchism would, by its very nature, coincide with the triumph of particularism. The absence of centralism would naturally strengthen attachments of a regional, local, family, ethnic, religious, cultural, or linguistic nature.[35] The marshalling of atomized individuals into a herd of identity-less masses at the mercy of the predations of whatever aberrant social engineering schemes the latest gang of thugs to achieve political power wishes to impose would no longer be possible. Particularistic attachments of the sort that serve as a vital bulwark against such predations would naturally blossom. A myriad of thriving communities would emerge, each with its own ideological, cultural, and economic foundations, organically rooted in the aspirations and evolved norms of its members. The sham of mass democracy, which sets all sorts of varied sectional interests at the throats of one another, and herds these diverse sections into party hierarchies where they may be safely divided and conquered at the hands of rootless and predatory elites, would be rendered obsolete.[36]

The triumph of philosophical anarchism as a sociopolitical meta-system would likewise mean the simultaneous victory of an enormous variety of subsystems. Against the fake "diversity" and "multiculturalism" offered by the liberal and neoconservative establishments and the reactionary left, whereby the total state rules in the name of "progressive" platitudes like Equality, Social Justice, and Humanity, in the place of more traditional platitudes like God, Family, and Country, a victorious anarchism offers an authentic pluralism consisting not only of genuine diversity in matters of culture, religion, and ethnicity, but also in questions of

---

35   This is a point Hans-Hermann Hoppe effectively argues in *Democracy: The God That Failed.*

36   Hoppe, *Democracy.*

politics and ideology. If the heart and soul of the anarchist ideal is a social order where autonomous individuals voluntarily choose those types of institutions, communities, or associations that are most suited to their own needs or desires, then virtually the entire panoply of dissident factions stand to gain through the victory of anarchism. The enemies of the current international ruling class and its rapidly encroaching New World Order include among themselves followers of the teachings of Karl Marx, Murray Rothbard, Osama bin Laden, John Zerzan, Eduard Limonov, Saddam Hussein, Emilio Zapata, Bo Gritz, Israel Shamir, Muammar Qaddafi, Mao Tse-tung, Noam Chomsky, Russell Means, R. J. Rushdoony, Mikhail Bakunin, Adolf Hitler, Anton Szandor LaVey, Elijah Muhammad, Julius Evola, Michael Oakeshott, Che Guevara, Edmund Burke, V. I. Lenin, Hilaire Belloc, Thomas Aquinas, Michel Foucault, Barry Goldwater, and many others.[37] Such a dazzling array of dissidents might be characterized as constituting a type of "diversity on steroids." With the disintegration of centralized power, all of these (and other) dissident communities would gain greater opportunities for self-determination.

Some anarchist factions, particularly the leftist ones, will no doubt denounce the aforementioned program as "authoritarian," "reactionary," or whatever. It is said by some in the anarchist milieu that a "true" anarchist must also reject "hierarchy," "authority," or even "organization" and "structure" of any kind. While one could certainly be an anarchist and oppose all of these things as well (though it is doubtful a community of such anarchists would be very productive or enjoy much longevity),

---

37   It goes without saying that someone, somewhere will use this passage as evidence that I endorse the particular views of all of these figures. Nothing could be further from the truth. Rather, I am simply trying to give reality its proper reverence. The elimination of a power structure, in this case the New World Order, automatically results in the filling of the power vacuum by the best organized opposition groups. I believe that a real-world society influenced by anarchistic ideas would amount to a collection of decentralized social systems spanning the entire cultural, ideological, ethnic, and religious spectrum, with widely divergent political and economic systems. Therefore, anarcho-communist, mutualist, syndicalist, Objectivist, Maoist, neo-Nazi, and Ba'ath Party communities might all exist within the broader decentralist framework.

the insistence by some anarchists that rejection of "hierarchy" or "authority" is mandated by the anarchist position actually betrays the authentic anarchist ideal of voluntarism (although it is necessary to distinguish between natural and artificial hierarchies and authorities). If one chooses to join a Tibetan Buddhist monastery and endure its accompanying rigors, then is it not authoritarian for an anarchist to denounce such a choice? If one such as John Walker Lindh decides for himself to adopt the ascetic ways of the Taliban, then who is another, particularly an anarchist, to attack his choice? Which is more authoritarian: a Nazi community on the top of a mountain whose members voluntarily choose their way of life or a massive, centralist, "democratic" state that seeks to impose the narrow values of a self-serving elite on the whole of society? Of course, it is a near certainty that a world dominated politically by anarchist ideals would produce many, many types of communities beyond the narrowly "conservative" ones described here. There might also be thriving homosexual communities, even communities where homosexuals constituted a privileged social class of the type Foucault once speculated about.[38] Just as there might be associations or communities of such a puritanical nature as to put Calvin or Khomeini to shame, so might there be communities of libertines whose principal economic base involved the commercial trade in drugs, alcohol, pornography, gambling, cockfighting, gladiatorial contests, or whatever. Of course, this by no means implies that all value systems are equally "true," valid, or likely to produce desirable or equal results. Some of the institutions that would form in an anarchist world might be hallmarks in human progress and achievement while others might be hellholes of incomparable ghastliness. This is what authentic liberty and authentic diversity are all about. Individuals and communities alike must be left to succeed or fail on their own terms.

---

38 I once came across an interview with Foucault where he challenged the legitimacy of the cultural Marxist view of homosexuals as a social class within the bourgeois order. He went on to speculate about a type of society where homosexuals might be a social class, although without much elaboration, if I recall correctly. Unfortunately, I have not been able to locate a transcript of this interview for reference.

The Economic Implications of Anarchism

It is important that the implications of such a decentralized and pluralistic political order for the realm of economics be properly understood if, for no other reason, to clarify the boundless confusion that has often existed among anarchists on economic matters. Within the rich history of anarchist thought, one finds both "individualist" and "socialist" traditions as far as economic questions are concerned. The spectrum of economic thought among anarchists includes "anarcho-capitalists" on one end and "anarcho-communists" on the other. Both sides often prefer to act as if the others are heretics and pursue the symbolic excommunication of their opponents. However, "socialist" and "communist" interpretations or applications of anarchism are not incompatible with "capitalist" or "individualist" ones. Anarchistic thought of the libertarian-individualist-capitalist variety frequently regards itself as the proper ideological heir of classical liberalism of the type espoused by Adam Smith or John Stuart Mill. However, as Noam Chomsky points out, the early classical liberals embraced many of the same criticisms of the bourgeois state as the classical socialists.[39] Hence, Chomsky regards traditional socialist-anarchism, or "libertarian socialism," as the logical outgrowth of classical liberalism. From the opposite end of the spectrum, the anarcho-capitalist godfather Murray Rothbard expressed sympathy for many of the criticisms of state capitalism advanced by the classical socialists, including Marx and Bakunin, but attacked them for blaming the market rather than the state qua state for the exploitation inherent in state capitalism. For Rothbard, the principal error of most of traditional socialism was its effort to achieve socialism by the reactionary methods of statism and militarism.[40]

Clearly, the conflicting economic tendencies within anarchist thought are sorely in need of some sort of reconciliation.

---

39   Noam Chomsky interviewed by David Barsamian, *Secrets, Lies and Democracy* (Tucson, AZ: Odonian Press, 2004), 17–18.

40   Murray N. Rothbard, "Left and Right: Prospects for Liberty," http://www.lewrockwell.com/rothbard/rothbard33.html

Fortunately, the work of Kevin Carson in the field of economics provides a means of doing so. Drawing upon both the Marxist and Austrian traditions within economics, Carson demonstrates that those who criticize the socialists for their carte blanche rejection of markets are correct in doing so.[41] After all, there is nothing inherently wrong, certainly not from an anarchist perspective, with the voluntary exchange of goods, services, and labor in the marketplace. Indeed, voluntary exchange is the cornerstone of anarchist social relations. Anti-market socialists have thrown out the baby with the bath water. However, pro-market, anti-state thinkers have quite frequently erred in failing to comprehend the degree to which market distortions resulting from state intervention are the source of genuine class exploitation. A principal problem is that many pro-market and anti-market observers alike consider the present system of international state capitalism to be an authentic product of the free market. The "left" tendency among anti-statists abhors this set of arrangements while the "right" tendency applauds it. Yet an authentic free market economy would produce institutional arrangements of a vastly different nature from those currently in existence.

The end of liberal democracy as a dominant political paradigm, and its replacement with philosophical anarchism, would naturally generate a brand new economic paradigm in the place of the current paradigm of state capitalism. Liberal democracy and state capitalism are considered by virtually all "mainstream" political theorists to be the natural corollaries of one another. Indeed, one often hears talk of "capitalist democracy" or "democratic capitalism" as some sort of ideal among establishment ideologists, particularly among (who else!) neoconservatives. On one hand, it is not exactly true that state capitalism and liberal democracy are natural complements to one another, as state capitalism preceded liberal democracy, and the mass democracy of the present era. Carson, following the lead of both Marx and

---

41   Kevin Carson, "Austrian and Marxist Theories of Monopoly
        Capital: A Mutualist Synthesis," http://kevin_carson.tripod.com/
        mutualistnetresourcesandinformationonmutualistanarchism/id10.html

Rothbard, explains how the declining feudal aristocracy of the latter Middle Ages sought to reverse its own fleeting fortunes by reinventing itself as a class of bourgeois capitalists by means of state interventionist tools of the mercantilist variety in order to preserve the centralization of wealth.[42] Hence, the birth of the paradigm of state capitalism that has come to dominate all of the industrialized nations. However, it is true that liberal democracy came to power largely through the efforts of a mercantile class, a middle class in the traditional European sense, who resented having to share power with the monarchy, the church, the landed nobility, and other relics of the feudal era. Subsequently, liberal democracy took the shape of mass democracy in order to justify the expansion of the state needed to effectively buy off and pacify newly emergent power groups (intellectuals, professionals, union bosses, political interest groups) who went on to comprise the "new class" of managerial elites of whom George Orwell and James Burnham provided penetrating critiques.[43] At the present time, the corporate elites of state capitalism and the bureaucratic elites of the welfare-warfare state (i.e., liberal democracy) have largely become intertwined with one another in the form of a state-corporate ruling class. This ruling class has become dominant in all of the advanced nations and is currently reconstituting itself on an international level in the form of the New World Order.

Conventional theories of political economy typically portray "Big Business" and "Big Government" as natural antagonists of one another. The "left" champions the state as the protector of the little guy from the predatory corporation while the "right" champions the corporation as the hapless victim of predatory government bureaucrats.[44] However, the present corporate system

---

42 Kevin A. Carson, *The Iron Fist Behind the Invisible Hand: Corporate-Capitalism as a State-Guaranteed System of Privilege*, rev. ed. (Montreal: Red Lion Press, 2002).

43 Kevin A. Carson, "Liberalism and Social Control: The New Class' Will to Power," http://attackthesystem.com/liberalism-and-social-control-the-new-class-will-to-power/

44 Keith Preston, "Reply to Brian Oliver Sheppard's 'Anarchism vs. Right-Wing Anti-Statism,'" http://attackthesystem.com/reply-to-brian-oliver-shepards-anarchism-vs-right-wing-anti-statism/

could not exist without the favors granted to corporations by the state in the form of subsidies, infrastructure, central banking, the state monopoly over the production of currency, tariffs, monopoly privilege, contracts, bailouts, guarantees, military intervention, patents, the suppression of labor, regulatory favors, protectionist trade legislation, limited liability and corporate personhood laws, and much else. Similarly, the state's legislative process and executive hierarchy is beholden to the corporate interests who fund the electoral system and provide the bureaucratic elite among the military, foreign policy, and "international trade" establishments. Condoleeza Rice's migration from Chevron to the National Security Council is no mere coincidence. The amalgam of Big Business and Big Government, consolidated on an international scale, represents a centralization of wealth and power of so great a degree as to jeopardize the future of humanity.

What sort of economic order would accompany the political victory of anarchism? Economic decentralization would naturally follow political decentralization. As the massive, bureaucratic nation-states currently being incorporated into the New World Order collapsed and disappeared, the corporate entities propped up and protected by these states would also vanish. Just as the dissolution of centralized political power would result in the sovereignty and self-determination of communities and associations, so would these entities be able to develop their own unique economic identities. Economic resources of all types, from land to industrial facilities to infrastructure to high technology, would fall into the hands of particular communities and popular organizations. Such entities would likely organize themselves into a myriad of economic institutions. It can be expected that workers would play a much greater leadership role in the formation of future economies as workers access to resources and bargaining power, both individually and collectively, would likely be greatly enhanced. The result would likely be an economic order where the worker-oriented enterprise replaces the capitalist corporation as the dominant mode of economic organization.[45]

---

45   Keith Preston, "What Would an Anarcho-Socialist Economy Look Like?," http://

The disappearance of massive, bureaucratic states would also result in the greater fluidity and dynamism of the marketplace, ushering in greater efficiency, more rapid innovation and, in the long term, rising living standards within the context of a more equitable overall distribution of wealth. Economic arrangements might include worker owned and operated enterprises, a proliferation of cooperatives and family businesses, mutual banks of the type envisioned by Greene, Proudhon, and Tucker, communal arrangements of the type envisioned by Kropotkin (and practiced, to some degree, by the kibbutzim of Israel), co-determined enterprises operating as a partnership between labor and management and industries operated by unions or workers councils in the manner envisioned by traditional anarcho-syndicalists, guild socialists, distributists, or council communists. The Mondragon workers' cooperatives of Spain have achieved some degree of success in this area.[46] Of course, if some groups of workers or entrepreneurs wished to organize themselves into giant, hierarchical formations similar to the traditional corporate model, that would be their prerogative. In addition, there would likely be an increase in the number of small to medium sized businesses of an individual or private nature, farmers, craftsmen, artisans, and the self-employed. The culture of particular regions or communities would shape the emerging economic arrangements. Land would be worked communally in those locations, such as central Africa, where traditions of communal ownership are strong. Open marketplaces would abound in regions where cultural precedent existed. There might also be municipalized industries or enterprises in some quarters, as well as such endeavors being owned by political parties of a particular stripe and operated by party members. There may be communities run by the Revolutionary Communist Party or the National Socialist Workers Revolutionary Party, each with their own factories or farms, with adherents of party ideology

---

attackthesystem.com/what-would-an-anarcho-socialist-economy-look-like/

46 William Foote Whyte and Kathleen King Whyte, *Making Mondragon: The Growth and Dynamics of the Worker Cooperative Complex* (Ithaca, NY: ILR Press, 1991); Roy Morrison, *We Build the Road as We Travel* (Philadelphia, PA: New Society Publishers, 1991).

providing the workforce. Still other communities might maintain economic arrangements modeled on the teachings of those figures their members find most inspirational, whether Gandhi or Qaddafi.[47] Kevin Carson provides a description of what a post-state capitalist economic order might look like:

1) an economy of self-employed artisans and farmers, small producers cooperatives, and worker-controlled large enterprises, all dealing with each other through the free market;

2) a money system based on labor exchanges or mutual banks, in which the producers associate to transform their own products into money and credit without relying on usurious banking monopolies;

3) a system of land ownership based on occupancy and use, with no enforcement of rights of absentee ownership;

4) a government based only on free association without initiating coercion against non-aggressors. This means all expenses are met by user fees and membership dues charged to willing participants. My own picture is . . . local government, minus compulsory payment for or consumption of its services.[48]

This vision is idealistic yet realistic, and Carson's overall economic analysis and objectives effectively reconcile the anti-statist traditions of classical liberalism and classical socialism. Of course, much variation on this broader theme is likely, as previously noted. For example, different sorts of communities might define "just" ownership or use of property in different ways, and the structure of local political institutions might be

---

47 Satish Kumar, "Gandhi's Swadeshi: The Economics of Permanence," http://caravan. squat.net/ICC-en/Krrs-en/ghandi-econ-en.htm; Muammar Qaddafi, *The Green Book* (Tripoli: The World Center for Studies and Research of The Green Book, 1987).

48 Kevin Carson, "The Left Libertarian Vision of the Good Society," http://groups. yahoo.com/group/LeftLibertarian/message/6821

highly varied. The collapse of the New World Order and the corporate-social democratic bureaucracies that govern its core provinces would inevitably lead to the coming to local power of a good many political or cultural elements disagreeable to the liberal elites who dominate the current world order and those who ape their values. For example, the disappearance of the nation-states across Europe would likely lead to the proliferation of a wide assortment of self-assertive communities and enclaves led by Communists, nationalists, monarchists, racialists, Catholic or Orthodox traditionalists, Islamic fundamentalists, neo-Nazis, warlords, or ordinary criminal gangs. Similarly, an end to Anglo-Zionist imperialism in the Middle East would inevitably lead to the removal of the region's current regimes and national borders alike, as these are nothing more than a legacy of previous imperial eras. However, it is quite doubtful that the sociopolitical institutions that would evolve in the Middle East following the dissolution of the present order there would be of a particularly "progressive" nature, as far as Western definitions of "progressive" are concerned. Already, the embarrassment of the neoconservatives, who have discovered unexpectedly that the people of Iraq prefer an ayatollah to a Tony Blair, has been witnessed.

Just as political decentralization would naturally result in the greater influence of those sociocultural and ideological elements most disagreeable to the values of modern liberalism, so would economic decentralization inspire a regeneration of those communitarian values that have been suppressed by the forces of global corporatism and its materialist/consumerist ethos. Although an end to the gargantuan bureaucracies of the current nation-state system and the overarching system of international state capitalism would on one hand result in a greater economic dynamism of the type sought by many "free market" libertarians, the absence of powerful corporate entities would allow the emergence of economic institutions that would be much more rooted in organic local and regional cultures and therefore much more beholden to the values and norms of those cultures.

Further, the wider dispersion of economic resources involved in economic decentralization would allow greater opportunities for self-determination and self-sufficiency among the neo-proletariat and provide the traditionally beleaguered classes with the means for self-emancipation.

The Death of the Nation-State System

The aforementioned predictions concerning what sort of politico-economic arrangements would follow the demise of the New World Order naturally assume an end to the five hundred year pre-eminence of the nation-state system. Simply put, the system of nation-states is one whose historical relevance has already expired. Traditional nations have largely devolved into provincial regions of the global order. Contrary to the sentiments of old-fashioned nationalists, this is not necessarily an unwelcome development. The principal function of the nation-state has been the greater concentration of political and economic power and the increased destructiveness of war and imperialism. Of course, the liberal "solution" to the horrors of international warfare has been even greater wars, imperialism, and centralization culminating in a Wilsonian global state that makes the world safe for corporate-mercantilist totalitarian-progressive "democracy." Against this liberal perversion, an authentic anarchism offers the radical dispersion of power as an antidote to the total wars generated by the modern state. As Joseph Sobran explains:

> . . . in the year 1500 there were about 500 distinct political entities in Europe; by 1800 the number had been reduced to a few dozen, and was soon further reduced by the unification of Italy and of Germany . . . Certain words, "secession" being one, are used in tones of horror that imply there is no point in discussing their possible merits. But, if secession is always bad, history can move in only one direction: toward a single global state, from which nobody must be allowed to withdraw, no matter how tyrannical it may become . . . In the twentieth century the great nation-

states (which were also empires) collided in the two most terrible wars of all time.

The explosion began with the assassination of a single man in Sarajevo in 1914. The alliances among the European states drew everyone into war, including, within three years, Midwestern farm boys who had never heard of the Archduke Ferdinand.

This would have been impossible if Europe had still consisted of those 500 independent political entities of the year 1500. Europe had seen many wars, but they had mostly been local. The "Great War" was something totally new, dwarfing even the Napoleonic Wars.

We have far more to fear from the consolidation of states than from secession and dispersion. With small states, there are sure to be local conflicts at almost all times, but it would be relatively easy to flee them. With only a few huge states, the danger of a general holocaust is constant.

Secession, small states, limited government, dispersion of power—these are the real paths to peace. The more political entities there are, the more rulers are forced to compete with each other for subjects, who can migrate to less oppressive domains. But when only huge states exist, with monopolies of power extending for thousands of miles, escape is difficult.[49]

One of the few positive features of the New World Order is that the enemy is now much more clearly identified.[50] It is pointless for contending political, economic, and cultural tendencies to continue to bicker among themselves when all are rapidly being

---

49 Joseph Sobran, "Small States Are Path to Peace," *Wake-Up Call America*, January–February 1999.

50 As Eduard Limonov says: "There's no longer any left or right. There's the system and the enemies of the system."

subjugated by the forces of globalism. As there is now really only one government, the system of international state capitalism, the task of anarchists has become much more simplified. Globalism may well be the final stage in the historical evolution of the state. The global superstate represents the consolidation of conventional nation-states into an ever-more powerful entity. The annihilation of the global superstate may well be the catalyst that ultimately leads to the realization of the reign of anarchism, just as the execution of the French monarch became the cornerstone of the ultimate triumph of liberal democracy and the supremacy of the bourgeoisie.

Separation of Law and State

No discussion of what the end product of a particular political or economic order might be can ever be complete without substantial reflection on what sort of laws and legal systems such arrangements might produce.[51] Thus far, it has been argued that the practical effect of the full implementation of the anarchist program would be the proliferation of countless voluntary communities and associations whose primary function would be the provision of the means to sovereignty for many different types of ideological or cultural tendencies. The internal structures of such associations would likely span the entire spectrum of political preferences. There might well be communities of monarchists, fascists, communists, liberal capitalists, liberal multiculturalists, theocrats, black nationalists, white nationalists, anarchists (of every possible stripe), neo-Aztecs, UFO enthusiasts, or whatever. Obviously, all of these elements would have very different views on the meaning of life, the role of the human species in the universe, the nature of human beings, the proper relationship between the individual and external institutions or collective entities, the proper means of reproduction and child-rearing, the methods of handling deviants from community norms, and much else. Consequently, the laws and legal institutions would differ greatly from community to community.

---

51   Keith Preston, "Law and Anarchism," http://attackthesystem.com/law-and-order

Many anarchists claim to categorically reject of the concept of "law," but this is simply a matter of semantics. Most anarchists believe that acts such as murder or robbery should be socially disallowed, although there may be considerable disagreement on what causes such antisocial behavior, and how offenders ought to be handled. Unless one prefers a hermitic existence in the Arctic or Andes (a reality that would be much more possible in an anarchist world), it is impossible for an individual to exist in the same manner as an asteroid floating about in the vacuum of space. As soon as a particular community is established, norms begin to develop concerning what is and what is not acceptable behavior. It is to be expected that the legal culture of a broader society organized along anarchistic lines would place a high emphasis on individual autonomy, or what the libertarians sometimes call the "non-aggression axiom." Such an emphasis would partly result from the prevalence of anarchistic thought in the broader society. However, it is to be expected, for reasons that will be explained below, that a radically decentralized politico-economic order would naturally evolve along such lines, regardless of the ideological inclinations of its inhabitants.

When surveying the history of past civilizations that eventually collapsed, it becomes clear political disintegration is rarely, if ever, accompanied by any sort of political liberation. The anarchist anthropologist Harold Barclay notes:

> Periods of so-called cultural or organizational decay in history may suggest this sort of trend [towards decentralization]. But what trends do occur in these situations is the creation of a number of petty despotisms out of one which had existed before. Decentralization is not accompanied by freedom. The revolutions and revolts of history and the decay of social systems have invariably entailed the replacement of one kind of despotism by another. Or what is a process of decay of one polity is the basis for the creation of another, so that, for example, the appearance of Clovis' Frankish kingdom and of the

Umayyad caliphate follow on the heels of the decline of Rome.[52]

It may be expected, then, that the eventual collapse and disintegration of the global superstate of the New World Order will result in the emergence of "petty despotisms" of various kinds as the new basis of political organization. Indeed, the parallels between the current era and Rome in its twilight period are obvious enough. Just as the end of the *Pax Romana* ushered in a whole new era of decentralized politics, technological regression (in the West but not quite so much in the East), and the coming to power of an apocalyptic otherworldly religious movement (Christianity), so might the end of the *Pax Americana* usher in a new era of decentralized politics, technological regression (at least initially) and the expanded influence of an apocalyptic otherworldly religious movement (Islamic fundamentalism). Just as it was the unwashed barbarians of the Germanic regions who sacked Rome, so it may well be the unwashed barbarians of the modern anti-globalization movement (accompanied by the barbarian hordes emanating from the trailer parks, ghettos, and barrios) who eventually sack Washington, D.C.

What are the implications of all this for the matter of law in an anarchistic social order? Following the collapse of the New World Order global superstate and the nation-states that comprise its provincial governments, the entire panoply of dissident factions who stand in opposition to the NWO will naturally achieve superiority or sovereignty in those geographic areas where they are best organized and have achieved the greatest level of popular support. These factions will then proceed to reorganize their internal political structures according to their own ideological inclinations. Such inclinations will range from the highly "liberal" or "progressive" on one hand to the very "conservative" or "reactionary" on the other. Remnants of the former system would likely continue in certain enclaves or be incorporated into newer

52   Harold Barclay, *People Without Government: An Anthropology of Anarchy* (London: Kahn and Averill, 1982), 148.

systems in the same manner that elements of contemporary American law include remnants of earlier English law. The laws of the communities, associations, and homelands that emerge following the demise of liberal democracy, state capitalism, the nation-state system, and the universalistic synthesis of these manifested by the New World Order will reflect the preferences and prejudices of organic regions and localities to a much greater degree than what is found in contemporary systems of parliamentary corporate-social democracy.

Fortunately, there exists in the contemporary world a working model of this type of decentralized legal order. The East African nation of Somalia experienced in the early 1990s the type of disintegration of central government that the entire world is likely to experience at some point in the future. Following this political collapse, the sixty clans that make up the Somali "nation" became largely sovereign entities unto themselves. The disappearance of the state has largely resulted in the resurrection of traditional society within Somalia. Political "leaders" are primarily the heads of extended families and religious leaders. Disputes among clans, families, businesses, and individuals alike are handled largely on the basis of mediation and arbitration. Crimes are dealt with in a manner similar to the handling of torts in Western society, with the emphasis being placed on compensating the wronged party. Since the implementation (or restoration) of this system, both economic prosperity and social peace have multiplied considerably in Somalia.[53]

While the laws regulating the subsystems to be found within an anarchistic meta-system would be highly diverse, certain common characteristics would likely evolve into a formally or customarily codified common law for the entire meta-system. This would stem from two factors. One, under a radically decentralized sociopolitical order migration from one polity to another becomes more feasible. If one finds a particular community unattractive, the natural solution is to find another

---

53   Michael van Notten, "From Nation-State to Stateless Nation," *Liberty*, April 2003.

community. This in turn means that communities that wished to prosper and preserve themselves would find it necessary to retain the allegiance of their more competent, productive, and valued members. Consequently, leaders of particular communities would be motivated to make their communities as attractive as possible to those whose loyalty they wished to obtain. Secondly, ordinary economic incentives would provide both individuals and collective entities with the desire to settle disputes in a cost-effective manner. Resolving conflicts through perpetual war is quite costly to polities that lack control over huge populations and resources that can be conscripted or taxed at will. Shifting the costs of obtaining advantages through political means (i.e., coercive legislation) onto a broader tax-paying public is also considerably more difficult in the absence of a centralized, tax-supported "democratic" state that can be lobbied towards such ends. This means that the residents of an anarchistic order will have every incentive to find both peaceful means of settling disputes between communities and individuals and limiting their own petitioning of legal institutions to matters of urgent self-interest, such as cases of violent or invasive crimes and serious breaches of contract.[54]

Although individual communities might maintain strong codified laws or informal social taboos and sanctions against behavior that departs drastically from community norms or ideals, the cultivation of an environment of stifling oppression would likely lead to little more than the departure of the communities' more desirable members. Consequently, the maintenance of communities as closed as those of the Nazis or the Taliban will take place only where ideological fervor is strong enough to trump virtually all other considerations, including prosperity and cordial relations with other communities. Likewise, communities would, out of the necessity of self-preservation, establish barriers to forms of social decay likely to be injurious to the overall stability

---

54 Bruce L. Benson, *Enterprise of Law: Justice Without the State* (San Francisco: Pacific Research Institute for Public Policy, 1990); Randy E. Barnett, *Structure of Liberty: Justice and the Rule of Law* (New York: Oxford University Press, 1998).

and prosperity of the community. As an example, predatory street crime of the type that the Western nations are increasingly famous for would likely find considerably less toleration among most communities in an anarchistic order, save those organized for the benefit of the criminals themselves, such as self-managed communities of exiles from other communities.[55]

It is likely that supra-community institutions or arrangements would eventually evolve for the purpose of resolving disputes between contending communities. This by no means implies the necessary re-emergence of the state in the traditional sense. Instead, it is more probable that evolved traditions would come into being according to which inter-community disputes might be dealt with through a process of negotiation, mediation, or arbitration. Such traditions might serve the same role as conventional "international law" in the current system. A process might also develop whereby individual citizens of one community would be able to effectively file grievances against citizens of another community. In traditional societies, such disputes are typically handled through the compensation of the injured party by the community of the offending party as a whole, thereby providing each community with the incentive to discipline their own members who act in injurious ways towards others, for the sake of preserving both the internal peace within their own community and external peace with other communities.

Disputes between communities or members of different communities would primarily involve ordinary conflicts over territory, resources, or common crimes (such as violence and theft) that are prohibited by all cultures and political entities out of necessity. As for the matter of deviation from community norms in a broader cultural sense, different types of communities would obviously handle such questions in their own ways. There already exists in modern states an endless amount of controversy over all sorts of social or cultural questions. Controversy of this

---

55   Keith Preston, "Dealing with Crime in a Free Society," http://attackthesystem.com/dealing-with-crime-in-a-free-society/

type would likely escalate in the absence of conventional states as more and more sociocultural groups would begin to establish sovereign enclaves of their own. These enclaves might maintain wildly divergent cultural, religious, or ethical norms. A seemingly endless list of questions arises. Is abortion a woman's sacred right or the callous murder of an unborn child? Is homosexuality a natural, healthy expression of human intimacy or a vile perversion? Should the ownership of weapons be allowed for all citizens or only for those charged with specific functions related to security and defense? Is the open criticism or even ridicule of leaders and authority figures a vital check on incompetence or malfeasance among leaders or simply an invitation to disorder and disrespect for natural hierarchies? Is the process of reproduction a matter of societal interests to such a degree that external authorities are to have a say in such matters or are these questions simply a private issue between consenting parties? What is to be the proper allocation of resources and how is the just possession and use of such resources to be defined? Are beliefs regarded as blasphemous a simple matter of individual conviction or do these invite the wrath of supernatural powers towards the entire community? To what degree, if any, can the individual be required to perform a service towards the greater good of the community at large?

The important issue for this discussion is not so much the matter of how different communities might answer these questions but rather the manner in which deviations from established norms in these and other areas might be handled. Although it is certainly possible, and indeed likely, that at the initial stages of the formation of various communities the sanctions enacted against deviants would be quite harsh, it is unlikely this will continue indefinitely without alteration or modification. Initially, religious fundamentalist communities might stone heretics or adulterers to death. Communities of political correctness lunatics might engage in the summary execution of racists, sexists, homophobes, anti-Semites, or vivisectionists in a manner emulating the Red Guards of the Great Proletarian Cultural Revolution or the

Khmer Rouge during the Return to Year One. In the polities that would follow the demise of liberal democracy and its institutional appendages, a wave of repression and bloodletting would likely accompany systemic collapse. However, the broader decentralized meta-system would allow the subjects of individual communities to once again "vote with their feet" in the absence of centralized nation-states or the global superstate. This arrangement would have a moderating effect on communities seeking to retain the allegiance of members and subjects. Decentralism, easy migration, and a polycentric legal order rooted in negotiations between communities and associations would produce an eventual scenario whereby "diffuse" sanctions would serve as the primary method of enforcing community standards. These might include everything from ostracism and economic reprisals ("discrimination") to "private" forms of violence (such as fighting, dueling, or vigilantism) to public censure and reprimand of a non-coercive nature (the so-called "bully pulpit").

The Death of Modernity

In the early period of the post-NWO world, occurrences resembling those that followed the collapse of Rome would likely transpire. During that period, roving bands of Christian zealots traveled about destroying pagan monuments and artifacts.[56] Similar behavior on the part of various anti-NWO elements is likely as well. A case in point is the destruction of Buddhist monuments by the former Taliban government of Afghanistan. Another example might be the zeal for the destruction of monuments to the late Confederate society of the American South found among the left-wing elements in my own community of Richmond, Virginia. While revolution is usually accompanied by chaos, and followed by a period of reaction, eventually stabilization begins to take place and the ordinary process of natural social evolution resumes. Therefore,

---

56 "The [Christian] zealots for conversion took to the streets or criss-crossed the countryside, destroying no doubt more of the [pagan] architectural and artistic treasure of their world than any passing barbarians thereafter." Ramsay MacMullen, *Christianizing the Roman Empire* (New Haven, CT: Yale University Press, 1984), 119.

the purges, bloodletting, and waves of repression that would naturally follow the disorder involved in the destruction of the NWO would eventually give way to the establishment of a new type of decentralized order such as that which developed in Western Europe during the post-Roman, medieval era. Indeed, the destruction of international state capitalism would in many ways be nothing more than the restoration of pre-modern traditional society with its emphasis on localism, regionalism, tribalism, particularism, religion, polycentrism, and the like. The rapid growth, on a worldwide basis, of Islam in general and Islamic fundamentalism in particular, and the corresponding explosion of Christianity in Asia, Africa, and Latin America (and to a lesser degree, the growth of Christian fundamentalism in North America), attests to this.[57] The specific civilization that is commonly referred to as "modernism" is already approaching a stage of advanced decay. Therefore, the eventual disappearance of modernism in a way that parallels the disappearance of Greco-Roman civilization can be predicted with relative safety.

If current demographic trends continue, it can be expected that a "post-modern" (not postmodernism in the popularized sense) world would exhibit certain predictable characteristics. Islam may well become the world's largest religion, and continue to dominate the Middle East and many other parts of Asia, and eventually come to dominate Europe and parts of North America as well. The future strongholds of Christianity will likely be found in the southern hemisphere and East Asia, particularly the Pacific rim region. The particularly primitive form of Christian fundamentalism found in North America may come to dominate much of that continent. These expanded or revitalized religions, along with revitalized regional or local organic communities or ethno-cultures, will likely be the basis of the social structures of

---

57   The disparity in birth rates alone render it virtually certain that Muslims will outnumber indigenous Europeans within a century. For an interesting look at the growth of Christian fundamentalism in North America, see Dean M. Kelley, *Why Conservative Churches Are Growing: A Study in Sociology of Religion* (New York: Harper and Row, 1972). For a look at African Christianity, see Harvey J. Sindima, *Drums of Redemption* (Westport, CT: Greenwood Press, 1994).

the future world. This too would be a development that paralleled the society of the medieval period. Once the stabilization of this order became seriously rooted, the foundation for further human social evolution of a genuinely progressive nature would be established. Substantial historical precedent can be found for this simply by looking at the progression of medieval society in the period leading up to the Enlightenment. If classical Greece at its height can be compared with the intellectual culture of the Renaissance, then contemporary modern civilization can be compared with Rome in its geriatric years.

The Enlightenment would have been impossible without the Middle Ages, for it was the decentralized and polycentric order of medieval Europe that inadvertently provided the cultural framework for the intellectual development that characterized the Enlightenment.[58] The most important characteristic of medieval society was the lack of a significant concentration of power. The monarchs had to share power with the popes and vice versa. Different manors, fiefdoms, feudatories, kingdoms, tribes, and other political entities had to share power with one another as none were ever able to acquire the upper hand. This decentralization allowed the individual more latitude with which to "vote with his feet" and placed an enormous check on the power of rulers in the manner previously discussed, and so limited their predations. Perpetual negotiations and renegotiations between kings and commoners and between rival kingdoms led to the intellectual conceptualization of such ideas as "freedom," "liberty," and "rights" that eventually became intertwined with Enlightenment political culture.

The Demographic and Cultural Implications of Anarchism

It has been argued that the current world civilization ("modernism") is on its deathbed in a manner resembling the expiration of

---

58   For a discussion of traditions of decentralization in Western culture, see Clyde Wilson, "Devolution," http://www.lewrockwell.com/wilson/wilson15.html

Greco-Roman civilization. It has been argued that the dominant political paradigm of modernism (liberal democracy) is doomed due to its own fatal contradictions. Drawing on the past historical experience of the collapse of Rome and the emergence of the decentralized polities of the medieval period, it has been argued that a similar decentralization is likely to transpire following the demise of the New World Order, which is simply the final stage of modernism, liberal democracy, the evolution of the modern state, and state capitalism. It has been argued that a principal characteristic of a post-NWO world will likely be the dramatic re-emergence of particularism. It has also been argued that out of this world order of decentralization and particularism, no matter how retrograde it may be in its initial stages, there might very likely evolve a new politico-economic paradigm whereby philosophical anarchism or voluntary association replaces liberal democracy and worker-oriented productive institutions come to replace capitalism and corporatism. Likewise, a decentralized political order and a polycentric legal order would generate a high level of individual autonomy and responsibility. The removal of parasitical state bureaucracies from human economic life would, in the long run, generate greater economic prosperity and corresponding increases in health and living standards and wider dispersion of economic resources. This type of scenario would then lay the intellectual, cultural, and material framework for the emergence of a new renaissance of human cultural achievement in a manner resembling that of the classical Greek or classical Renaissance periods, and a new revolution in science, philosophy, and politics of the type that occurred during the early stages of the Enlightenment.

There are still other interesting questions regarding sociological, cultural, and demographic matters that are certainly worth considering. One of these involves the matter of immigration.[59]

---

59 For a discussion of the implications of anarchist theory for ethnic matters, see my "A Calm Anarchist Look at Race, Culture and Immigration," http://attackthesystem. com/a-calm-anarchist-look-at-race-culture-and-immigration/. Interestingly, within contemporary anarchist thought two diametrically opposed schools have developed concerning the question of race. One of these, situated on the Far Left, has adopted

This is an issue that is becoming increasingly more controversial in the Western nations. Broadly described, immigration opponents regard unwanted migrants as a source of increased crime, competition for scarce employment opportunities, dilution and erosion of established culture, burdens on tax-financed social services and, in some instances, depletion of particular ethnic or regional identities. Pro-immigration forces regard immigration as a source of cultural diversity and enrichment, cheap labor for business interests, a source of strength for favored ethnic groups, humanitarian asylum for refugees from political oppression or deplorable socio-economic conditions, individual freedom of movement and travel, and economic progress derived from the importation of foreigners possessing valuable skills. Both sides on this conflict have a habit of oversimplifying the issues involved. Whatever one's views on the matter of immigration, it is interesting to look at how this issue might have been handled under anarchistic institutions and what the results would be.

As for my own views on the subject of immigration, let me say that I am in favor of the free migration of peoples. I oppose border police, passport laws, visa requirements, and customs inspectors.

---

neo-Leninist doctrines rooted in the latter New Left of the 1960s such as "white skin privilege," "whiteness" theory, and other similar perspectives of questionable intellectual character. On the other end, national-anarchism (or at least a subset of it), originating from the European Far Right, maintains a belief in racial separatism and ethnic "identity" theories more commonly associated with neo-Nazis and certain fundamentalist religious perspectives such as Christian Identity. As to which side is more authentically anarchistic, it would appear that national-anarchists are more strongly committed to the practice of voluntarism, wishing to set up their own sovereign ethnically homogeneous enclaves and allowing for similar communities among other ethnic groups and non-racial ideological tendencies. Left-wing anarchists frequently seem to have no conception of the principle of voluntarism when it comes to questions of social relations and often seem committed to eliminating those who oppose their rabid integrationist/left-multiculturalist agenda by violence. In many ways, these two diametrical opposites may be necessary counterparts to one another within the broader realm of anarchist theory. This conflict also illustrates the degree to which most contemporary anarchist factions are derived from the cultural fringes. Most people are neither racists nor racial separatists or "anti-racist" multicultural fanatics. Presumably, once the New World Order is defeated and modernism disappears, communities and regions will emerge that reflect the entire panoply of racial and ethnic identity. There will likely be homelands for racial separatists and/ or supremacists, authoritarian multiculturalists, militant integrationists, and racially neutral persons such as myself alike.

I regard the INS as just another police state organization of the same type as the FBI, DEA, and BATF. However, I also believe that a system of genuine free migration would produce results more favorable to contemporary anti-immigration advocates. The current international system is about as far removed from a system of free migration as it could possibly be. The existence of passport laws or border police is only a minor aspect of the overall statism that currently dominates international travel. Indeed, current migration patterns represent the influence of the broader imperialistic and social engineering schemes of international state capitalism. First and foremost, it must be recognized that many Third World immigrants into First World nations are in fact refugees from political and economic conditions created by the imperialist policies towards the Third World established by the First World.

The legacy of the colonialism of Old Europe has been the disruption and destruction of organic social structures of the indigenous societies of the Third World. Africa is an excellent case in point. The strategy of the colonialists was to destroy indigenous forms of self-rule on that continent and play off different ethnic factions against one another in a classic "divide and conquer" maneuver, thereby eradicating any and all popular resistance to the pillaging of the continent. The enduring legacy of this has been perpetual instability, bloody ethnic conflict, and terminal poverty on a continent with the greatest abundance of natural resources in the world. Similarly, much Latin American immigration into the United States has been inspired by the poverty and civil war perpetuated or aggravated by nearly a century of American imperialism in that region. Persons in First World nations are justified in criticizing Third World immigration into their own regions only to the degree that they recognize and oppose imperialist efforts on the part of their own states towards the Third World. The best bet for those wishing to reduce Third World immigration into the northern hemisphere would be the achievement of political, economic, and cultural sovereignty and eventual stability for the Third World.

It is also necessary to recognize the degree to which the domestic states of the First World encourage immigration into their own territories by means of social, as well as foreign, policy. As most Third World immigrants are poor and uneducated, their increased presence automatically necessitates the expansion of social and educational services, thereby justifying the further expansion of the state and higher levels of taxation. As poor immigrants are disproportionately prone to street crime, increased numbers of police, the construction of new prisons, and the expansion of the state's apparatus of control (the so-called "criminal justice system") can be sold more easily to the general public. Immigrants create an expanded demand for social welfare-related entitlements and therefore a larger social welfare bureaucracy with greater employment security for welfare bureaucrats.

Various ethnic lobbies understandably wish to increase the size of their constituencies and push for increased immigration by members of their own ethnic, racial, or national group. Corporate lobbies view immigrants willing to work for lower wages as a means of reducing labor costs and the overall individual and collective bargaining power of workers and push for pro-immigration policies alongside left-wing "multiculturalists" who associate any and all opposition to immigration with fascism, Nazism, slavery, genocide, et al., *ad nauseum*. Additionally, the embarrassingly low quality of American education, particularly in the arts and sciences, virtually necessitates the importation of skilled technical and professional workers from other regions into the United States. The interests of the central state are served by the immigration of peoples possessing a drastically different cultural identity into the host nation. The standard tactic of states everywhere who rule over diverse populations— "divide and conquer"—can be employed must more easily and effectively in such a scenario. Of course, this can only work for so long. Eventually, such systems collapse and the ethno-cultural or religious antagonisms which have been kindled by the prior ruling elite ignite.

Those who favor "liberal" immigration policies on civil libertarian or humanitarian grounds have a point. As the international power of the New World Order continues to be consolidated and the First World nations degenerate into ever-greater authoritarianism, it is likely that attacks on those who dissent from the dictates of the Establishment will continue to expand. Being able to flee from one political jurisdiction to another is a vital means of countering such attacks. As the policing systems of the corporate-social democratic states of the West continue to more closely resemble paramilitary occupational forces, it can be expected that police units of this type charged with the enforcement of immigration law will be increasingly incorporated into consolidated state security units along with those charged with investigation or enforcement with regards to "terrorism," "diversity," "drugs," "firearms," "public morality," "sedition," and the like. Whatever one's views on immigration, it is not strategically advantageous to favor the expansion of the state's current enforcement apparatus as a means of curbing it.

Opponents of the New World Order and the state-corporate ruling class include both staunch anti-immigration and stanch pro-immigration thinkers. Anarchistic politics offers a way of dealing with this conflict. The first order of business would be to deny state entitlements to non-citizens or require a long waiting period (say, fifteen years) before immigrants could become eligible for such entitlements. This would go a long way towards resolving the pressures on social services resulting from massive immigration. Such a policy would also be very likely to generate overwhelming popular support, although much of the radical left would falsely regard such an effort as racist or xenophobic. Cultural conflicts and social antagonisms generated by immigration could be handled more effectively simply by removing legal barriers to "discrimination" against immigrants. Forced integration only exacerbates hostility between social groups. Allowing different groups to practice mutual self-segregation and sovereignty may be a partial way out of this predicament. Again, the liberal establishment and the reactionary left will regard such ideas as heresy, but this only demonstrates the intellectual bankruptcy of these elements. Another idea might be to decentralize the immigration and naturalization process to the local level, as is currently the case in Switzerland. This way, different communities could adopt for themselves immigration policies that were as restrictive or as permissive as they desired. Of course, such a decentralized immigration policy could only work if politics in general were to be decentralized. Otherwise, different regions and localities would simply view immigrants as a means of expanding the voting bloc for their own territory in order to obtain more subsidies and favors from the central government.

Economic decentralization would also help to stabilize international migration patterns. An economy ordered on the basis of localized production for local use would not involve the relocation of productive facilities to regions with more easily exploitable labor. If workers owned or operated their own economic institutions they would not be particularly inclined to fire themselves in favor of cheap imported labor or to ship their jobs abroad. Also, solidarity and cooperation among workers on an international level against the corporate powers that be, would improve the situation of workers everywhere by preserving the economic stability of First World workers and reducing the exploitability of Third World workers. International labor unions and cooperatives organized on the old anarcho-syndicalist model might be the proper path with regards to these questions. There is also the matter of the responsibility of communities and private groups in the broader sense. Those who champion immigration on humanitarian grounds should be prepared to put their time and money where their mouth is. During the 1980s, the "sanctuary" movement in the Southwestern United States, composed mostly of Catholic and evangelical churches, provided asylum to refugees from the wars that were then raging in Central America, largely as a result of the imperialistic policies of the US regime. This was often done in defiance of US law, and those being assisted were genuine victims of political persecution and military aggression. At the same time, "asylum" laws in some countries are simply a means of creating clients for social welfare agencies and granting safe haven to criminals who happen to belong to favored social groups. Such abuses might be curbed by transferring responsibility for such matters to non-governmental organizations. Likewise, in some communities large-scale immigration is the source of a genuine crime problem. Reliance on local militias rather than the state's immigration enforcement and policing systems would likely prove to be more productive.

Immigration is only one issue in the broader "culture wars" that are currently being waged in the Western states, particularly America. Typically, the scenario is described as an impending showdown between "conservative" or "reactionary" forces on one end and "liberal" or "progressive" forces on the other. The stereotypical combatant on the liberal side is a tofu-munching, unkempt, unwashed neurotic railing hysterically against racism, sexism, homophobia, looksism, transphobia, producerism, et al., with his conservative counterpart being a flag-waving, Bible-banging, pious prig who issues warnings to Middle Americans concerning the imminent homo-doper menace to their children by day, while cruising for teenage male prostitutes by night. Somewhere in between is the stereotypical libertarian with his credit cards in one pocket and crack cocaine in the other. Stereotypes are usually derived from the generalization or exaggeration of perceptions that have some basis in actual facts. Unfortunately, the types of human waste material being discussed here are also very easy to find in various opposition movements from the Left and the Right. I suspect one of the reasons that anti-Establishment elements in American politics enjoy so little success is the tendency of these to adopt the most small-minded perspective on cultural matters imaginable. Populist-oriented tendencies have been more influential in European than American politics in recent times, probably because of the efforts of populist figures in Europe to transcend the conventional left/right cultural-ideological boundaries. Whatever one thinks of Jean-Marie Le Pen, he comes across as an educated, worldly man unafraid to address working class issues and make common cause with the Left on such matters, as his attraction of considerable Communist cross-over votes demonstrates. The closest thing in American politics to Le Pen is Patrick Buchanan, a man who combines many sensible and thoughtful ideas with the standard right-wing American hysteria over the alleged threat posed by dirty books, flag-burners, and unisex toilets.

Even more interesting is the case of the late Pim Fortuyn, a truly original political figure who might have seriously shaken up the Establishment had he survived to do so.[60] It is indicative of the nature of the reactionary left that a man who sought to curb immigration from backward, feudal, theocratic Islamic nations into liberal Northern European nations, where gays and feminists enjoy considerable influence, would be assassinated, ironically, not by a Muslim but by a reactionary leftist, political correctness fanatic, who equated the gay libertarian Fortuyn with Adolf Hitler. This action as much as any other demonstrates that the guiding values of the reactionary left are absurdity, nihilism, and masochism rather than socialism or liberalism. Nevertheless, the Left includes many sincere and reasonable people in addition to riff-raff, just as the Right includes many authentic populists alongside Know-Nothings. A new political synthesis that transcends boundaries of Left, Right, and Center is necessary if the international ruling class is to be successfully combated. The first step is to begin to work around the cultural differences to be found among anti-Establishment elements. The key is to focus on issues that concern ordinary working people rather than the cultural fringes. Most people do not think that Nazis or Commies or homosexuals or homophobes are hiding under every bed. Most of the current anarchist factions originate from extremist elements of one kind or another. This situation is not wholly undesirable as it provides fertile ground for the evolution of a Left-Right anarcho-fusionism. Yet, for such a synthesis to reach its full potential, the Centrist perspective, particularly on cultural

---

60   For background on the Fortuyn phenomenon, see Tjebbe van Tijen, "The Sorrow of the Netherlands," http://www.opendemocracy.net/democracy-newright/article_382.jsp

matters, has to be included as well. Most people are cultural and social moderates rather than hard leftists or hard rightists. Any authentic populism has to appeal to the sensibilities of ordinary people and, as populism and anarchism are closely related, any authentic anarchism must do so as well.[61]

Anarcho-Populism: A New Political Force?

An effective political outlook or strategy requires the development of a certain hierarchy of priorities. Those issues that are the most pressing and on which there is the most common agreement should be the primary focus. Issues of this type come in two categories: those that are the most serious for the world as a whole but are often recognized only by the small number of people who are actually capable of independent thinking beyond the influence of peers and leaders, and those that are foremost on the mind of the common man.[62] The most important issue in the contemporary world is the consolidation of an international

---

61   Keith Preston, "Canning Reactionary Leftism," http://attackthesystem.com/canning-reactionary-leftism/

62   The adoption of some pseudo-Nietzschean concepts may be useful here. Nietzsche tended to categorize persons as slaves, masters, and "*Übermenschen.*" A heterodox adoption of these categories may provide us with certain insights into modern social psychology. Most people appear to fall into the category of the "slaves," demonstrating an inability to think or act independently of group norms, directions provided by authority figures, and the values of their particular culture of origin. The dominant instincts for this category are those of survival and the herd. They are concerned primarily with obtaining their own day-to-day sustenance and look to peers and leaders for a sense of security and identity, hence the reflexive, non-reflective, and often quite irrational attachment of those in this category to particularistic notions like religion, tradition, "morality" as defined by their culture of origin, nationality, ethnicity, family, the orthodoxy of the official ideology of the state to which they are subjects, and so on. The category of the "masters" includes those who are more intelligent and perceptive than others, and also more ruthless and cunning. This element tends to see through established cultural, political, religious, national, or moral myths, and instead devote themselves to the pursuit of power, wealth, and pleasure. It is from this category that societal leaders in the political and economic realms are typically drawn. The final category, the Nietzschean "*Übermenschen,*" are those genuinely superior individuals who find base concerns like the pursuit of wealth and power for its own sake to be unsatisfying. For this element, knowledge, creativity, and discovery are the highest values. It is from this category that the greatest achievers in the arts, sciences, and philosophy are drawn. It is those in this category who become the innovators and instigators of genuine human progress.

Leviathan in the form of the proto-state of the New World Order under the boot of American imperialism and its Anglo-Zionist allies. This is an issue that is more commonly recognized in the Eastern world and in those Western nations outside of the Anglosphere. Consequently, serious opposition to the New World Order will have to originate from those parts of the world. The international trend towards the universalization of American-style "capitalist democracy" (welfare-warfare corporate statism) should be countered by the emergence of an Eastern bloc whose members assert their common independence from Washington and are supported by an alliance of dissident forces within the Anglosphere itself. The American conquest and annexation of Iraq under direct colonial administration has been vehemently opposed by most of the world, particularly France, Germany, Russia, Belgium, and the Islamic world. Therefore, the natural leadership of an international resistance to American imperialism should come from these nations. The question is the matter of what type of strategic-ideological formulation would get the job done.

Larry Gambone argues that a principal source of division between the Anglosphere on one hand and the nations of continental Europe and Asia on the other is the ideology of neoconservatism. It is only in the Anglo nations that this peculiar tendency has thrived. This is a highly elitist ideology whose adherents are numerically small but whose core tenets have become standard policy for the Anglo nations, particularly the United States. Gambone attributes this to the "winner take all" structure of Anglo-American electoral systems as opposed to the proportional systems of the European continent.[63] This may be true, but I suspect the success of the neocons is more likely the result of their efforts to work their way into positions as court intellectuals and the close-knit, cult-like, often family and kinship based nature of the internal structure of their movement. Many in the paleoconservative milieu (Paul

---

63   Larry Gambone, "Neocons, Parts 2 & 3," http://www.attackthesystem.com/neocons2&3.html

Gottfried, for instance) argue that the globalist ambitions of the neocons originate from the Marxist or Trotskyist roots of some of their leading theoreticians.[64] According to this view, the neocons simply substitute global capitalist democracy for international socialism as the motivation for their messianic zeal. Gambone argues that the neocons have more in common with another messianic ideology from the twentieth century: fascism. Says Gambone:

> In its eclectic nature, its authoritarianism, militarism, statism, hostility for real democracy, centralism, Jacobinism, mercantilism, corporatism and Big Lie propaganda, neoconservatism is very similar to fascism. But of course, it is not fascism in the true sense, with its ambiguity about nationalism, and the lack of the party-army, mass mobilization of the population, leader-concept and a popular corporatist ideology. It could be seen as a moderate substitute for fascism . . .[65]

In other words, neoconservatism is as close to fascism as Anglo-American political culture will accept.

My own studies of the nature and origin of neoconservative ideology lead me to the conclusion that the Jewish ethnicity of most of the intellectual exponents of this perspective is essential to understanding their ambitions and beliefs. For the sake of avoiding the usual misunderstandings and accusations, let me say that I am not an "anti-Semite" and generally hold Judaism in higher regard than the other religions originating from the Near East.[66] Nor do I have any special objection to the nation

---

64   Paul Gottfried, "The Trotsky Hour," http://www.lewrockwell.com/gottfried/gottfried46.html

65   Larry Gambone, "Neocons in a Nutshell (Where They Belong)," http://www.attackthesystem.com/neoconnutshell.html

66   Ancient Hebraic religion seems to me to be more closely related to pre-biblical paganism than either Christianity or Islam. First, it is considerably more particularistic, the Jews having their god, Yahweh, with each of the other ethno-cultures having theirs, whether it be Shamash, Baal, Moloch, Zeus, or whomever. Also, biblical Judaism in considerably more "this-worldly" than its two offshoots,

of Israel, beyond its vile oppression of the Palestinian people and its maintenance of a fifth column within domestic American politics. Yet to avoid the discussion of real and immensely important questions out of fear of giving the appearance of impropriety is foolish. Considering the ethnic or religious motivations of those pursuing particular aims is indispensable to sound political analysis. If there is any issue on which the neocons can be counted on to behave with absolute consistency, it is their rabid Zionism. It seems relatively unimportant as to whether the neocons draw their greatest inspiration from Robespierre, Trotsky, or Mussolini. Those who seek absolute power are likely to resemble all of these in certain ways. The more serious question involves the matter of why they seek such power in the first place (beyond ordinary pathology) and what they intend to do with it.

Since the neocons' takeover of the foreign policy apparatus of the United States, their political opponents have begun to examine the influence of Leo Strauss on the neoconservative world view. Virtually all of the leading neoconservative intellectuals, from Irving Kristol to David Horowitz, cite Strauss as a major influence. Some, like Paul Wolfowitz, are his former students. The left-wing scholar Shadia Drury describes Straussian thought as extremely elitist in nature, rooted in a belief in the unfitness of the masses for self-determination and the need for political authority to be vested in Machiavellian leaders whose principal function is to preserve those myths and fairy tales, whether religious or national, by which the masses can be rallied to the defense of the state. The role of the intellectual is to serve as a court advisor to such leaders. Strauss' adoption of such views seems to be rooted in his experience as a German-Jewish refugee from the Hitler regime. Strauss blamed the liberal political climate of the Weimar Republic for allowing the

---

with this life and the nation of Israel being where the action is. Christianity seems to be little more than an apostate, apocalyptic spin-off from Judaism intertwined with various ideas lifted from paganism—virgin births, savior gods, resurrections from the dead, etc. Islam has always seemed to me to be a cheap imitation of Christianity, albeit one with superior warrior traditions.

ascendancy of the Nazis. In his view, this discredited political pluralism as a means of achieving sanctuary for the Jews. While he may not have said so directly (a not surprising fact given his taste for esotericism), Strauss seems to have developed the idea that the best course for Jews would be to develop authoritarian states that they would either rule directly, such as Israel (Strauss was a rabid Zionist), or serve as court intellectuals and thereby influence the practice of statecraft, as in America. Hence, the development of neoconservative ideology by the students and admirers of Strauss.[67]

Of course, the neoconservatives could have never achieved their present level of power without accomplices, primarily the traditional right wing of the US ruling class—oil barons, armaments manufacturers, elite banking interests, etc.—and the Christian Zionist dullards who serve as their ground forces and shock troops. It might be said that the neocons play the role of the NSDAP with Halliburton, Boeing, et al., filling the position of Krupp and I. G. Farben. Perhaps the Christian Zionists are playing the role of the SA.[68] Just as the world united for the defeat of Fascism and National Socialism sixty years ago, so must the world unite for the defeat of the neocons and the New World Order of whom they are the most militant proponents. Outside the Anglosphere, the most successful opponents of the New World Order thus far have been adherents of what Kenneth J. Schmidt refers to as "populist nationalism":

In Europe, these days particularly, nationalism has replaced communism as the threat which unites the center-right and the center-left. In recent days all one needs to do is pick up a newspaper and the names jump out at you: Le Pen, Fortuyn, Haider, Kajarrlstad.

What are the reasons for the rise of a populist-tinged

---

67 Shadia B. Drury, *Leo Strauss and the American Right* (New York: St. Martin's Press, 1997).

68 Preston, "Canning Reactionary Leftism."

nationalism? In the so-called western world, a great rift has developed between the ordinary people and the elites that rule over them.

The fact that the elites and the common people have always had different worldviews is a given. I contend, however, that never in the history of European civilization has there been such a large gap in the way our elites see the world and how the common folk see the world. The historian and social thinker Christopher Lasch had a term for this, he called it a "Revolt of the Elites." The people that rule over us—the big business managerial elite, the media barons, the Zionists and the Manhattan intelligentsia—adhere to values that are strongly at variance with those of working and middle-class whites.[69]

Schmidt notes that populist-nationalist parties in Europe have primarily eclipsed the radical left rather than the center-right. The center-right and center-left parties have essentially identical positions: neo-liberal economics and left-egalitarian cultural values. It is for this reason that, despite the relative vibrant nature of the anti-globalization movement, the far left will fail as a revolutionary force against the international ruling class. On cultural matters, the Far Left differs from the left wing of capital only with regards to the question of degree. The Libertarians are in a similar position, differing from the neo-liberal economics of the Establishment only on questions of degree rather than principle. Some have even gone so far as to endorse flagrantly mercantilist arrangements such as NAFTA. It should also be noted that most rank-and-file supporters of "populist nationalism" throw their allegiance behind those whom they perceive as representing their own interests, rather than some grand principle. While "populist nationalism" may have its roots in the Far Right, its ability to attract sympathy from

---

69   Kenneth J. Schmidt, "Populist Nationalism Developing Across the Western World,"
      The Barnes Review 9, no. 3 (May–June 2003), http://www.barnesreview.org/
      May_2003/Populist/populist.html

mainstream working people, crossover leftists, and even some libertarians, such as those of the paleo variety, establishes it as a force with considerable potential.

I am not a nationalist and I regard the principal flaws in nationalism to be its tendency towards chauvinism and its usually inadequate critique of the state.[70] Leaders like Le Pen, Fortuyn, Haider, and Buchanan may have laid an important foundation but much, much more work needs to be done. I have argued in this article that philosophical anarchism represents a potential alternative paradigm to the contemporary paradigm of state-capitalist liberal democracy. Elsewhere, I have argued that populism is likely to be the proper means to anarchism.[71] Hence, what I am proposing is a new strategic paradigm and, to a certain extent, a new school of anarchist thought that I call "anarcho-populism." This new brand of anarchism would draw on the other schools in various ways. The classical anarchism originally developed by Proudhon would be its foundation. Like anarcho-socialism, anarcho-populism would be anti-capitalist and pro-class struggle. Like anarcho-capitalism, anarcho-populism would endorse property, markets, and the independent sector as an antidote to statism, corporatism, and welfarism. Along with leftist-anarchists, this new anarchist tendency would support political freedom and cultural self-determination for racial minorities, women, gays, and the like, but it would not seek to mindlessly glorify or privilege these groups or demonize white males. Along with primitivists and eco-anarchists, anarcho-populism would seek to preserve the natural environment, but without the misanthropy and anti-tech hysteria of much of modern environmentalism. Like national-anarchists, anarcho-populism would endorse the right of traditional racial, ethnic, religious, or cultural groups to self-preservation and political sovereignty and cross-cultural, cross-ideological alliances against

---

70   Keith Preston, "Conservatism Is Not Enough: Reclaiming the Legacy of the Anti-State Left," http://attackthesystem.com/conservatism-is-not-enough-reclaiming-the-legacy-of-the-anti-state-left/

71   Preston, "Canning Reactionary Leftism."

the NWO, but would seek to branch out into "mainstream" society rather than seek out reclusive isolation from the modern world. The objective is revolution rather than withdrawal. On cultural matters, anarcho-populism would endorse social organicism evolved and historic traditions, and natural evolution in opposition to either "cultural conservatism" (which implies stasis or chauvinism) or "progressivism" (with its incipient universalism or utopianism). Our icons would be Aristotle, Burke, Jefferson, Stirner, Proudhon, Nietzsche, Mencken, Dennis, Hayek, Nisbet, and Kirk, rather than Rousseau, Marx, and Adorno, or William F. Buckley, Margaret Thatcher, and Rush Limbaugh.[72]

Resisting the Empire

It has been mentioned that leadership in building a consensus and alliance against the New World Order and American imperialism would necessarily have to come from outside the Anglosphere. While admirably opposing imperial aggression against the Islamic nations, the nations of continental Western Europe are too influenced by American cultural values, political correctness being largely an American export, and their elite classes are too intertwined with American capitalism to initiate consistent leadership against these things. These nations are in a process of social and economic decay and are militarily weak. Also, their lengthy history of formal alliances with the US regime will be altered only with considerable struggle and difficulty. The Arab nations are too poor to lead such a resistance and the Asian nations are more interested in buying American consumer goods than resisting American imperialism. Ideally, leadership in the development of an anti-NWO, anti-Anglo-Zionist bloc would

---

72 From Aristotle, we derive the core principles of logic against mysticism and irrationalism. From Burke and Jefferson, we understand the relationship of community to anti-statism. From Stirner and Nietzsche, we recognize the importance of the superior individual in the shaping of history. From Proudhon, we adopt the classical anarchist alternative to state-capitalism. From Mencken, we understand that no totems should be spared attack. From Lawrence Dennis, we know the importance of operational as opposed to ideological thinking. From Hayek, Kirk, and Nisbet, we champion evolved traditions, organic society, and natural social evolution against centralist social engineering schemes of any kind.

come from Russia. First, Russia is second only to the United States in military strength. Second, Russia has a long history of serving as a counterbalance to Western, particularly American, imperialisms, even if it was done under the decaying, backward regimes of the tsars or the political deformation of communism. Archonis, a national-anarchist commentator, observes:

> The Russian people and politicians must forge ahead in the "Red-Brown" alliance of Left and Right populism and decentralization, and return Russia to a nation of small institutions, but with adequate defenses and an agrarian economy. The civil institutions must be made small . . . along the lines of farming and guild socialism. The military defenses including nuclear weapons must be built up.

> Russia should forge alliances with China and the Middle East, along with Europe, and be the center of power in a domain that embraces both the East and West . . . guard the resources of its former satellites . . . and . . . maintain control of the oil and mineral reserves . . . [T]he economic survival of Eurasia as a whole is predicated on the interdependence on all of the countries of Europe as well as China and India. . . . Without Europe unifying with Russia and Asia, along with the Middle East, . . . [these nations] will end up being a "Client-State-Network," dominated by U.S. hegemony.

> A united Eurasia could pressure [the Anglo-American-Zionist axis] with trade sanctions and disinvestment, . . . form an intra-net and cut off these countries from their portion of the Internet. The only recourse imperialist nations could turn to would be war, but as long as Eurasia has weapons of mass destruction this will not happen. U.S. imperialists . . . are greedy, decadent cowards who only care about keeping their wealth and nothing else. They cannot comprehend the honor-concept of war. They only understand war as a tool of "gunboat" diplomacy. . . .

Even in conventional warfare, Russia and the large Eurasian landmass has an advantage over the balkanized sea-surrounded lands. Movement is quicker and there are more options for strategic deployment. There are hosts of areas with strange peoples and terrains in the former Soviet Asia, and Chechens and the Turkic peoples . . . have training in unconventional warfare. In the event of war against Eurasia by the imperialists, Russia and China and the peoples of the former Soviet Asia could provide the fighting forces, whereas the European flank can levy diplomatic and economic sanctions . . .[73]

While the downfall and disintegration of the USSR was, for the most part, a positive occurrence, one of its negative side effects has been the creation of power vacuum that American imperialism has been all too eager to fill, thereby generating an even greater concentration of power on a global scale. The sort of revitalized Russia that Archonis hopes for, a Russia rooted in its own traditional culture, a culture that produced Tolstoy and Dostoevsky and Bakunin and Kropotkin, and minus the crackpot ideology of Soviet communism and its accompanying bureaucratic monolith, might indeed be the force needed to successfully challenge the hegemony of the Anglo-American-Zionist triumvirate, the genuine "Axis of Evil." Such an effort within the Russian nation would require visionary leadership founded on recognition of the necessity of looking beyond conventional ideological, cultural, or national boundaries towards the creation of an anti-imperialist bloc. The Russian philosopher and political figure Alexander Dugin postulates the concept of "Eurasianism" as the means to such ends. Dugin explains:

To whom are we addressing the call to enter and to back our movement? To each Russian, educated or not, influential and the last of the dispossessed, to the worker and to the manager, to the needy and the well-off, to the Russian and

---

73   Archonis, "Onward Eurasia," http://www.rosenoire.org/essays/eurasia.php. See also
     Archonis, "The Hammer of Nihilation," http://www.rosenoire.org/essays/hammer.php

the Tatar, to the Orthodox and the Jew, to the conservative and the modernist, to the student and the defender of the law, to the soldier and the weaver, to the governor and the rock musician.... The movement "Eurasian" is founded on the principles of the radical centre. We are neither leftists nor rightists, we are neither slavishly compliant to the authorities, nor oppositionists barking with a reason and without at any costs . . .

Russia will seriously be faced with the purpose of rescuing itself and the rest of the world from the terrible threat which creeps from the West . . .

In the religious sphere it means constructive and solid dialogue between the traditional creeds of Russia: Orthodoxy, Islam, Judaism, Buddhism . . . In the sphere of foreign policy, Eurasianism implies a wide process of strategic integration . . . spread to wider areas—to the countries of the Moscow-Teheran-Delhi-Beijing axis . . . priority relations with the European countries . . . active cooperation with the countries of the Pacific region . . . active and universal opposition to globalization . . .

Eurasianism defends the blossoming complexity of peoples, religions and nations . . . a combination of strategic unity and ethno-cultural (in definite cases, economic) autonomies. Different ways of life at the local level . . . Eurasianism is primarily addressed to the youth, to the people whose consciousness has not yet been spoiled by random leaps from one inadequate ideological pattern to another, even less adequate . . . [74]

Dugin mentions a number of ideological tendencies that are involved in the struggle against New World Order imperialism. These include Orthodoxy, Islam, Traditionalism,

---

74   Alexander Dugin, "Manifesto of the Eurasia Movement," http://arctogaia.com/public/
        eng/Manifesto.html

the Conservative Revolution, National Bolshevism, Third Positionism, Russian nationalism, Socialism, Islamic socialism, Eurasianism, Nationalism (in general), Anarchism (in its various manifestations), the New Left, the New Right, and a good number of others.[75] While it is true that there is a vast array of tendencies struggling against the common imperial enemy, and that tactical alliances between these forces are necessary and legitimate, there remains the practical matter of how such differences within the revolutionary ranks can be accommodated. Fortunately, the "national-anarchist" theories of Troy Southgate and David Michael provide some clues as to how to proceed.[76] Whatever one's views on the state, the ideal formation of the state, and the proper role of the state in human political or civil society, it is abundantly clear that, as a matter of expediency, statist centralization is simply incompatible with the formulation of solid tactical alliances against the common imperial enemy. The establishment of strong states in ostensible opposition to the NWO, but where the state is ordered on the basis of bitter factionalism with an ongoing danger of internal cannibalization, will inevitably have a corrupting effect on the resistance forces whereby one or another contending faction can be induced to stab the others in the back by means of bribery and offers of greater power on the part of the enemy. One need only look at the ruling classes of the so-called "moderate" Arab nations to see a graphic illustration of this point.

The conventional nation-state system has been rendered obsolete by the consolidation of the NWO global superstate. Therefore, old-style nationalisms are irrelevant. The proper form of social organization to be offered in opposition to the global superstate is the organic local, regional, cultural, or ideological community. Within all traditional nations, many tendencies stand in opposition to the NWO, from the Far Left to the Far

---

75   From the Arctogaia website at http://www.arctogaia.com/public/engl1.htm

76   For a look at the works of David Michael, visit his website at http://www.nationalanarchist.com. For an overview of national-anarchism, visit http://www.rosenoire.org and http://terrafirma.rosenoire.org.

Right to the Radical Center, to libertarians, anarchists, religious communities, Greens, "Beyond Left and Right," and others. Single-issue unity on the part of these forces for the purpose of pulling their respective nations out of the imperial system seems to be the way to go. Points of contention can be dealt with more effectively through decentralization. For example, in the nation of France, opponents of American imperialism and the NWO include the Communists and Greens from the left, nationalists on the right along with Muslims and Catholic traditionalists. Yet there is considerable disagreement among these divergent forces on many issues, particularly immigration. Conversion to a decentralized political infrastructure, such as the Swiss canton system or the federalism of Old America, might allow different factions autonomy and self-determination within their own enclaves. There could be towns and cities governed by the National Front, the Greens, Islamists, Communists, or whomever. In many nations, forces such as these constitute a majority against the center-left/center-right, pro-NWO ruling classes.[77]

What about the fate of those countries currently enduring the greatest assault at the hands of the imperialists? The resistance forces in both Iraq and Afghanistan are notoriously divided and on the verge of civil war, and collaborators and traitors exist within their ranks. How much different would the fate of Iraq be, if the Sunnis, Shiites, and Kurds each agreed to sovereignty within their own historic regions, with internal sovereignty for individual tribes and clans, additional enclaves for minorities like the Assyrian Christians, and common unity and resistance to the imperial conqueror? If the contending tribes, religious, and ethnic factions of Afghanistan adopted a polycentric order of the Somali variety, Afghanistan's current status as a colony of Western oilmen might be drastically altered. Likewise, the relegation of the Palestinian people to the "One Big Concentration Camp" that the West Bank has become might be reversed if Anglo-Zionist imperial power

---

77   Jaroslaw Tomasiewicz, "An Alternative to the American Empire of the New World Order," http://www.attackthesystem.com/alternative.html

had a decentralized but confederated Eurasian bloc, organized on the basis of a defensive, diplomatic, and economic tactical alliance, to contend with.

What about the struggle within the "belly of the beast" itself, the nations of the Anglosphere? If, as Kenneth J. Schmidt argues, the ideology of the ruling class is "libertarian in its economic views and left-wing multiculturalist in its social policies,"[78] then it stands to reason that the natural opposition would be the reverse: libertarian in social matters but "left-wing" (radical and revolutionary) in economics, i.e., "libertarian socialism." By "libertarian," I am not referring to utopian universalism of either the left-progressive or liberal-consumerist variety. Rather, I am referring to an authentic cultural diversity rooted in such anarchistic principles as individual autonomy, voluntary association, mutual aid, and decentralism. By "socialism," I do not mean statism of either a Marxist or nationalist variety but something more consistent with the original meaning of socialism—an economy of the producers, by the producers and for the producers. "Producerism," as the reactionary leftist Chip Berlet might call it.[79] The established schools of anarchism each have something to offer, as I pointed out earlier. However, there remains the question of how anarchism is to break out of its various ideological ghettos and into mainstream society. From classical anarchism and anarcho-syndicalism, we derive the class struggle. From libertarian-individualist anarchism, we champion the individual against the state. From eco-anarchism, we approach material and technological development with a watchful eye. With neo-anarchism, we champion the downtrodden and marginalized. With national-anarchism, we seek the preservation of indigenous cultures and ideological diversity. But the point remains that most people care little, if anything, about any of this.

---

78   Schmidt, "Populist Nationalism Developing Across the Western World."

79   For an unintentionally comical discussion of "producerism" by a reactionary leftist, see "Right-Wing Populism in America: Too Close for Comfort," http://www.publiceye. org/tooclose/producerism.html

To develop an effective anti-ruling class strategy, the structure and tactics of the ruling elite must first be understood. The Anglo nations, particularly America, are dominated by two largely identical parties that represent contending factions of the corrupt elites. The right wing of the ruling class consists primarily of "old money," i.e., banking, oil, agricultural cartels, arms merchants, etc. The left wing of the ruling class consists of newer, high-tech, capital-intensive industries such as media, entertainment, medical, and computer related corporate interests. Both principal factions cement their support base by appealing to contending cultural factions—"social conservatives," the dominant ethnic group, and religious fundamentalists on one end, and elite members of minority groups, union bosses, public sector workers, and environmentalists on the other end. Zionists appear to be rather influential within both camps. The key to building any sort of successful opposition would be to disrupt and neutralize existing ruling class coalitions.[80]

For an Anarchist Vanguard

It is interesting to note that existing ruling class factions and their constituencies include some rather bizarre alliances. What exactly do aristocratic country clubbers have in common with backwoods religious fundamentalists? Yet both are a part of the Republican coalition. What do traditional working class union members have in common with militants from the homosexual counterculture? Yet both are a part of the Democratic coalition. An effective oppositional coalition would draw away certain elements from both of the enemy coalitions, yielding them ineffectual. To achieve this objective, several strategies might need to be simultaneously employed. First, there is the question of leadership. Mark Gillespie postulates the idea of an "anarchist

---

80 Noam Chomsky has developed an interesting "investment theory" of US politics. Chomsky argues that the US political system operates on the basis of shifting coalitions of investors. These investors have previously acquired enough private wealth and power to make the acquisition of political power feasible. See Anthony Gancarski , "Does Noam Chomsky Hate America?," http://www.antiwar.com/gancarski/ gan102403.html

vanguard" whose primary function is the construction of an anti-ruling class coalition. Says Gillespie:

> Anarchists can work to foster alliances between disparate groups. As mediators and vision-holders, we can help each group to see that uniting for the common goal of freedom, trumps their own agendas. After all, once the government is gone, no one will care if you set up an all-black, all-white, all-Jew, all-Muslim, all-socialist, all-capitalist community. We should pick up the torch of unity and educate people into respecting the diverse views of others. I may not like what you're doing, saying, being, etc. but I will defend to the death your right to do, say or be it.[81]

This kind of modern Voltairean outlook might serve as the core principle of the anarchist vanguard. In a sense, we should seek to emulate our deadly enemies, the neoconservatives, in an effort to become a highly influential element in great disproportion to our actual numbers. David Michael suggests that such an effort might be done through non-traditional political strategies such as resource acquisition, alliance building, and community formation.[82] This could include the establishment of self-sufficient intentional communities, alternative media, alternative economic institutions, and even alternative legal institutions or defense organizations as some in the US militia/patriot/constitutionalist movement have sought to do. Such communities and institutions might eventually develop a cultural presence and identity of their own in the same manner that the divergent ethnic groups in large cities currently do. These could in turn be the building blocks of localized political movements and, eventually, full-blown local and regional secessionist or autonomist movements.

---

81 Mark Gillespie, "The Vanguard Idea," http://www.attackthesystem.com/the-vanguard-idea/. See also Keith Preston, "Smashing the State: Thoughts on Anarchist Strategy," http://attackthesystem.com/smashing-the-state-thoughts-on-anarchist-strategy/

82 David Michael, "On Strategy," http://www.nationalanarchist.com/strategy.html

Hans-Hermann Hoppe argues that the proliferation of independent or semi-independent free cities, such as those that emerged in the latter Middle Ages, might be the core institutional foundation for the subversion of modern centralist, imperialist states.[83] A core idea within the national-anarchist milieu is the creation of anti-establishment communities functioning on a largely autarchic basis, highly diverse in their cultural and ideological orientation, but mutually supportive of one another against the common enemy.[84] In this way, a common alliance of those wanting out of the System could develop. Divergent forces might form a common agreement to work to gain political pre-eminence in their own areas of influence with each agreeing to support the others in their efforts to do so as well. Thus, communities formed by the All-African Peoples' Revolutionary Party in the inner-city regions might be tactically aligned with similar communities formed by the Militia of Montana in rural areas.

While efforts of these types might go a long way as far as dealing with "extremist" elements within the ranks of various oppositional tendencies, and such elements might form the core constituencies of an anti-ruling class coalition, there remains the question of how to reach mainstream working people not inclined towards any sort of clearly articulated ideological structures or any particular aspect of peripheral cultures. Troy Southgate argues that a tactic known as "entryism" might be appropriate as far as creating an organizational infrastructure that can be utilized as a political vehicle. Says Southgate:

> Entryism is the name given to the process of entering or infiltrating bona fide organizations, institutions and political parties with the intention of either gaining control of them for our own ends, misdirecting or disrupting them for our own purposes or converting sections of their memberships to our cause. . . . So what are we looking

83   Hoppe, *Democracy*.

84   David Michael, "Unity in Diversity," http://www.nationalanarchist.com/unity.html

for? Any organization with a weak, apathetic or elderly leadership. An organization that has a youth section or a youthful membership . . . What we need is an organization that has idealists, people motivated by ideology and an organization that has—or could have—some sort of influence, given the right leadership in the community . . . It is the case that many organizations currently dominated by both Left and Right simply need turning away from their present ideology . . .[85]

Organizations of this type might include dissident or minor political parties, neighborhood or grassroots community organizations, single-issue pressure groups, territorial secession movements, labor unions, and educational institutions, particularly university humanities departments. Cadre of anarchists would seek out seats on the board of directors of the National Rifle Association, or the American Civil Liberties Union. Anarchists would obtain positions on the executive committees of "third-parties" or local civic organizations. Anarchist educators would be teaching the history of the United States during the twentieth century from the perspective of Murray Rothbard, William Appleman Williams or Lawrence Dennis rather than Arthur Schlesinger Jr. at the local university. Anarchists sitting on the advisory boards of local business associations, churches or charities would do much more for the broader struggle than anarchist agitators who throw rocks through Starbucks windows currently do, although the latter is not necessarily without its place as well.

It is through achieving control of the kinds of institutions being described here, using the methods that Troy Southgate suggests, that anarchists could work their way into positions to influence the broader public. Indeed, a precedent for this does exist. In an excellent essay on the ideas of the classical anarchist godfather Pierre-Joseph Proudhon, Larry Gambone describes how the values of libertarian socialism had at one time begun to enter mainstream society:

---

85 Troy Southgate, "The Case for National-Anarchist Entryism," http://www.rosenoire. org/articles/entryism.php

Proudhon's criticism of the credit and monetary systems were an influence upon the Greenback Party. His concept of mutual associations and the Peoples' Bank were forerunners of the credit union and cooperative movements. . . . Support for labor and even "socialism" was found among the upper classes. The British Prime Minister, Disraeli, expressed sympathy for the workers, Lincoln corresponded with the International [Workingmen's Association] and the editor and publisher of the world's largest newspaper, the *New York Tribune*, Charles Dana and Horace Greely, were followers of Proudhon and Charles Fourier.[86]

Beyond Left and Right

The initial way for this new, modernized, revitalized version of traditional anarchism to publicize itself, once it has secured its position in the manner previously suggested, would be to vocally proclaim to be an alternative to the liberal establishment, the reactionary left, and mainstream "conservatism" alike. First, the matter of the culture wars has to be dealt with. This seems to be more of an issue in America that in other Anglo nations like England or Canada and, as I am an American and most familiar with the political landscape of my own country of origin, I will address this question from the perspective of the internal politics of America. A mainstream "conservative" commentator, Dennis Prager, describes some of the controversies that define the culture war:

> The Left believes in removing America's Judeo-Christian identity, e.g., removing "under God" from the Pledge, "In God We Trust" from the currency . . . The Right believes that destroying these symbols and this identity is tantamount is to destroying America.

> The Left regards America as morally inferior to many

---

86   Larry Gambone, "Proudhon and Anarchism: Proudhon's Libertarian Thought and the Anarchist Movement," http://www.spunk.org/library/writers/proudhon/sp001863. html

European societies with their abolition of the death penalty, cradle-to-grave-welfare and religion-free life; and it does not believe that there are distinctive American values worth preserving. The Right regards America as the last best hope for humanity and believes that there are distinctive American values, the unique combination of a religious (Judeo-Christian) society, a secular government, personal liberty and capitalism—that are worth fighting and dying for.

The Left believes multiculturalism should be the ideal for American schools and American policy. The Right believes that the Americanization of all its citizens is indispensable to the survival of the United States.

The Left believes that "war is not the answer." The Right believes that war is often the only answer to governmental evil.[87]

Prager goes on to describe other aspects of the whole moronic "liberal-conservative" divide including condoms in schools, silicone breast implants, gays in the Boy Scouts, yadda, yadda, yadda. Some of Prager's assertions are absurd to the point of comedy, such as his claim that "capitalism" is worth fighting and dying for. Yes, we can all envision the troops marching into battle singing: "If I die, at least I know, I gave my life for Texaco." Then there is the assertion that America is "the last best hope for humanity." Yes, an ethos of materialist-consumerism, false egalitarianism, and totalitarian therapeutic statism is most assuredly the road to Paradise.

Essentially, these culture wars are between those who prefer that the New World Order take on a distinctively "Americanist"

---

87 Dennis Prager, "The Second American Civil War: What It's About," http://townhall. com/columnists/dennisprager/2003/10/14/the_second_american_civil_war_what_ its_about/page/full, and "The Second American Civil War: What It's About—Part II," http://townhall.com/columnists/dennisprager/2003/10/21/the_second_american_ civil_war_what_its_about_part_ii/page/full

identity and those who prefer a global superstate with a more overtly internationalist face. Should the United States rule the world through the United Nations or through the Pentagon? The discrepancies are not nearly as significant as the partisans to this intramural battle insist. Joseph Sobran points out that the constitutional order that the allegedly "right-wing" or "conservative" Bush regime seeks to impose on Iraq includes provisions for ". . . democracy, non-violence, diversity and a role for women."[88] This sounds like something out of the mouth of Morris "Dildo" Dees or Hillary "It Takes a Police State to Raise a Child" Clinton. This is to be the conservative "solution" for a highly patriarchal, religious, militaristic society? Even Trotsky, who claimed that under Marxism the average man would reach the level of an Aristotle, would likely have been more practical.

The relevance of all of this for those of us who are involved in the struggle against the US regime is the question of which side in the "culture wars" will eventually win and, therefore, be our greatest enemy in the long run. I predict that the liberal-internationalist-multiculturalist wing of the US ruling class will win hands down. Even some of the proponents of the "Americanist" perspective agree. For example, John Fonte, a columnist for "Front Page Magazine," edited by the arch-propagandist for Anglo-Zionist imperialism David Horowitz, speculates:

> Thus, it is entirely possible that modernity—thirty or forty years hence—will witness not the final triumph of liberal democracy, but the emergence of a new transnational hybrid regime that is post-liberal democratic and, in the American context, post-Constitutional and post-American.[89]

The simple reason that the "Americanists" are destined to lose is that their ideology is even more utopian and constructivist than

---

88   Joseph Sobran, "A New Constitution—Coming Up!," http://www.sobran.com/columns/2003/030930.shtml

89   John Fonte, "The Ideological War Within the West," September 9, 2002, http://www.frontpagemag.com/Articles/ReadArticle.asp?ID=2853

that of the "progressives" whom they so ardently despise. There is not, and can never be, an authentic American nationalism. Nationalism must be rooted in the organic culture of the people. This is impossible in a state whose common identity is rooted in abstract ideological concepts, with the debate being over how these concepts are to be applied, and where whatever passes for a common culture is simply a constantly changing amalgam of all sorts of fractious and contradictory tendencies.[90] This is the so-called "melting pot." Some "Americanists" at least implicitly understand this. Robert Locke, a cynical but candid expositor of Straussian jingoism, observes:

> [T]he Constitution . . . is a curious mixture of Greco-Roman ideas, Christian ideas, Lockean natural-rights ideas, plus a few other odds and ends from Montesquieu and other sources . . . The idea that America was founded foursquare on liberty and inalienable rights is the Platonic noble lie of our republic, and as such is entirely appropriate for schoolchildren and most of the rest of us. It is not, however, the truth.[91]

Locke regards the ideological nationalism promulgated by most "Americanists" to be inadequate as a source of national cohesion and prefers to attempt to construct an American nationalism rooted in more conventional nationalist concepts like ethnicity (in a nation where nearly a third of the population are minorities), Judeo-Christian religious traditions (where did the "Judeo" part come from?), language (in an increasingly bilingual society), and "middle class values" (when most of the constituents of political correctness are middle class professionals and intellectuals). Like most crackpot reactionaries, Locke wants to return to an America that may have existed briefly in the early nineteenth century, if it ever existed at all. Modern America is an imperial empire, not a nation. Even the American state itself more closely resembles the

---

90   Joseph Sobran, "The Empire and Its Denizens," *The Wanderer*, May 15, 2003.

91   Robert Locke, "Why America Is Not a Propositional Nation," Front Page Magazine, June 4, 2002, http://archive.frontpagemag.com/readArticle.aspx?ARTID=24240

old USSR than anything—a continent-wide regime composed of all sorts of sub-cultural and sub-national groupings absorbed into a bureaucratic monolith ordered on the basis of an imposed ideology. Like the Soviets, the Americanists wish to impose a regime of ideological homogeneity on a society ordered on the basis of extreme cultural diversity. It doesn't work that way.

It is likely, then, that the prevailing future ideology of the United States and therefore the international ruling class will be overt liberal corporatism, globalism, and multiculturalism. All contemporary trends point in that direction. Consequently, the primary target of the anarchist intellectual vanguard should be the liberal establishment and the reactionary left. The David Horowitzes and Ann Coulters are an amusing sideshow to the main event, the professional wrestling of the political/media elite. The liberal orientation of the supposedly "conservative" Bush administration—Keynesian economics, nationalized education, massive subsidies to "curing AIDS in Africa," the liberal "constitution" to be imposed on Iraq, proposed amnesty for illegal immigrants—attests to this. An interesting parallel might be invoked from certain pages in classical anarchist history. The classical anarchists fought for generations against the capitalists, only to be stabbed in the back by their Marxist arch-enemies when the "socialist" revolution actually came. This is the primary fight that authentic anarchists are in today. Old-style capitalism no longer exists. Modern societies are ruled by the "new class" or "managerial elite" observed by Burnham, Orwell, and Dennis. This class has long since made its peace with both capitalism and socialism (in the form of corporate-social democracy and neo-mercantilist "free trade") and has adopted "cultural Marxism" (whether of the neo-conservative or neo-liberal variety) as its social outlook. It is this element that is our principal enemy.

Tradition, Revolution and Anarchism Without Hyphens

Whatever else could be said about the Straussians, one thing they get right is their understanding of the utility of national and cultural myths as a potent force for political mobilization. Although an actual American nationalism is contradictory and impossible, an appeal to classical American revolutionary ideals is entirely appropriate for opponents of the current American regime. Such venerable notions to be derived from historic Americana as inalienable rights, criticism of state power, decentralism, anti-imperialist revolution, authentic cultural and ideological pluralism (mythically personified by the "First Amendment"), anti-taxation protest, self-reliance, agrarianism, populism, "the right to bear arms," "give me liberty or give me death," and symbolized by such events as the Boston Tea Party, Lexington and Concord, the Whiskey Rebellion, the Confederate secession, the Underground Railroad, Haymarket, and much else provides a virtual fountain of cultural resources for modern enemies of the state to draw on. Larry Gambone provides instruction on how to begin:

> Anarchists should organize at the local level, i.e., neighborhood, village, municipality or county, around issues that affect the population . . . A city-wide organization could fight to decentralize the city government to the neighborhood level and gain greater autonomy for the municipality.[92]

In such an effort, we might look to the example of Norman Mailer's 1969 New York mayoral campaign. Mailer remembered:

> I ran for mayor of New York in the hope that a Left-Right coalition could be formed and this Left-Right pincers could make a dent in the entrenched power of the center . . . So, we called for Power to the Neighborhoods. We suggested that New York City become a state itself, the fifty-first. Its

---

92   Larry Gambone, *Sane Anarchy* (Montreal: Red Lion Press, 1995), 12.

citizens would then have the power to create a variety of new neighborhoods, new townships, all built on separate concepts, core neighborhoods founded on one or another of our cherished notions from the Left or the Right. One could have egalitarian towns and privileged places, or, for those who did not wish to be bothered with living in so detailed (and demanding) a society, there would be the more familiar and old way of doing things—the City of the State of New York—a government for those who did not care—just like old times.[93]

A number of local and regionalist movements have emerged in the United States in recent years. The ideological and cultural content of these is quite diverse. Some from the Left have suggested secession by the city of San Francisco, the Northeast corridor, and other bastions of "liberal" cultural values. The libertarian-capitalist Free State Project is working to become politically dominant in New Hampshire and radically scale back that state's government. Similar independence, separatist, or autonomist movements exist in the South, Texas, Alaska, Hawaii, New England, the Northwest, Puerto Rico, and elsewhere, including many localities. Some within the patriot/ constitutionalist milieu have sought to set up an alternative infrastructure, usually based on local or populist themes that can be put into place once central power is eradicated. Anarchists should get involved with these kinds of tendencies, and seek to influence the intellectual content and ideological orientation of such movements. It is of the utmost importance to recognize the need for authentic cultural and ideological diversity within the ranks of such resistance efforts. In the tradition of Voltairine de Cleyre, Larry Gambone calls for an unhyphenated anarchism where particular cultural, economic, or theoretical differences are subordinated to the struggle against the common enemy:

Read even the most superficial book on anarchism and

---

93   Norman Mailer, "I Am Not for World Empire," *The American Conservative*, December 2, 2002, 18.

you will discover that many forms of anarchism exist—anarchist-communism, individualist-anarchism, anarcho-syndicalism, free-market anarchism, anarcho-feminism and green-anarchism. This division results from people taking their favorite economic system or extrapolating from what they see as the most important social struggle and linking this to anarchism. . . . The hyphenation presents a danger. Like it or not, everyone, without exception, compromises, modifies or softens their beliefs at some point. Where they compromise is what is important. Do they give up on the anarchism of the other aspect? You can be sure that most hyphenated anarchists will prefer to drop the libertarian side of the hyphen. There are plenty examples of this occurring.[94]

Most existing anarchist tendencies tend to promote their preferred set of sociocultural, economic, or issue-based views over the broader struggle against the state. For example, anarchists with leftist cultural views seem to be more interested in anti-racism, feminism, and "gay liberation" than anarchism. At the other end, anarchists with nationalist or racialist tendencies are often likely to emphasize the latter rather than the former. Eco-anarchists are typically environmentalists first and anarchists second, or last. Anarcho-socialists and anarcho-capitalists usually put socialism or capitalism before anarchism. To some degree, this is understandable. Most people, including anarchists, tend to identify more strongly with their own culture and others who share their personal values than with ideological abstractions. One anarchist tendency, the national-anarchists, has attempted to deal with this problem. David Michael distinguishes between "core" issues and "peripheral" issues. Core issues involve the common struggle against the New World Order global superstate and the regional/national elites who are its benefactors and beneficiaries. Peripheral issues involve one's preferred cultural, intellectual, economic, or lifestyle interests.[95] These could include

---

94 Gambone, *Sane Anarchy*.

95 David Michael, "National Anarchist FAQ," http://www.nationalanarchist.com/faq.

communism, capitalism, black nationalism, white nationalism, environmentalism, socialism, feminism, Christianity, Islam, monarchism, Satanism, injecting heroin, or whatever. Divisions of this type are certainly important, and cannot merely be swept under the rug for the sake of some fractious "unity," yet nothing will ever be achieved if these sorts of differences allow the opposition forces to be divided, conquered, or co-opted by the international ruling class. David Michael provides us with one poignant example after another of how the NWO imperialists have done just this to nations, cultures, and religions all over the world, including the communist countries of Eastern Europe, the Islamic nations of the Middle East, and the peoples (both white and black) of southern Africa.[96] As Larry Gambone says:

> . . . try as much as you like, you can't ignore the big one— Leviathan—the central state. Eventually it must be tackled head on and this can only be done by a nation-wide mass movement [or a global movement in the case of the NWO and opposition between local organizations and the larger movement, on the contrary, the latter must be based upon the former. This must be a single issue movement, uniting everyone with a grievance against the state into a movement for the decentralization of power. It must not be allowed to be bogged down by secondary and therefore divisive issues. These can be dealt with by other groups.[97]

Indeed, domestic American politics tends to be driven by single-issue movements and organizations rather than ideological ones. Raw ideology pushers tend to find little success in US politics. With this consideration in mind, the question becomes one of how to best formulate a successful single-issue anti-state movement. Several possible constituents for such a movement have already been discussed. The emergence of a single-issue anti-state party or organization that included the agendas of

---

html

96   Michael, "Unity in Diversity."

97   Gambone, *Sane Anarchy.*

each of the various local and regionalist movements would likely be a good start. There is no reason why there cannot be a party, or alliance of parties, that simultaneously favors the independence of Puerto Rico, Hawaii, Texas, the South, numerous local communities, and religion/ethnicity based separatists like the Nation of Islam, Christian Identity, Aztlán, indigenous peoples, and others. Such advocacy of regional/local autonomy should be accompanied by an emphasis on populist structural changes. Norman Mailer's suggestion of decentralizing the governments of large metropolitan areas down to the neighborhood level coincides nicely with the objective of sovereign townships or county supremacy found in the patriot/constitutionalist milieu.

The efforts of the American Civil Liberties Union to defend the civil rights of all sorts of groups which come under attack from the state, ranging from neo-Nazis to pornographers, might be emulated. There are many such groups who are currently ignored by mainstream political organizations. These include home schoolers, "cults" or marginal religious denominations, intentional communities, so-called "hate" groups, prisoners and their families, opponents of the war on drugs, gun rights militants, tax resisters, and many others. It is important to remember that a movement for political decentralization should employ a decentralized strategy. This means that the same tactics will not be appropriate in all situations. For example, anarchists working in urban or metropolitan areas should naturally take a political line that is considerably further to the left than anarchists working in rural areas or among more conservative population groups. The cultural paradigm of anti-racism, feminism, and gay rights that dominates the modern left might well be applicable in those communities that it is suited for, such as large cities with huge minority populations and where the prevailing values are cosmopolitan in nature. However, this would clearly not be an appropriate model for rural Kansas. For anarchists to persistently push "the right to bear arms" in liberal Connecticut would probably be a waste of time. For anarchists to agitate for gay causes in small Tennessee towns would likewise be rather futile.

Philosophical Anarchism and the Death of Empire

So-called "extremists" from all points on the political spectrum might be rallied as the core constituents of the anti-System forces. It is essential to remember that the anarchist movement itself (properly and constructively organized) is not necessarily a mass movement per se but only the intellectual and activist vanguard of a broader populist movement containing many different tendencies. The role of the anarchists is to serve as the coordinating mediators conceived of by Mark Gillespie or the principled militants envisioned by Mikhail Bakunin. The decentralized organizational efforts of the anarchists would necessarily involve a scenario where the character of the anti-System movement varied considerably in its specific ideological, cultural, religious, or ethnic orientation on a geographical or institutional basis. Across the American heartland, in the Deep South and in the mountainous regions, the anarchists might assemble a coalition of tax resisters, home schoolers, gun nuts, conspiracy theorists, pro-lifers, Christian fundamentalists, common law enthusiasts, farmers rights advocates, land rights advocates, "cults," racists, libertarians, militiamen, and other elements common to the political culture of right-wing populism. In large metropolitan centers, inner cities, border areas, and coastal regions, a similar coalition might include militants and separatists from the various minority groups, advocates for all sorts of class-based social issues (gentrification, housing, environment), gays and other sexual minorities, all sorts of countercultural groups, students, street gangs and other official outlaws, communists, left-wing "anarchists," and others.

Among the affluent elements of American society, such as the realm of suburbia, it is probably best if the ranks of the revolutionaries draw heavily from the youth population. Opposition to the great oppressor of youth—the state's school systems—may well be the key issue. It is also important to note that class distinctions in modern liberal democratic states are somewhat more blurred than they may have been in previous times. Any authentic populist revolutionary movement would naturally have to include persons from all classes. The task of the genuine anarchists, who will always be a small minority, even in Official Anarchist circles, is to coordinate and guide formal and informal alliances among such disparate groups. The kinds of issue and ideology based constituent groups being described here would provide the grassroots base for the broader anarchist agenda. But there remains the question of how to appeal to the broader public. A party/organization that combined local and regional autonomy, defended social groups under attack by the state, recruited disparate elements from the cultural fringes as its activist/support base, and maintained a decentralized infrastructure would also have to develop a populist program for the masses.

Popular Front Anarchism and the Defense of Culture and Civilization Against Nihilism

It is essential to remember that not everything the state does is equally pernicious or equally in need of abolition. The most important issue is the need to defeat the New World Order internationally and the creeping police state domestically. All other considerations should be subordinated to these concerns. The ultimate objective is to bring down the corrupt, tyrannical US regime and to consequently implode the New World Order. The issues that motivate those on the margins— radical environmentalism, gun rights absolutism, racial nationalism, socialism, radical feminism, queer power, religious fundamentalism—mean nothing to most people. The ordinary citizen is concerned only with his own day-to-day business. His issues are unemployment, housing, taxes, health care, provisions for old age, and education.[98] Some people may also have one or two social issues like abortion or the environment that they are interested in or have strong opinions about. Most Americans have received something of a libertarian education from the Jeffersonian strand of traditional American politics. For this reason, populist rhetoric denouncing "big government" resonates well with the commoner. A populist movement that combined

---

98   *Ibid.*

both libertarian and socialist themes, without explicitly describing itself as such, would likely go over well with the broad American working class.

Populist structural changes with a libertarian bent might be the first item on the agenda. Larry Gambone comments:

> In order to make significant structural changes to society, one must have a program consisting of, say, half a dozen or so key items which the majority of the population might support. The most important point, and the point upon which all populists agree, is the need to empower the ordinary person and their communities and the concurrent weakening of the authority of the politico-economic elite. This can be done by combining the traditional populist structural political reforms of proportional ballot, referenda, initiative and recall with radical decentralization of political power down to the natural community. The power of the economic elite can be clipped by the abolition of corporate welfare and all other government-granted privileges. All populist groups either do or would agree with these principles. Once empowered, the people and their communities could then seek any other social, political or economic reforms they chose, since they would now have the ability to make those decisions.[99]

This proposal seems to be as cogent as any. As the recent recall of the governor of California illustrates, populist fiscal reforms are also quite popular, even in havens of leftward-leaning politics. As taxes are the lifeblood of the state, and as the average American is familiar with the partial origins of the American Revolution in anti-taxation protest, a radical assault upon the state's taxing system seems warranted. Depicting Establishment politicians as corrupt squanderers of the public treasury is a tried and true American political tactic, and could almost certainly be utilized to the advantage of anarchists.

---

99   *Ibid.*

Kevin Carson provides us with a possible economic program.[100] On economic matters, an anarcho-populist, libertarian-decentralist, left-right, radical-center alliance should assert itself as a populist alternative to both the neoliberal economics of the Anglo-American New Right (as opposed to the more populist New Right of the European continent) and the New Class welfare statism of the reactionary left. Carson offers three principal targets for such an alliance: the state's monopolistic currency and banking legislation, the monopoly privilege imposed by patent laws, and the concentration of control over land through the enforcement of absentee ownership. Elimination of barriers to the formation of credit unions, organization of tenants of public and private rental housing into unions organized on the old anarcho-syndicalist model, demands for the recognition of squatters rights, establishment of the right of local and regional political units and "private" groupings to issue alternative units of exchange, and the establishment of mutual aid societies for the provision of unemployment, medical, and old-age insurance might be a first step. These can be followed by the elimination of licensing regulations designed to prevent competition with established corporate or professional monopolies from small businesses and the self-employed and to concentrate control over the media. The elimination of all corporate welfare and the establishment of worker cooperatives as an antidote to corporatism and the conversion of social or municipal services to consumer cooperatives should accompany the dismantling of the corporate-social democratic welfare state.[101] Measures such as these have been proposed by a wide variety of radical thinkers and would be fairly consistent with both the ideals of the "small is beautiful" social activist left along with the "anti-big government" right. Furthermore, the emerging presence and popularity of radicals advocating such a program would have the effect of further discrediting the common left/right divide. The reactionary left would be forced to abandon any populist

---

100 Kevin Carson, "A 'Political' Program for Anarchists," http://attackthesystem.com/a-political-program-for-anarchists/

101 *Ibid.*

or decentralist pretensions it might otherwise display and position itself as the defenders of the welfare state. Likewise, the reactionary right would be forced to abandon its libertarian pretensions and become the open, unabashed defenders of corporatism. Also, the anarchist/populist forces would include a genuine cross-section of the cultural spectrum, ranging from patriarchal fundamentalists and racialists to gay, feminist, countercultural anarchists and communists, with each of these seeking sovereignty within their own communities. In response, the totalitarian multicultural left would likely gravitate towards the corporatists. The ruling class enemy would be more greatly consolidated in the form of the corporate-social democratic welfare-warfare state, with reactionary multiculturalism and totalitarian progressivism as its ideological orientation, and would therefore be easier to identify and attack.

There remains yet another consideration regarding programmatic concerns. Any movement that aims to break up ruling class coalitions needs to recognize the importance of "wedge" issues to such efforts. These involve issues for which there is a constituency but where all established parties are committed to the other side.[102] Probably the most significant wedge issues in American politics are drug prohibition and the relationship between the United States and Israel. A growing and militant opposition is brewing on both of these matters, yet the political establishment cannot budge a bit as the "war on drugs" is an essential component of the police state apparatus, and involves a vast array of vested interests, and the Zionist lobby has a firm grip on both the center-left and the center-right. Anti-Zionism and anti-prohibition both have a considerable number of enthusiasts from across the spectrum of opinion and on the Far Left and Far Right alike.

The one-time US Speaker of the House Thomas P. "Tip" O'Neill once remarked that "all politics is local." Localism as both a

---

102 Opposition to the drug war as a wedge issue has been repeatedly suggested by R. W. Bradford of *Liberty* magazine.

means and an end seems consistent with a broader anarchist perspective. Ideological and programmatic considerations aside, there remains the immensely complicated question of how the US regime is to be effectively challenged. Most of the "third-party" formations in the United States are oriented towards some particular ideological or cultural constituency that is sizable enough to form a minor party but not large enough to actually challenge the status quo. Examples of this include the theocratic "Constitution" Party and the highly ideological "Libertarian" Party. These types of party formations ultimately fail because of their inability to transcend ordinary cultural, ideological, ethnic, or religious boundaries. For an example of how to best proceed with this task, we might look to a nation with a long tradition of authentically progressive politics, the Netherlands, and the phenomenon of Pim Fortuyn. A Dutch commentator, Tjebbe van Tijen, observes:

> The shake-up . . . had its first expression in local elections, with many locally initiated parties—often called Leefbaar (Livable) followed by the name of a village or town. The issues raised by these parties varied depending on the particular area. But in general they focused on "quality of life"issues: recurring elements were environmental, housing, and traffic problems, and sometimes also questions about "foreigners," be it the influx of refugees or lamentations about the lack of adaptation of other nations, religions and cultures to Dutch society.

> After the success of such Leefbaar parties in some bigger cities in the mid-1990s, an initiative was made to try to bundle this locally dispersed force into a national Leefbaar Nederland party.

> The bundling of loose parts implies the use of a binding element, and little coherence could be found in the diverse assembly of many of those local parties. . . . So . . . they started looking for a leader . . . in the person of a commentator on

Dutch social and economic affairs, a former professor of sociology . . ., a . . . homosexual, and a provocative public debater: Pim Fortuyn.[103]

It should be noted that Fortuyn's primary significance was rooted in his role as a symbolic figurehead of a grassroots, authentically populist movement. His appeal seems based on the fact that, as a gay, Marxist, social liberal opponent of immigration, he found a hearing among both the liberal cultural elite and the instinctively nationalist and xenophobic common people as well. Some might argue that Fortuyn's subsequent assassination by a reactionary leftist ideologue is indicative of his political failure. However, the martyrdom of John Hus did not prevent the Protestant Reformation.

Anarchist militants should begin to assemble diverse coalitions in local communities across the United States, tailoring their specific programs to the culture of the local community. Anarchists, as the intellectual and activist vanguard, should maintain communication with one another irrespective of local boundaries and formulate a common agenda and plan. The first goal is to become the dominant force at the local level, whether by electoral means, strikes, boycotts, armed insurrection, or whatever. Once established in local communities, the next step would be to issue formal declarations condemning central government as some communities have already done regarding such matters as the US invasion of Iraq and the USA PATRIOT Act. Alliances between such communities should then be formed with the eventual goal of secession from the national regime. Larry Gambone describes how such a revolution might take place:

> People begin taking control at the local level, developing or re-instituting forms of self-government and ignoring the state. Certain politicians at the national level become cognizant of the anti-statist sentiment, and for genuine

or opportunist reasons, will help prevent the regime from attacking the decentralists. They may also pass certain "de-fanging" legislation which will weaken the state. Demonstrations accompanied by mass strikes will occur on an almost daily basis in the capital cities in support of the local movements and as means to keep up the pressure on the politicos. [Allies] . . . in other countries will also be developed to insure a massive outcry should the state choose to repress the libertarian upsurge. The outcome will be the development of genuine federal institutions.[104]

If history is any guide, such an insurgence is likely to occur following both an unpopular and failed war and a series of scandals leading to the loss of perceived legitimacy on the part of the state in the eyes of the public. One needs only to look at the loss of prestige suffered by the US regime following the combined Vietnam/Watergate fiasco and the fall of the Soviet Union in the aftermath of the disastrous Afghan war. The US regime is currently moving into such a scenario once again, thanks to the imperial ambitions of the neoconservatives, brewing scandals in the Bush administration, and impending economic collapse resulting from currency devaluation and outrageous levels of both private and public debt. In the likely scenario that armed confrontation with the regime becomes necessary, popular militias formed at the community level combined with defector units from the state's military forces will become the basis of the armed struggle. The task of anarchist and populist leaders will be to redirect the apparent natural zeal for war among the commoners towards the war against the illegitimate ruling class, appealing to American revolutionary traditions, and to redirect the natural patriotic inclinations of the masses towards the struggle against the state in defense of their own communities, regions, cultures, and religions.[105] Such efforts are apparently not

---

104 Gambone, *Sane Anarchy.*

105 One thing that will certainly be necessary in the broader struggle against the New World Order, particularly in the Western countries, is the cultivation of a warrior ethic appropriate to the battle at hand. Thus far, most Western radicals are heavily under the influence of the delusions of liberalism, humanism, pacifism, democratism, and

as impossible as they may seem. After all, if a former *National Review* conservative like Joseph Sobran can be converted to the anarchist position, who couldn't be?[106]

The struggle against the Anglo-American-Zionist empire, the authentic Axis of Evil, is not simply a matter of idealism, advancing one's own social or political aesthetics, or humanitarian concern. Rather, it has become a matter of planetary survival (in a human, rather than eco-doomsday, sense). The conservative commentator Paul Craig Roberts points to the real agenda of the Empire and its neoconservative court intellectuals:

> . . . influential advisors at the Pentagon are backing the development of a new generation of low yield nuclear weapons . . . In the place of bad old nuclear weapons, the new good nukes will be easier to use and more "relevant to the threat environment" . . . The Pentagon report designates "terrorists" as the targets of the mini-nukes. New nuclear weapons are said to be necessary in order to destroy deeply buried biological weapons caches, terrorist cells and hidden weapons of mass destruction. Such weapons caches will exist wherever neoconservatives declare them to be. Obviously, nuclear weapons of any size are too destructive to use against terrorists . . . The only purpose of the "small nuclear weapons" is to incinerate Muslim cities. It looks as if the neocons intend a final solution to their "Muslim problem" and are organizing genocide for Arabs.[107]

The use of such weapons by the US regime will necessitate the development, deployment, and use of such weapons by other

---

other perspectives that look askance at any sort of warrior ethic. Traditions and cultural phenomenon we might look to for inspiration include the gladiators of ancient Rome, the Spartan warriors, the chivalry of medieval knights, the New Model Army, the Taiping rebels, the bushido warrior ethics of the samurai and the kamikaze, and, of course, modern Islamic jihadists.

106 Joseph Sobran, "The Reluctant Anarchist," http://www.lewrockwell.com/orig3/sobran-j1.html

107 Paul Craig Roberts, "A Holocaust in the Making," http://www.antiwar.com/cs/roberts3.html

states, and the provision of such weapons to freelance military organizations by states. The neoconservatives' ambitions amount to little more than worldwide nuclear holocaust. Larry Gambone perceptively describes the neocons as "an American version of the Khmer Rouge . . . The possible roots of neocon nihilism? A mad desire to revolutionize the world, not for socialism, but for global corporatism, the Zionazi hatred of everything Arab, and the 'Christian' fundi's world-hating lust for an apocalypse."[108]

Whatever one's perception of Islamic "terrorists" and "suicide" bombers, the Muslims are fighting for the defense of their culture, religion, and homelands. The neocons have no excuse. Eminently destructive weaponry in the hands of such fanatics constitutes the greatest danger to the world yet to emerge, surpassing even the looming nuclear holocaust of the Cuban missile crisis and the apocalyptic showdown between the imperial powers during the Second World War. Therefore, the defeat of Empire and the development of a new political paradigm that is antithetical to Empire has become an imperative. Hopefully, philosophical anarchism will help to show the way.

---

108 Larry Gambone, Porcupine Blog, May 17, 2003.

Zionism and the Power Elite

Any discussion of the relationship between Zionism and the "power elite" in Western countries must inevitably begin with a qualification of meanings, as these terms have been used in ways as to imply multiple definitions. For purposes of this discussion, the term "Zionism" is meant to describe an outlook that prioritizes the defense and promotion of the state of Israel as a bastion of Jewish nationalism, and which more broadly and implicitly favors a Jewish ethno-nationalism that spans the spectrum of the Jewish diaspora. The term "power elite" is being utilized in the manner suggested by the sociologist C. Wright Mills, who coined the term in order to describe those holding the dominant positions in the dominant institutions in society, such as government, business, industry, finance, military, education, religion, and the mass media. The central question involved in the analysis of this relationship is the matter of to what degree political decisions are shaped by the influence of Zionist sympathies. The evidence indicates that Zionists exercise considerable influence over the process of political decision-making in many Western countries, and particularly in the United States.

Mearsheimer, Walt and the Israel Lobby

In 2006, John Mearsheimer, a professor of political science at the University of Chicago, and Stephen Walt, a professor of international relations at the Kennedy School of Government at Harvard, issued a paper titled "The Israel Lobby," which defined the Israel lobby as "a loose coalition of individuals and organizations who actively work to steer U.S. foreign policy in a pro-Israel direction." The authors published a book under the title "The Israel Lobby and U.S. Foreign Policy" the following year and provoked a storm of controversy in the process, including predictable accusations of anti-Semitism and claims that the authors were promoting age-old fantasies about a "Jewish conspiracy" of the kind reminiscent of "The Protocols of the Elders of Zion."

However, the authors specifically stated that "the boundaries of the Israel lobby cannot be identified precisely," that "not every American with a favorable attitude to Israel is part of the lobby," that not all American Jews were a part of or sympathetic to the Israel lobby, that the lobby also included non-Jews such as the Christian Zionists, and overlapped extensively with the neoconservatives, whose ranks include both Jews and non-Jews. Mearsheimer and Walt did insist that the U.S. Israel lobby "has a core consisting of organizations whose declared purpose is to encourage the U.S. government and the American public to provide material aid to Israel and to support its government's policies, as well as influential individuals for whom these goals are also a top priority."

James Petras and the Power of Israel in the United States

Another important work analyzing Israel's influence over American foreign policy was also published in 2006. A book titled "The Power of Israel in the United States," was issued by James Petras, a professor of sociology at Binghampton University. While Mearsheimer and Walt regard themselves as foreign policy "realists," and are within the mainstream of American foreign policy scholarship, Petras is a scholar of the radical Left and a long time critic of U.S. imperialism. Petras argued extensively that the Israel lobby has embedded itself in virtually the entire range of U.S. institutions, including government, business, academia, the media, and organized religion (particularly the zealously pro-Israel Christian Zionist contingent among American evangelical fundamentalist Protestants).

Petras noted that as of the early 2000s, sixty percent of the fundraising for the Democratic Party originated from Jewish-organized or funded Political Action Committees, and that thirty-five percent of Republican fundraising likewise originated from Jewish sources. Petras further argued that no other lobbying network in U.S. politics exercises comparable influence, not even major industrial or business interests such as the pharmaceutical industry, the oil industry, or agribusiness firms. The reason that pro-Israel interests have been able to obtain such power has to do with the concentration of American Jews within the ranks of the elite. While Jews are only slightly more than two percent of the U.S. population, between one quarter and one third of the wealthiest families and individuals are Jewish, including Jewish billionaires with extraordinary amounts of power and influence.

J.J. Goldberg and Jewish Power in the United States

In 1996, the liberal Jewish author J.J. Goldberg, presently the editor-at-large of *The Forward*, published "Jewish Power: Inside the American Jewish Establishment." In this work, Goldberg enthusiastically celebrated the potency of Jewish influence in the United States. In the introduction to his book, Goldberg candidly described the role of Jewish power in American politics:

As for concrete evidence of the Jewish community's clout, it is not hard to find. There is, to begin with, the $3 billion foreign-aid package sent each year to Israel. Fully one fifth of America's foreign aid has gone to a nation of barely 5 million souls, one tenth of 1 percent of the world's population. Analysts commonly credited this imbalance to the power of the Jewish lobby.

Coupled with financial aid is the familiar fact of Washington's staunch support for Israel in the diplomatic arena, at what sometimes seemed like great cost to America's own interests. And there have been threats to those in

Washington who opposed Israeli policy: the senators and representatives sent down to defeat, like Charles Percy and Paul Findley, for defying the Jewish lobby.

But American Jewish power does not begin and end with Israel. Even more dramatic than foreign aid, perhaps, was the Jackson-Vanik amendment. Passed by Congress in 1974, it made U.S.-Soviet trade relations conditional on the Soviets' treatment of their Jewish minority. The amendment remained on the books even after the Soviet Union collapsed in 1990, effectively giving the Jewish community a veto over America's commercial links with Moscow.

Jewish power is felt, too, in a wide variety of domestic spheres: immigration and refugee policy, civil rights and affirmative action, abortion rights, church-state separation issues, and much more. Local Jewish communities from New York to Los Angeles have become major players on their own turf, helping to make the rules and call the shots on matters from health care to zoning.

Yes, by the end of the twentieth century, American Jewry has come to be viewed around the globe as a serious player in the great game of politics, able to influence events, to define and achieve important goals, to reward its friends and punish its enemies.

To be sure, plenty of political interest groups representing all kinds of opinions on issues also play important roles in American politics, and this certainly includes Jewish-oriented ones. There is nothing inherently wrong with this as it is simply a manifestation of the way a modern, pluralistic, liberal democracy works. However, the relevant question involves the degree to which Jewish power and influence translates into American institutional policies being guided by organized Zionist objectives.

The Mass Media

The question of Jewish ownership and influence in the mass media is a controversial one, and the alleged Jewish control of the media is a point that is consistently promoted by genuine anti-Semites, ranging from neo-Nazis to Islamic fundamentalists to a range of conspiracy theorists. It is certainly true that Jewish presence in the media is greatly disproportional to the actual number of Jews among the wider public, and this long has been the case. For example, in 1988 author Neal Gabler published "An Empire of Their Own: How the Jews Invented Hollywood," which documented the role of Jewish movie producers and film moguls, many of whom were Eastern European immigrants, in shaping the American film industry. Regarding claims that "Jews control the media," the Jewish left-wing scholar and pro-Palestinian activist Jeffrey Blankfort argues:

> As to Jews owning the media (as opposed to "the Jews),"
> being a myth...that "myth" has legs...(T)he owners of
> the Washington Post, Newsweek, the New York Times,
> Boston Globe, NY Daily News, the Los Angeles Times,
> the Chicago Tribune, and a number of others happen to
> be Jewish as are the owners of CBS, ABC, and all of the
> major Hollywood studios. They don't all have the same
> politics but they do share the same religious background.
> As for (Rupert)Murdoch (owner of FOX and the Wall
> Street Journal), he considers himself to be an honorary
> Jew, having received numerous awards as a friend to Israel
> by major Jewish organizations and he has openly stated
> his unqualified support for Israeli government policy many
> times and his Wall Street Journal certainly reflects that.

Likewise, a Jewish journalist and blogger, Philip Weiss, observes:

> Do Jews dominate the media? This is something I know
> about personally. I've worked in print journalism for
> more than 30 years. I've worked for many magazines and
> newspapers, and for a time my whole social circle was

editors and writers in New York... My sample is surely skewed by the fact that I'm Jewish and have always felt great comfort with other Jews. But in my experience, Jews have made up the majority of the important positions in the publications I worked for, a majority of the writers I've known at these places, and the majority of the owners who have paid me. Yes, my own sample may be skewed, but I think it shows that Jews make up a significant proportion of power positions in media, half, if not more.

The real issue is, Does it matter? Most of my life I felt it didn't...Now I think it does matter, for two reasons. Elitist establishment culture, and Israel. As to elitism, I worry when any affluent group has power and little sense of what the common man is experiencing...The values of my cohort sometimes seem narrow: globalism, prosperity, professionalism. In Israel the values are a lot broader. None of my cohort has served in the military, myself included. A lot of our fathers did; but I bet none of our kids do. Military service is for losers–or for Israelis.

So we are way overrepresented in the chattering classes, and way underrepresented in the battering classes. Not a great recipe for leadership, especially in wartime.

Then there's Israel. Support for Israel is an element of Jewish religious practice and more important, part of the Jewish cultural experience. Even if you're a secular Jewish professional who prides himself on his objectivity, there is a ton of cultural pressure on you to support Israel or at least not to betray Israel. We are talking about a religion, after all, and the pressures faced by Jews who are critical of Israel are not that different from what Muslim women who want greater freedom undergo psychically or by evangelical Christians who want to support gay rights. It is worth noting that great Jewish heretics on the Israel question suffer anger or even ostracism inside their own families...

Conversations about Israel even inside the liberal Jewish community are emotionally loaded, and result in people not speaking to one another. I lost this blog at a mainstream publication because the editor was Jewish and conservative on Israel and so was the new owner, and the publisher had worked for AIPAC. And all of them would likely call themselves liberal Democrats.

The result is that Americans are not getting the full story re Israel/Palestine...

Weiss further observes that even sectors of the Israeli press have been far more forthcoming in reporting on atrocities committed by the Israeli regime in the occupied territories than the American press with its disproportional Zionist influence:

Why does the American press behave differently from the Israeli press? I think the answer is guilt. The Jewish cohort of which I am a part has largely accepted the duty... of supporting Israel. This duty is rarely interrogated, and yet consciously or not we all know that American public opinion/leadership is critical to Israel's political invulnerability; and we think that if we take their fingers out of the dike, who knows what will happen. That is a ton of responsibility. This responsibility is not executed with special care. Generally, my cohort hasn't been to Israel, hasn't seen the West Bank. But they do feel kinship with Israeli Jews, and—above all—have guilt feelings about the Holocaust, or the American Jewish silence about it during the event, the Jewish passivity; and they are determined not to be passive during Israel's never ending existential crises. And thus they misunderstand Israel and fail to serve their readers.

Clearly, the American mass media claims within its ranks many Jewish Israeli partisans (and no doubt plenty of Gentile collaborators) who provide journalistic cover for Israel.

The Growth of Zionist Power in the United States

Zionist power in the United States has grown considerably, indeed almost exponentially, in recent decades. While the U.S. along with England was instrumental in the formation of the state of Israel in 1948, Zionist interests did not dominate U.S. foreign policy in the Middle East during subsequent years. For example, during the crisis over the Suez Canal in 1956, the U.S. sided with the Arab nations against not only Israel, but also France and England. However, the turning point began with the Six Day War in 1967 which had the effect of galvanizing the pro-Zionist elements of the American Jewish community, and the Israel lobby began exercising considerable influence over U.S. policy in the region. Remarkably, the U.S. failed to retaliate when Israel sank the American naval vessel the *USS Liberty* during the same year. Zionist power was demonstrated once again when America sided with Israel during the Yom Kippur War in 1973, and which resulted in a costly petroleum embargo being imposed on the U.S. by the OPEC nations.

Meanwhile, the cultural openings and civil rights revolution of the 1960s opened the door for greater participation of traditionally excluded minorities in American institutions. These cultural changes were especially beneficial to Jews, who were already a prosperous, affluent, and educated minority group. While American Jewish intellectuals typically leaned very strongly to the Left politically, this began to change during the 1970s as many Zionists began to defect from the New Left over questions involving both Israel and the Cold War. The New Left tended towards pro-Palestinian views, and regarded the Cold War merely as a clash between rival imperialisms. However, many American Zionists regarded American power as a safeguard for Israel, and vociferously opposed the Soviet Union in large part because of Russian anti-Semitism. Jewish intellectuals and defectors from the Left such as Irving Kristol and Norman Podhoretz were instrumental in developing the neoconservative movement. The neoconservatives began developing a relationship with the American conservative movement that had begun during the postwar period under leadership of such figures as William F. Buckley, and moving away from the Democratic Party towards the Republican Party.

During this same period, the American Christian Zionist movement also began to grow considerably due to the resurgence of evangelical Christianity that occurred in the United States during the 1970s. While not all evangelical Christians are Christian Zionists, a significant subset of American evangelicals adhere to a theological tendency known as "dispensationalism," which believes that the restoration of Israel is a fulfillment of biblical prophecy and is a necessary step towards the eventual Second Coming of Jesus Christ. American evangelical leaders espousing such views began to become politically influential during the rise of the "religious right" in the late 1970s. By the time of the so-called "Reagan Revolution" of the 1980s, these three forces-the postwar conservative movement, the neo-conservatives, and the religious right, had converged with foreign policy hawks and economic conservatives to form the basis of the Republican Party and American conservatism generally, a trend that largely continues in the present.

Scott McConnell: The Republican Party is the Party of Zionism

During the 1980s and 1990s, tensions occasionally existed between the Zionist partisans and other factions within the American conservative coalition. While the leadership of right-wing Zionism in the U.S. had shifted towards the Republicans, the majority of rank and file Jews still tended to vote for the Democratic Party, which is the case with minority groups in the U.S. generally. During the Republican presidency of George H. W. Bush in the late 1980s and early 1990s, then Secretary of State James Baker III threatened to withhold American loans to Israel in response to Israel's settlement efforts in the occupied territories. During a private meeting, Baker earned the permanent ire of the Israel lobby when he remarked, "Fuck the

Jews. They don't vote for us anyway." However, the Republican Party has since become devoid of any voices that dare to defy the wishes of the Israel lobby.

Scott McConnell of *The American Conservative* identifies the process by which the Republicans became the "party of Israel," and how the party aligned itself with the most right-wing faction of domestic Israeli politics, the Likud Party. He cites the work of various researchers who trace the dominance of the Republican Party by Israeli interests to the increased dependence of the Republican Party on wealthy Jewish billionaire donors, the ongoing importance of Christian Zionist evangelicals as a Republican voting bloc, the view of Israel as an important ally against Islamic terrorism during the post-September 11 era, and the ardently pro-Israel and quasi-evangelical views of former President George W. Bush. McConnell adds to this the strengthening of Zionist control over the U.S. broadcast media through the establishment of FOX News, the emergence of neoconservative publications such as *The Weekly Standard*, the neoconservative takeover of the conservative movement's flagship magazine *The National Review*, the effective ostracism of anti-Israel voices such as Patrick Buchanan from the conservative milieu, and the proliferation and growing influence of Zionist organized or funded think tanks.

The Israel Lobby and the American Political Class

This is not to say that the Israel lobby only exercises influence within the Republican Party. Nothing could be further from the truth. The Republican Party normally holds to positions that align with the furthest right-wing sectors within Israeli politics. However, the most influential pro-Israel organization in the United States, the American Israel Public Affairs Committee (AIPAC), considers itself to be a bipartisan organization and is firmly embedded in both major American political parties. For example, AIPAC holds an annual policy conference that is normally attended by a cross-section of the American political elite. Attendees and speakers at the conference have included Presidents Bill Clinton and Barack Obama, Secretaries of State John Kerry and Hillary Clinton, former Speaker of the House Nancy Pelosi, House Majority Leader Harry Reid, and a vast array of current and former Senators and Congressmen.

The principal and considerably less influential rival to AIPAC is J Street, a more moderate organization founded in 2008, and which has been funded by the multi-billionaire George Soros. While AIPAC is supportive of the Likud Party, J Street is oriented towards the centrist Kadima Party. The principal differences between the two groups is that the Likud Party is an overtly Israeli imperialist party that opposes Palestinian sovereignty, favors the continued expansion of Israeli colonial settlements in the occupied territories, and assumes a hawkish stance towards Iran. Kadima is more moderate only when compared with Likud, having been a strong supporter of former Prime Minister Ariel Sharon, and Kadima's leadership has actually described itself as more right-wing than J Street. The entire American political class exhibits extreme subservience to the Israel lobby, as was illustrated during the summer of 2014 when Israel launched its attack on Gaza. The U.S. Senate voted unanimously in favor of an AIPAC-backed resolution endorsing the attacks, including ostensible "progressives" Elizabeth Warren and Al Franken, "socialist" Bernie Sanders, and "libertarian" Rand Paul.

The Israel lobby also exercises power outside of the United States to a considerable degree. An Israel lobby similar to the U.S. Israel lobby exists in the United Kingdom, although it is more loosely organized and not quite as powerful. Israel also exercises considerable influence in the European Union, due to the fact that Israel and the EU are primary trading partners. Canada has even threatened to use its hate speech and hate crimes laws against organizations that advocate a boycott of Israel, similar to the international boycott of South Africa that existed during the apartheid era.

The Fate of Critics of Israel

On May 27, 2010, eighty-nine year old journalist Helen Thomas, a veteran White House Reporter remarked when asked for comments on Israel during an impromptu interview, "Tell them to get the hell out of Palestine…Remember, these people are occupied and it's their land. It's not Germany, it's not Poland" and that the Israelis should "go home to Poland or Germany or America and everywhere else. Why push people out of there who have lived there for centuries?" Thomas' remarks were met with a round of termination of employment contracts and revocation of previously bestowed awards. She subsequently resigned from her position with Hearst Newspapers. However, Thomas refused to retract her remarks saying, "I paid a price, but it's worth it to speak the truth…Congress, the White House, Hollywood, and Wall Street, are owned by Zionists. No question, in my opinion…I just think that people should be enlightened as to who is in charge of opinion in this country." Coming to Thomas' defense, Ralph Nader observed the irony that Thomas would be attacked for such comments, noting that "ultra-right wing radio and cable ranters" promoted "bigotry, stereotypes and falsehoods directed wholesale against Muslims, including a blatant anti-Semitism against Arabs" hold a substantial presence in the American media.

Not only journalists but also politicians and academics that have dared to expose or challenge the power of the Zionists over U.S. politics have been subjected to professional ruin. Among the American elected officials whose careers were destroyed or undermined by the Israel lobby have been Paul Findley, Jim Trafficant, Cynthia McKinney, Pete McCloskey, JamesMoran, Charles Pearcy, Earl Hilliard, William Fulbright, Mike Gravel, Roger Jepson, and James Abourezk. DePaul University denied tenure to the distinguished Jewish scholar Norman Finkelstein, the son of Holocaust survivors and a leading critic of Israel's treatment of the Palestinians, after a campaign against Finkelstein was organized by the Zionist attorney Alan Dershowitz.

A Turning of the Tides?

Traditionally, authentic anti-Zionist, anti-imperialist, or pro-Palestinian voices have been completely absent from both the U.S. media and the political class. Such voices have existed only on the left-wing or right-wing fringes of American politics. However, a rather remarkable event occurred in March of 2015. The Congressional leadership of the Republican Party invited former Israeli Prime Minister and Likud Party leader Benjamin Netanyahu, then seeking re-election which he would successfully achieve, to address the U.S. Congress for the purpose of denouncing President Obama's nuclear negotiations with Iran, and in defiance of ordinary protocols. Nearly sixty members of Obama's Democratic Party retaliated by boycotting Netanyahu's address. The key question regarding this occurrence involves what this unprecedented defiance of the Israel lobby means for the future of U.S. politics.

The division between the two major political parties in the United States is now wider than at any point in the past century, and the same is true of both cultural and socioeconomic divisions. It may be that these divisions are now so great that the Zionist currents among the power elite are increasingly unable to control the political process. The willingness of President Obama to negotiate with Iran and avoid war may represent a growing division between the Zionist elites and important sectors of the wider American ruling class. Indeed, a sharpening of divisions between among the Zionist elite may be developing, as illustrated by the emergence of J Street. Evidence indicates that Americans, both Jewish and Gentile and especially younger people, are becoming increasingly unsympathetic to Israel, as evidenced by the rise of the "Boycott, Divestment, and Sanctions" movement concerning Israel, and the emergence of such groups such as Jewish Voice for Peace.

A War with Iran?

The power of Israel in the United States and in other nations has rendered these nations into accomplices to the carnage that occurs in the occupied territories. There can be no denying that Likud's primary allies in the United States, the neoconservatives, were the driving force behind the war in Iraq with its hundreds of thousands of deaths, and millions more maimed, displaced, or subjected to the dystopian tyranny of the Islamic State that has emerged in more recent times. In a similar vein, Colonel Lawrence Wilkerson, a one-time aide to former Secretary of State Colin Powell, recently observed that the Republican Party, "the party of Israel" as Scott McConnell describes the GOP, is apparently zealous for an eventual war with Iran, a war that will have an even more devastating outcome than the war with Iraq. Further, Zionist partisans in the United States appear to be constructing a false rationale for a war with Iran that is comparable to the false rationale that led to the war with Iraq. Just as it was wrongfully claimed that Iraq was in possession of "weapons of mass destruction," against the insistence of an actual experts on international disarmament, so it is being claimed that Iran is developing nuclear weapons in defiance of the consensus of actual scholarly opinion on the question. If the present push for war on the part of the Likud Party and its arguably even more extreme partisans in the United States is successful, a voluminous amount of entirely needless death, destruction, and human suffering will result.

Anti-Imperialists of the World, Unite!

Towards an Anarchist Theory of Geopolitics

In the century and a half that modern anarchist movements have been in existence, anarchism has thus far passed through two distinct phases. The first of these was the era of classical anarchism, a movement inspired by the thought of Pierre-Joseph Proudhon, Mikhail Bakunin, and Peter Kropotkin, which arose out of the rebellions of 1848 and came to position itself as the most militant wing of the international workers movement. The orientation of classical anarchism towards proletarian socialism was appropriate given that the "labor question" was the dominant political struggle of the time. This embryonic era of anarchist history lasted for nearly a century before meeting its end after the defeat of the anarchists at Kronstadt and in the Spanish Civil War, the achievement of hegemony by Communism on the Left, the massive strengthening of states during the "managerial revolution" of the mid-twentieth century, and the unrivaled levels of militarist bloodshed and statist repression perpetrated by the rival imperialist powers during the two world wars.

The second phase of modern anarchism, what might be termed "neo-anarchism," had its roots in the student rebellions of the late 1960s. Neo-anarchism reflected the general trend within the New Left milieu in which it was born by shifting its focus away from workers' struggles and the proletarian class towards an agglomeration of both privileged class youth and members of traditional social and cultural outgroups, such as racial minorities, feminist women, homosexuals, immigrants, and the like, all the while becoming intertwined with the growing ecological consciousness, pop psychology, and therapeutic culture of the time. This ideological formula continues to dominate anarchist movements at the present juncture nearly a half century after it emerged.

The proletarian socialist orientation of classical anarchism may continue to possess considerable value in those nations and regions where the level of economic and technological development continues to approximate that of the West during the classical anarchist era. Likewise, the orientation of neo-anarchism towards social justice for racial minorities, women, gays, and other outgroups, preservation of the natural environment, and critiquing cultural barriers to self-actualization may retain its relevance in those regions where the cultural revolution of the 1960s and 1970s has not taken root or become particularly entrenched. However, both the orientation of the classical anarchist movement towards the proletarian class and the orientation of neo-anarchism towards the cultural margins have become anachronistic in the modern Western nations where the working class has become integrated into the political mainstream, where labor unions have become respectable public institutions, and where criticism of cultural or demographic sectors regarded as traditionally excluded or disadvantaged has become a taboo subject to severe social opprobrium and, in some cases, legal repression.

If anarchism is to regain the political status that it held in the late nineteenth century, that of the premier revolutionary movement in the West that simultaneously arose on the periphery as the vanguard of anti-colonialist struggles, it will be necessary to construct a theoretical paradigm, ideological formulation, and strategic orientation for twenty-first-century anarchist movements that possesses a contemporary analysis and factual understanding of the nature of the institutions that actually dominate modern societies. If the orientation of previous anarchist movements towards proletarian socialism or cultural radicalism is inappropriate in societies where the state reflects both social democratic and multicultural values, then the question arises of what the primary focus of contemporary anarchist movements should actually be.

The Nature of Contemporary Imperialism

Anarchist anti-imperialism of the classical era had its roots in resistance to the European colonial empires that were in turn outgrowths of the conquests that followed the meeting of European civilization and the societies of Asia, Africa, and the Americas during the Age of Discovery, the commercial revolution, and the development of capitalism as the dominant mode of production. European colonialism reached its zenith at the end of the nineteenth century but went into decline following the decimation of the European nations by the two world wars and the overthrow of the traditional monarchies and aristocracies in these nations by the rising liberal, democratic, and socialist movements of the early twentieth century.[1]

The decimation of the European and Asian continents by war and the resulting destruction of the traditional colonial empires created the international geopolitical conditions for the achievement of American hegemony as the United States had been the only major power that had not experienced the two world wars within its internal boundaries and had therefore avoided the destruction inflicted on the European and Asian powers. For the first four decades following the conclusion of the Second World War, the "First World" hegemony of the United States and its Western European allies and protectorates was countered with a limited degree of effectiveness by the regional imperialism of the "Second World" Soviet Union and its modest efforts to aid anti-colonial struggles in the pre-industrial "Third World." However, the collapse of the Eurasian empire of the Soviet Union in the late 1980s and early 1990s allowed for the full achievement of global American hegemony.[2]

---

1 William S. Lind, "That Old Romanov Feeling," *The American Conservative*, April 9, 2012.

2 Noam Chomsky, *Deterring Democracy* (New York: Hill and Wang, 1992).

The American model of imperialism during the postwar era was not the traditional model of formal acquisition of colonies through direct military conquest. Rather, the form the American empire began to assume in the mid-twentieth century was one largely predicated on the informal domination of other nations by means of economic hegemony, the cultivation of local elites as clients, cultural imperialism exercised by the increasingly dominant American mass media, destabilization and counter-insurgency campaigns fought with local forces but financed and given diplomatic cover by the American state, proxy wars fought by mercenary armies, and small scale military interventions often conducted under the guise of "police actions." Large-scale warfare was utilized only in extraordinary circumstances, such as American intervention on the Korean peninsula, in the former French colonies of Indochina, and in the Persian Gulf. Though the degree of overt militarism displayed by the American state has escalated since the historic events of September 11, 2001, the general structure of mid to late twentieth-century American imperialism outlined above largely continues as the *modus operandi* of the American empire and the client states and network of international institutions through which its hegemony is maintained.[3]

Our Enemies: Marxism and Totalitarian Humanism

Any serious analysis of anti-imperialist resistance movements during the twentieth century must necessarily seek to address the unquestionable fact that Marxism eventually eclipsed anarchism as the prevailing ideology of those with a radically anti-imperialist perspective. Why was this so? Surely, it was not due to the ability of Marxism to provide a more comprehensive theoretical critique of imperialism than anarchism. The actual

---

3   William Blum, *Killing Hope: U.S. Military and CIA Interventions Since World War II* (Monroe, ME: Common Courage Press, 2003); James A. Lucas, "Deaths in Other Nations Since WWII Due to U.S. Interventions," Countercurrents.Org, April 24, 2007, http://www.countercurrents.org/lucas240407.htm (accessed September 23, 2012).

historical contrasts between the perspectives of classical anarchism and Marxism regarding imperialism have been aptly summarized by Michael Schmidt:

> It cannot be overemphasised how for the first 50 years of its existence as a proletarian mass movement since its origin in the First International, the anarchist movement often entrenched itself far more deeply in the colonies of the imperialist powers and in those parts of the world still shackled by post-colonial regimes than in its better-known Western heartlands like France or Spain. Until Lenin, Marxism had almost nothing to offer on the national question in the colonies, and until Mao, who had been an anarchist in his youth, neither did Marxism have anything to offer the peasantry in such regions—regions that Marx and Engels, speaking as de facto German supremacists from the high tower of German capitalism, dismissed in their *Communist Manifesto* (1848) as the "barbarian and semi-barbarian countries." Instead, Marxism stressed the virtues of capitalism (and even imperialism) as an onerous, yet necessary stepping stone to socialism. Engels summed up their devastating position in an article entitled "Democratic Pan-Slavism" in their *Neue Rheinische Zeitung* of 14 February 1849: the United States' annexation of Texas in 1845 and invasion of Mexico in 1846 in which Mexico lost 40% of its territory were applauded as they had been "waged wholly and solely in the interest of civilisation," as "splendid California has been taken away from the lazy Mexicans, who could not do anything with it" by "the energetic Yankees" who would "for the first time really open the Pacific Ocean to civilization . . ."

So, "the 'independence' of a few Spanish Californians and Texans may suffer because of it, in some places 'justice' and other moral principles may be violated; but what does that matter to such facts of world-historic significance?" By this racial argument of the "iron reality" of inherent national virility giving rise to laudable capitalist overmastery, Engels said the failure of the Slavic nations during the 1848 Pan-European Revolt to throw off their Ottoman, Austro-Hungarian and Russian yokes, demonstrated not only their ethnic unfitness for independence, but that they were in fact "counter-revolutionary" nations deserving of "the most determined use of terror" to suppress them.

It reads chillingly like a foreshadowing of the Nazis' racial nationalist arguments for the use of terror against the Slavs during their East European conquest. Engels' abysmal article had been written in response to Mikhail Bakunin's *Appeal to the Slavs by a Russian Patriot* in which he—at that stage not yet an anarchist—had by stark contrast argued that the revolutionary and counter-revolutionary camps were divided not by nationality or stage of capitalist development, but by class.[4]

Clearly, Marxism possessed no greater intellectual force in its critique of imperialism than anarchism. Indeed, Marx and Engels were demonstrably pro-imperialist in their geopolitical outlook. It is also abundantly clear from the pervasiveness of anarchist tendencies throughout the world during the classical anarchist era that Marxism traveled with no greater ease than anarchism. Schmidt goes on to describe the vastness of the anarchist presence throughout the colonized world:

By 1873, when Bakunin, now unashamedly anarchist, threw down the gauntlet to imperialism, writing that "Two-thirds of humanity, 800 million Asiatics, asleep in their servitude, will necessarily awaken and begin to move," the newly-minted anarchist movement was engaging directly and repeatedly with the challenges of imperialism, colonialism, national liberation movements, and post-colonial regimes. So it was that staunchly anti-imperialist

---

4   Michael Schmidt, "South Asian Anarchism: Paths to Practice," Anarkismo.net, July, 27, 2012, http://www.anarkismo.net/article/23404 (accessed September 23, 2012).

anarchism and its emergent revolutionary unionist strategy, syndicalism—and not pro-imperialist Marxism—that rose to often hegemonic dominance of the union centres of Argentina, Brazil, Chile, Colombia, Cuba, Mexico, Paraguay, Peru and Uruguay in the early 1900s, almost every significant economy and population concentration in post-colonial Latin America. In six of these countries, anarchists mounted attempts at revolution; in Cuba and Mexico, they played a key role in the successful overthrow of reactionary regimes; while in Mexico and Nicaragua they deeply influenced significant experiments in large-scale revolutionary agrarian social construction.

The anarchist movement also established smaller syndicalist unions in colonial and semi-colonial territories as diverse as Algeria, Bulgaria, China, Ecuador, Egypt, Korea, Malaya (Malaysia), New Zealand, North and South Rhodesia (Zambia and Zimbabwe, respectively), the Philippines, Poland, Puerto Rico, South Africa, South-West Africa (Namibia), and Venezuela—and built crucial radical networks in the colonial and post-colonial world: East Africa, Eastern Europe, the Middle East, Central Asia, Central America, the Caribbean, South-East Asia, and Ramnath's chosen terrain, the South Asian sub-continent.[5]

So why did Marxism or Marxist-inspired movements come to achieve hegemony in the great majority of anti-imperialist struggles during the mid to late twentieth century, in nations throughout Asia, Africa, and Latin America? Two primary explanations for this phenomenon would seem to be the most plausible.

The first is the international prestige of the Soviet Union following the Bolshevik coup of 1917 and the subsequent achievement of a position of dominance on the international Left by Communism,

---

5   *Ibid.*

a position that was strengthened by the key role played by the Soviets as a member of the Allied coalition during the Second World War. As mentioned, the regional empire extending across the Eurasian landmass established by the Soviet Union at the conclusion of the war became the principal source of opposition to the international hegemony achieved by the United States as the neo-colonialism of the latter eclipsed and essentially replaced the traditional colonial empires previously maintained by Great Britain and the continental European nations. As part of its geopolitical strategy during the Cold War, the Soviet Union would aid anti-American resistance forces throughout the Third World with the hope of cultivating future revolutionary regimes in these countries as client states (ambition that was of course actually achieved in some instances, for example, in Cuba).

The Soviet efforts at cultivating Third World revolutionary movements as the foundation for future client states in the Cold War with America fit well with the opportunistic ambitions of the leadership of Third World anti-colonial movements, which typically consisted of alienated intellectuals drawn from the ranks of the middle classes and who considered their ambitions to be frustrated by the static, traditional feudal regimes which dominated their own countries. Marxism had the same appeal to late nineteenth, and twentieth-century, alienated middle class intellectuals as liberalism and Jacobinism had in the eighteenth century, and the statism of Marxism had a greater appeal to these ambitious opportunists drawn from the privileged classes than the decentralist and libertarian ideals of anarchism.[6]

The second major reason for the eclipsing of anarchism by Marxism during the twentieth century must be understood within the context of what James Burnham described as the "managerial revolution" that occurred during the same era. Burnham observed that all of the industrialized societies of the time, whether capitalist America, socialist Russia, or fascist

---

6   Eric von Kuehnelt-Leddihn, *Leftism Revisited: From de Sade and Marx to Hitler and Pol Pot* (Washington, DC: Regnery Gateway, 1990).

Italy and Germany, were undergoing a transformation towards a new form of bureaucratic rule that transcended their respective ideological differences and defied categorization as far as traditional labels of "capitalist" or "socialist" were concerned. The trend of the time was towards ever-greater centralization, statism, and bureaucracy, meaning that the anarchists were swimming against the tides of the era. Marxism, with its orientation towards state-managed command economies, appeared to be progressive and forward-looking while anarchism took on the appearance of an archaic romanticism.[7]

The defeat of the fascist powers in the Second World War along with the collapse of the Soviet Union and the discrediting of Communism at the end of the Cold War meant that only the form of the managerial revolution that had emerged in the capitalist countries continued to give the appearance of legitimacy or viability. Indeed, the Western model of the managerial revolution (so-called "democratic capitalism") was even touted by some, most notably Francis Fukuyama, as representing the final stage in human political evolution. The disappearance of any effective opposition to the American empire following the demise of the Soviet Union allowed the American state and its international junior partners to arrogantly assert the universality of their own claims to legitimacy. Hence, the post-Cold War acts of military aggression taken by the United States and its allies in the name of democratization and the universal imposition of Western ideological conceptions of "human rights."[8]

This geopolitical framework of "human rights imperialism" provides the foreign policy component of the wider ideological foundations of the contemporary Western ruling classes, the core elements of which also include the previously discussed bureaucratic managerialism, plutocratic liberalism, and welfare capitalism in the economic realm. In the social and cultural

---

7   James Burnham, *The Managerial Revolution: What Is Happening in the World* (New York: John Day, 1941).

8   Francis Fukuyama, *The End of History and the Last Man* (New York: Free Press, 1992).

arena, the contemporary ruling class ideology exhibits such characteristics as multiculturalism, a general social egalitarianism (feminism, gay rights, "anti-ablism," etc.) which is regarded as necessary for a larger, better integrated, and better trained labor force, therapeutic statism (for example, the obsessive fixation on health represented by neo-puritan campaigns against smoking, fatty food, sugar-laden beverages, and the ongoing war on drugs), mass democracy (with public elections serving as the ritualistic means of political class self-legitimization), media pre-eminence, and educationism (with the mass media and educational institutions serving as the primary means of inculcating ruling class ideology and training subordinate classes to function in a complex, technologically advanced society), infantilization (for instance, the nanny state's perpetual obsession with "protecting the children"), and the ever-expanding police state. Each of these ideological elements in turn reflects a general world view rooted in notions of universalism, egalitarianism, and a linear-progressive view of history that might be collectively labeled as "totalitarian humanism."[9]

The Decline of the State and the Prospects for an Anarchist Renaissance

A rather fascinating convergence of two historical trends has emerged over the last two decades. The first of these is the previously discussed achievement of global hegemony by the American empire following the end of the Cold War. The second is the decline of the state as an institution, the beginning of which Martin van Creveld traces to the period between the conclusion of the Second World War through the economic downturns and backlash against the Vietnam War during the mid-1970s. The decline of the state is itself the product of a convergence of multiple forces, including the prohibitive cost of mass warfare due to the destructive capabilities of modern weaponry, the failure of the state to fully entrench itself in the

9   Keith Preston, "The New Totalitarianism," LewRockwell.Com, January 22, 2007, http://www.lewrockwell.com/orig8/preston1.html (accessed September 23, 2012).

lesser developed parts of the world and the subsequent spread of disorder from those regions to the West, a prevailing cultural ethos which deemphasizes or even denigrates martial values, the exorbitant costs of modern welfare states and its resulting fiscal difficulties, the growth of the global economy, an increase in the private provision of security, and the inability of contemporary states to inspire or retain the loyalty of their citizens.[10]

This accelerating decline of the state would indicate that conventional nationalism is becoming an anachronism. Classical nineteenth-century nationalism and its later ideological descendents are themselves the ideological and institutional outgrowths of the centralizing tendencies of the French Revolution and the subsequent nation-state system that eventually eclipsed the older royal empires. Indeed, a core insight of fourth generation warfare theory is that the loyalty of populations is being transferred away from conventional nation-states and towards non-state entities and that contemporary warfare is becoming increasingly dominated by non-state actors. Further, the ruling classes and national regimes of most of the world's nations, save a few so-called "rogue" nations (as termed by the overlords of the empire), have positioned themselves as component parts and territorial prefects within the empire's expanse.

Many of the component nation-states within the empire practice their own internal imperialisms. No greater example can be found than that of the "mother country" of the empire itself, the United States, whose domestic, continent-wide, "fifty state" empire includes the captive nations of the former Hawaiian kingdom, the scattered African-American communities, the Alaskan natives, the American Indian nations, the former Mexican territories of the American southwest, Texas, Vermont, and the southeastern territories (so-called "Dixie") that were incorporated into the American empire following the defeat of the Southern independence efforts during the American Civil

---

10   Martin van Creveld, *The Rise and Decline of the State* (Cambridge: Cambridge University Press, 1999).

War. A comparable analysis could be applied to, for example, the nation-states of India, China, the British Isles, or the continental European nations. Clearly, the most appropriate ideological foundation for contemporary anti-imperialist struggles is not a reactionary nation-state-centered nationalism but an orientation towards self-determination for all peoples that only anarchism can provide. It is not sufficient to merely liberate national entities from the wider imperial order but to also liberate regions, provinces, communities, ethnicities, tribes, cultures, linguistic groups, and religions that are often held captive to these nation-state systems. Nor is an authentic anti-imperialist struggle consistent with the mere replacement of the global imperialism of the American empire and international plutocracy with an agglomeration of regional imperialisms of the kind practiced by the United States under the guise of the "Monroe Doctrine" during the nineteenth century.

If conventional nation-state nationalism has become archaic, the anti-Europeanism and racist denigration of white ethnicity exhibited by the Left in its present-day incarnations has likewise become anachronistic. The Left's anti-Europeanism and anti-white racism is a reactionary backlash against past events and past social orders that no longer exist, notably America's historic racial caste system, South African apartheid, Nazism, the Holocaust, and the chauvinistic presumptions utilized as a means of self-legitimization by classical European colonialism. However, the European nations and historic white homelands are today colonies of the international plutocratic order grounded in America's neo-colonial political, military, economic, and cultural hegemony, and the national regimes of the white nations are themselves de facto puppet states of the American empire and global plutocratic oligarchy. The struggle against this empire and oligarchy is likewise a global struggle and one that transcends the boundaries of race, nation, culture, religion, political ideology, and socio-economic class. The overlords of the empire seek the subjugation of all races, all nations, all religions, all philosophies, all cultures, and all classes.

Beyond the End of History

The most appropriate ideological foundation for a twenty-first-century anarchist movement would be one that advances beyond both the class determinism and economism of classical anarchism and the counterculturalism and the racial, class, and gender reductionism of the postwar and late twentieth-century Left that has been incorporated into neo-anarchism. Rather than defining the anarchist struggle in terms of either a class conflict between the international working classes and the capitalist classes within their respective nations, or in terms of traditional outgroups versus traditional ingroups, a contemporary anarchism possessing the most penetrating analysis of imperialism and the global plutocratic order would define the struggle as one pitting all subjugated peoples, regardless of race, class, nation, or culture, against the imperial overlords. Therefore, twenty-first-century anarchists, regardless of their sectarian identity (e.g., syndicalist, anarcho-communist, individualist) should position themselves as the most militant wing of international anti-imperialist struggles just as the classical anarchists were the most militant wing of the historic labor struggles. Likewise, just as the classical anarchists became the leadership of mass syndicalist labor organizations, so should contemporary anarchists aspire to become the leadership of anti-state populist movements whose principal aim is resistance to imperialism, the destruction of the national regimes and ruling classes that are its component parts, and the achievement of self-determination for all peoples exhibiting all forms of cultural identity.

At present, the majority of contemporary anarchist movements maintain an orientation towards the most extreme forms of cultural leftism and counterculturalism. This may be fine by itself when expressed as a form of tribal or particularistic identity, but it becomes extraordinarily self-limiting as far as the ability of anarchist movements to grow beyond the level of existing merely as a type of youth subculture or as a sect within the ranks of the reactionary Left. To truly become the vanguard of anti-imperialist struggles, anarchists will necessarily have to cultivate allies and constituents far beyond those towards which they are presently oriented. Anarchists must out of necessity reach out to people of all cultures, classes, political ideologies, and value systems as part of the project of building the anti-imperialist struggle.

The recognition of these issues additionally requires the rejection of the conventional left/right model of the political spectrum in favor of alternative models that define the anti-imperialist struggle as one pitting not the Left against the Right, but pitting the forces of decentralization against centralism or pitting the periphery against the center in the manner suggested by Alain de Benoist.[11] Anarchists should subsequently strive to become the leadership of movements within their respective nations that seek national independence from the empire and international oligarchy. Such movements would possess three primary ideological elements: anti-statism, populism, and anti-imperialism. This anarchist-led anti-state populism might potentially be organized on the basis of nation-by-nation anarchist federations with a synthesist/pluralist outlook. Such federations might be internally layered and decentralized in such a way that anarchists would constitute an ideological center and leadership corps that emanates outward into the ranks of political and cultural forces from across the spectrum and drawing towards itself equally from the ranks of conservatives, nationalists, liberals, progressives, socialists, libertarians, Christians, Muslims, atheists, environmentalists, and others.

While an anarchist-led anti-state populism would transcend class boundaries, it might also be expected that the "vanguard classes" within each respective nation would be the poorest or most marginalized classes (e.g., the urban lumpenproletariat, rural neo-peasantry, and déclassé sectors, and spreading out into the sinking middle classes). Likewise, it would be expected that the "vanguard nations" would be those nations most under the boot of the international imperial order and the nation-states

---

11   Daniel McCarthy, "Left, Right, and Le Pen," LewRockwell.Com, April 30, 2002, http://www.lewrockwell.com/dmccarthy/dmccarthy31.html (accessed September 23, 2012).

which are its component parts, such as the native, indigenous, or aboriginal peoples within each respective nation-state. With regards to the relationship of the anarchist-led anti-imperialist movements to anti-imperialist so-called "rogue states," the most consistent and farsighted position for anarchists to assume would be one of support for the independence and sovereignty of such states against attacks from the empire while favoring ever-greater decentralization within the rogue states themselves and greater autonomy for their own internal regions, communities, and specific cultural identities.

Postmodernism and Cultural Relativism

A final consideration involves the need to respond to those anarchists who would criticize many of the ideas outlined thus far as not fully representing "true" or "authentic" anarchism, however defined, particularly the rejection of the left/right model of the political spectrum, the rejection of class determinism, and the pluralist and accommodating stance assumed towards cultural conservatives, traditionalists, nationalists, and others with whom anarchists have been in conflict with in the past. Such criticisms are well represented and summarized in Michael Schmidt's comparison of the Sarvodaya movement of Gandhi with classical anarchism. As Schmidt observes:

Gandhian Sarvodaya falls outside of the anarchist current, but initially appears, like anarchism, to be part of the larger libertarian socialist stream within which one finds the likes of council communism. There are some parallels between Gandhi's vision of "a decentralized federation of autonomous village republics" and the anarchist vision of a world of worker and community councils. Yet this should not be overstated. Gandhi's rejection of Western capitalist modernity and industrialism has libertarian elements, but . . . Gandhi's opposition to both British and Indian capital seems simply romantic, anti-modern and anti-industrial, a rejection of the blight on the Indian landscape of what

William Blake called the "dark Satanic mills." Absent is a real vision of opposing the exploitative mode of production servicing a parasitic class, of seeing the problem with modern technology as lying not in the technology itself, but in its abuse by that class.

This contradiction is at the very heart of the Gandhian Sarvodaya movement. On the one hand, it has a healthy distrust of the state. On the other, it retains archaic rights and privileges, traditional village hierarchies and paternalistic landlordism—in line with Gandhi's own "refusal to endorse the class war or repudiate the caste system" . . . Gandhi's embrace of caste, landlordism, and opposition to modern technologies that can end hunger and backbreaking labour, is diametrically opposed to anarchist egalitarianism.

Moreover, the mainstream of the anarchist tradition is rationalist, and thus opposed to the state-bulwarking mystification of most organised religion, whereas Gandhian Sarvodaya explicitly promoted Hinduism as part of its uncritical embrace of traditionalism. So what do we make of Gandhi himself? . . . On balance, in his völkisch nationalist decentralism, I would argue for him to be seen as something of a forebearer of "national anarchism," that strange hybrid of recent years. Misdiagnosed by most anarchists as fascist, "national anarchism" fuses radical decentralism, anti-hegemonic anti-statism (and often anti-capitalism), with a strong self-determinist thrust that stresses cultural-ethnic homogeneity with a traditional past justifying a radical future; this is hardly "fascism" or a rebranding of "fascism," for what is fascism without the state, hierarchy and class, authoritarianism, and the führer-principle?[12]

---

12 Schmidt, "South Asian Anarchism."

These comments contain far more insight than their author likely recognizes. For while the general thrust of classical anarchism was rationalist, modernist, and egalitarian, and Gandhi's philosophical premises were largely oriented towards traditionalism, mysticism, and a romantic anti-modernism not dissimilar to that of Catholic anti-modernists such as Hilaire Belloc and G. K. Chesterton, these dichotomies become problematic only within the context of a universalist framework derived from the liberal-rationalist premises of the latter Enlightenment period. Yet these premises have largely been eclipsed by the critiques of them offered by a diverse array of thinkers including Nietzsche, Weber, Heidegger, the theoreticians of the neo-Marxist Frankfurt School, pioneer postmodernists such Foucault, Lacan, and Derrida, and the intellectuals of the New Right. As the liberal-rationalist principles of the Enlightenment have slowly receded and postmodernism has become the dominant mode of contemporary thought, so has the cultural universalism derived from eighteenth - and nineteenth - century liberalism (which in many ways reflected a kind of Western ethnocentrism in a more secularized and ostensibly progressive form) given way to cultural relativism.[13] Hence, the growing conflict between proponents of "universal human rights" and radical multiculturalists.[14]

As a consequence of this paradigm shift in Western philosophy, the seeming conflict between the rationalist-modernism and egalitarian-universalism of the classical anarchists and the traditionalism, romanticism, anti-modernism, and mysticism of, for instance, Gandhi disappears if each of these are recognized as representing merely the particular values of specific cultural, regional, tribal, or philosophical identities with the claims to "truth" or legitimacy of each being contingent upon and

---

13   Martin Jay, *The Dialectical Imagination: A History of the Frankfurt School and the Institute of Social Research, 1923–1950* (Berkeley, CA: University of California Press, 1996 [1973]).

14   Johann Hari, "How Multiculturalism Is Betraying Women," *The Independent*, April 30, 2007, http://www.independent.co.uk/voices/commentators/johann-hari/johann-hari-how-multiculturalism-is-betraying-women-446806.html (accessed September 23, 2012).

relative to their own unique sets of historical, geographical, tribal, and social-psychological circumstances. A twenty-first-century, postmodern, and culturally relativist anarchism with an orientation towards the particular would be fully capable of incorporating into its political framework elements of each of these seemingly polar opposite perspectives in ways such as that represented by the National-Anarchist tendency described by Schmidt. Indeed, such "strange hybrids" are the likely wave of the future in anarchist thought.

References

Barrett, Kevin. "The Courageous Legacy of Journalist Helen Thomas: 'Zionists Go Home!'" *Final Call*, August 14, 2013. http://www.finalcall.com/artman/publish/Perspectives_1/article_100663.shtml

Benjamin, Medea. "10 Reasons to Pray for AIPAC's Decline." *Common Dreams*, February 27, 2015. http://www.commondreams.org/views/2015/02/27/10-reasons-pray-aipacs-decline

Bennis, Phyllis. "Why Opposing Israel is No Longer Political Suicide." *The Nation*, July 15, 2014. http://www.thenation.com/article/180653/room-criticize-israel-grows-are-policy-changes-table#

Domhoff, G. William. "Mills's *The Power Elite* 50 Years Later." *Contemporary Sociology*, November, 2006. http://www2.ucsc.edu/whorulesamerica/theory/mills_review_2006.html

Fantina, Robert. "Anti-Israel and the Myth of Anti-Semitism." *Counterpunch*, April 3-5, 2015. http://www.counterpunch.org/2015/04/03/anti-israel-and-the-myth-of-anti-semitism/

Gabler, Neal. *An Empire of Their Own: How the Jews Invented Hollywood*. Crown,1988.

Goldberg, Jeffrey. "Is it Time for the Jews to Leave Europe?" *The Atlantic*, April 2015. http://www.theatlantic.com/features/archive/2015/03/is-it-time-for-the-jews-to-leave-europe/386279/

Goldberg, J.J. *Jewish Power: Inside the American Jewish Establishment*. Addison-Wesley, 1996.

References

Kreiger, Hilary Leila. "J Street's Ben-Ami: Our stance is like Kadima's." *The Jerusalem Post*, October 28, 2009.

Maltz, Judy. "American Jewish Population Rises to 6.8 Million." *Haaretz*, September 30, 2013. http://www.haaretz.com/jewish-world/jewish-world-news/.premium-1.549713

MacDonald, Neil. "Ottawa cites hate crime laws when asked about its 'zero tolerance' for Israel boycotters." *CBCNews.Ca*, May 11, 2015. http://www.cbc.ca/news/politics/ottawa-cites-hate-crime-laws-when-asked-about-its-zero-tolerance-for-israel-boycotters-1.3067497

McCauley, Lauren. "Nearly 60 Lawmakers Boycott Netanyahu Speech." *Common Dreams*, March 3, 2015. http://www.commondreams.org/news/2015/03/03/nearly-60-lawmakers-boycott-netanyahu-speech

McConnell, Scott. "How the GOP Became the Israel Party." *The American Conservative*, April 8, 2015. http://www.theamericanconservative.com/articles/how-the-gop-became-the-israel-party/

Mearsheimer, John and Stephen Walt. *The Israel Lobby and U.S. Foreign Policy*. New York: Farrar, Straus, and Giroux, 2007. Original essay http://www.lrb.co.uk/v28/n06/john-mearsheimer/the-israel-lobby

Myers, Winfield. "Norman Finkelstein Denied Tenure at DePaul." *Campus Watch*, June 8, 2007. http://www.campus-watch.org/blog/2007/06/norman-finkelstein-denied-tenure

Nader, Ralph. "A Deep Regard for People's Right to Know, The Scourging of Helen Thomas" *CounterPunch*, June 16, 2010. http://www.counterpunch.org/2010/06/16/the-scourging-of-helen-thomas/

Newell, Jim. Jeb's "James Baker" problem: Why hawks are turning on the "anti-Israel" Bush. *Salon.Com*, March 25, 2015. http://www.salon.com/2015/03/25/jebs_james_baker_problem_why_hawks_are_turning_on_the_anti_israel_bush/

Petras, James. *The Power of Israel in the United States*. Black

Point, Nova Scotia: Fernwood Publshing, 2006.http://www.coalitionoftheobvious.com/17112929-Petras-J-The-Power-of-Israel-in-the-United-States-2006.pdf

Plessix, Caroline. "The European Union and Israel: A Lasting and Ambiguous 'Special Relationship.'" *Bulletin du Centre de recherche français à Jérusalem* [En ligne], 22 | 2011, mis en ligne le 31 décembre 2011, Consulté le 08 mai 2015. URL : http://bcrfj.revues.org/6675

Porter, Gareth. "The Israel Lobby Shows Its Clout." *ConsortiumNews.Com*, February 2, 2015. https://consortiumnews.com/2015/02/02/the-israel-lobby-shows-its-clout/

Raimondo, Justin. "Netanyahu, the George Wallace of the Middle East,' *Antiwar.Com*, March 20, 2015. http://original.antiwar.com/justin/2015/03/19/netanyahu-the-george-wallace-of-the-middle-east/

Shamee, Maureen. "US Congress Acts Against European Boycotts of Israel." *European Jewish Press*, April 29, 2015. http://ejpress.org/index.php?option=com_content&view=article&id=52096&catid=17

Tamir, Nadav. "Europe is Not Hostile to Israel." *Haaretz*, February 10, 2015. http://www.haaretz.com/opinion/.premium-1.641641

Thomas, Martin. "Zionism, Anti-Semitism, and the Left." *Solidarity 3* (166), February 4, 2010. http://www.krisis.org/2010/zionism-anti-semitism-and-the-left

Verbeeten, David. "How Important is the Israel Lobby?" *Middle East Quarterly*, Fall 2006, pp. 37-44.

Warikoo, Niraj (2010, December 9). "Helen Thomas says Anti-Defamation League is intimidating her." *Detroit Free Press*. http://www.freep.com/article/20101209/NEWS05/12090446/Helen-Thomas-says-Anti-Defamation-League-is-intimidating-her

Weiss, Philip. "A Jewish journalist is not sincere about Jewish ownership of media." Mondweiss.Net, September 4, 2009. http://mondoweiss.net/2009/09/a-jewish-journalist-is-not-sincere-about-jewish-ownership-of-media

Weiss, Philip. "Bowing to AIPAC, Senate unanimously passes resolution supporting Israel." Mondoweiss.Net, July 18, 2014. http://mondoweiss.net/2014/07/resolution-supporting-israel

Weiss, Philip. "Do Jews Dominate in American Media? And So What if We Do?" Mondoweiss.Net, February 17, 2008. http://mondoweiss.net/2008/02/do-jews-dominat#sthash. xlaGwLrx.dpuf

Willies, Egberto. "Republican Col. Lawrence Wilkerson: I know what my political party wants-They want war." Daily Kos, April 3, 2015. http://www.dailykos.com/story/2015/04/04/1375506/-Republican-Col-Lawrence-Wilkerson-I-know-what-my-political-party-wants-They-want-war#